China's Fiscal Policy

Fiscal policy has always been a primary measure of macroeconomic control. Fiscal revenue and expenditure can influence the operation of all economic and social activity by changing the existing GDP distribution pattern, affecting consumption and investment of enterprises and people, etc.

Within the framework of macroeconomic analysis, this book reviews the evolution of China's fiscal policy and the main changes China's economy has experienced since the 1990s. To begin with, it makes an empirical research of China's national debts, including their relationship with macroeconomic regulation and total social demand. Besides, it examines the economic effect mechanism of national debts issuance. Then it focuses on the taxation issues, elucidating the sources of tax revenue growth and the judgments on tax burden. The issue of tax reduction is also covered, especially its complexity in China. Lastly, it provides insights into China's fiscal tendency, changes in macroeconomic policies and financial operation in the context of the "New Normal".

Scholars and students of economics, finance and Chinese economic studies will be attracted by this book. Also, it will appeal to readers interested in modern Chinese economic history.

Gao Peiyong is the director of Institute of Economics, Chinese Academy of Social Sciences. His main research interests include theoretical research, policy analysis and institution design in the field of public finance and taxation.

China Perspectives

The *China Perspectives* series focuses on translating and publishing works by leading Chinese scholars, writing about both global topics and China-related themes. It covers Humanities & Social Sciences, Education, Media and Psychology, as well as many interdisciplinary themes.

This is the first time any of these books have been published in English for international readers. The series aims to put forward a Chinese perspective, give insights into cutting-edge academic thinking in China, and inspire researchers globally.

Titles in economics currently include

Internationalization of the RMB
Establishment and Development of RMB Offshore Markets
International Monetary Institute of the RUC

Chinese Macroeconomic Operation
Liu Shucheng

The Chinese Path to Economic Dual Transformation
Li Yining

Hyperinflation
A World History
Liping He

Game Theory and Society
Weiying Zhang

Structure and Changes of China's Financial System
Jie Zhang

China's Fiscal Policy
Theoretical and Situation Analysis
Gao Peiyong

For more information about this series, please visit: www.routledge.com/series/CPH

China's Fiscal Policy

Theoretical and Situation Analysis

Gao Peiyong

Routledge
Taylor & Francis Group
LONDON AND NEW YORK

中国社会科学出版社
CHINA SOCIAL SCIENCES PRESS

This book is published with financial support from Innovation Project of CASS

First published 2018 by Routledge

2 Park Square, Milton Park, Abingdon, Oxfordshire OX14 4RN
52 Vanderbilt Avenue, New York, NY 10017

Routledge is an imprint of the Taylor & Francis Group, an informa business

First issued in paperback 2020

Translated by Yang Limeng

Published in Chinese by China Social Sciences Press, 2013

British Library Cataloguing-in-Publication Data
A catalogue record for this book is available from the British Library

Library of Congress Cataloging-in-Publication Data
A catalog record for this book has been requested

ISBN: 978-1-138-89958-2 (hbk)
ISBN: 978-0-367-59057-4 (pbk)

Typeset in Times New Roman
by Apex CoVantage, LLC

Contents

Figures

Tables

Foreword to the Chinese edition

The Presidium of CASS (Chinese Academy of Social Sciences) Academic Division organizes the publication of Collections of the Committee Members of CASS Academic Division in order to uncover their findings of special researches on specific subjects and professions, as well as exhibit their dynamic research tracks and academic understandings after a long-term focus on a specific profession or subject. For myself, this publication is not just about the committee members of CASS academic division, but is a good opportunity to review what I have done over my scholarly research, organize my thoughts and improve my research level and quality.

After sorting out and editing my representative papers published in recent years, I locked on two clues and composed two corresponding symposiums, *Fiscal and Tax Reforms after 1994* and *Fiscal Policies in the Macroeconomic Analysis*.

The *Fiscal Policies in the Macroeconomic Analysis* presented here centers on the clue of fiscal policies decided in macroeconomic situation. It consists of my representative papers on macroeconomic climate and fiscal policies published since the 1990s.

To pick up such a research angle, I have my own reasons. Starting from my undergraduate, graduate and doctoral studies, then my teaching in Tianjin University Finance & Economics and Renin University of China and then my research work at CASS, I have never left the specialty of finance. I'm an academic with professional training in the finance and anchored in finance for long. After years of nurture even baptism of the finance, I've shaped the following perceptions.

Comprehensiveness is a unique quality for which finance distinguishes itself from other economic categories. As fiscal revenue and expenditure provides the base for all government activities, and also links governments, enterprises and people most directly, it can cover all government functions, departments and activities and extend to all enterprises and people, all consumption and investment segments and all economic and social sectors. It means the research on the finance cannot be only about finance but be done out of its professional limit and from a wider view.

Finance is an academic discipline of pragmatism, even for more practical purposes than any other economic disciplines. All arrangements related to fiscal revenue and expenditure always get down to business by directly changing the existing interest groups, improving people's well beings, affecting economic and social development and ensuring an ever-lasting political stability of the state. To this end, finance has never stood alone but has been closely associated with the fervent reality throughout its development. It has never been content with theoretical ideas but emphasized the practical application of ideas by acting on them to solve real problems throughout the building of its discipline. It means research on finance cannot be only about academic theories but perceive the practices outside of theoretical limits.

Basically fiscal revenue and expenditure activities are always taken as an aggregate included in the list of the general equilibrium elements, even in the planned economy age. In the market economy time, when people are more aware of the universally true proposition that the total supply and demand are in balance, not only do fiscal revenue and expenditure become a more important weight in the macroeconomic equilibrium, but the macroeconomic analysis is more liable to host the discipline of finance. We should base ourselves on the macroeconomy, discuss the finance issues from the macro perspective and study the financial resource allocation by macroeconomic analysis in order to obtain a sustainable and healthy development of the national economy. These are increasingly becoming the dominant orientation of the development and building of the discipline of finance. It means the research on finance cannot be done without macroeconomic awareness and thoughts but break the limit of general financial researches and enter into the new era of macroeconomic analysis.

As a very important macroeconomic variant in the command of governments, fiscal revenue and expenditure can change the existing GDP distribution pattern, profoundly affect the consumption and investment of enterprises and people and the total supply and demand of the society, and even influence the operation of whole economic and social activities; therefore, the fiscal policy is always a primary measure of macroeconomic control under the framework of macroeconomic analysis. Rare buffer zones are left for the decisions and overall arrangements regarding fiscal policies, as they determine the success of macroeconomic policies. In some sense, the analysis of fiscal policies among macroeconomic policies is the priority among priorities in the scope of finance. It means the research on finance cannot but be done by specialized and professional economists who are admitted for truly excellent learning, pursue practical problem solving and think outside the box of general academics.

Given the aforementioned, I've always focused on and devoted myself to researches on the macroeconomy and fiscal policy for years. The dominant course of my academic studies is to import the fiscal policy into the framework of macroeconomic analysis, and based on that, keep updated on the macroeconomic ups and downs, systematically look into the implementation effects of macroeconomic policies, outline how the fiscal policy is operated and put forward the fiscal policy arrangement plans in appropriate time.

All papers collected in this symposium are compiled in publication order. They unfold all major changes in China's macroeconomy after the 1990s and the evolutionary progress of fiscal policy decision making, the main measure of macroeconomic control, and basically reflect my thoughts about fiscal policy among the macroeconomic decisions.

I would like to take this opportunity to express my gratitude to the leaders and editors of China Social Sciences Press, whose great support and help have given rise to the publication of this book, and I would like also to ask for advice from peers and readers.

Gao Peiyong
July 10, 2013

Acknowledgments

This book is a collection of evidence-based studies funded by the Innovation Program of the Chinese Academy of Social Sciences (CASS). It contains my experience regarding both the practices and the theoretical studies of China's economic development.

Here I would like to express my sincere gratitude to Mr. Yang Limeng, translator of this book, for his painstaking efforts devoted to translating and polishing the book; I also thank all of the colleagues at China Social Sciences Press for their professional and energetic support.

My particular thank you goes to the CASS Innovation Translation Fund for having the book translated and published.

December 2017

1 National debts management and macroeconomic regulation

In recent years, the increasing issuance and accumulative scale of Chinese national debts have become a topic of common concern. For instance, there are doubts about whether we can bring under control the increasing year-by-year scale of national debts and to what extent China can achieve this at least in the reasonably near future. It is also argued that China will be at high risk if repayments of principal and interest for national debts keep occupying an overly high proportion of the national fiscal expenditure as a result of the expanding scale of national debts. Such arguments are too numerous to mention one by one. However, the relationship between national debts management and macroeconomic regulation has not been discussed as often as the foregoing, and may be in effect a task of top priority and of greater practical importance.

1 Scientific definition of NDM's connotation and extension

Correctly understanding the connotation and extension of the economic concept of "National Debts Management (NDM)"is a prerequisite for discussing the relationship between NDM and macroeconomic regulation.

At first appearance, NDM may look like something familiar because all economic activities financed by national debts maybe included into items under NDM and because NDM seems a general term of a series of activities carried out by the State government to decide, organize, envisage, direct, supervise and regulate the operation of national debts. Nevertheless, there always exist some ever-elusive intricacies in our mind. In the case of fiscal deficit, for instance, offsetting the deficit by way of borrowing debts should be deemed as a NDM activity; however, the deficit offset policy is usually taken as a part of fiscal policy by the government, so it is obviously inappropriate to treat this deficit offset method that falls within the scope of fiscal policy as a NDM activity. Furthermore, in addition to national debts, the deficit offset methods available also include other fiscal revenue forms such as taxation and fiscal overdraft, which certainly doesn't exclude national debts as a deficit offset method. However, it is illogical to include the choice among various fiscal revenue forms offsetting fiscal deficit into the scope of NDM activities.

Further studies show that the occurrence of fiscal deficits is always accompanied by borrowing debts but at no time will it lead to the assertion that national debts are borrowed only to offset the fiscal deficit, and that the earnings from taxation and other fiscal revenue forms can't be used for the same purpose. The reason is very simple: it is hard to make clear whether the fiscal deficit results from one or more items of fiscal expenditure because it is almost impractical to attribute fiscal deficit to certain fiscal revenue forms. In fact, despite different forms, the fiscal revenue itself is unified and undifferentiated in its very nature. It will make no sense if the deficit reduction method is included in the NDM's scope.

For another example, there are some questions about the borrowing of national debts: how to use the financial funds raised by issuing national debts, in what sectors the funds will be invested, how to assess the returns on such investment, etc. If these questions are covered by NDM, they will mingle with the fiscal expenditure policy that theoretically pertains to the scope of fiscal policy.

One more example: the so-called Open Market Operations (OMO) initiated by the Central Bank to implement monetary policy and regulate money supply is also relevant to national debts. Similarly, if the Central Bank's OMO business is considered as an activity of NDM, it will be harder to define the boundary between national debts and monetary policy.

Fundamentally, the effect of NDM on macroeconomic regulation can be identified in the analysis of its similarities to and differences from other means of macroeconomic regulation. Only on this basis will the position of NDM be established in the government's macroeconomic regulation system and be efficiently applied in practice.

It is thus argued in this paper that all economic activities in relation to national debts are classified into several levels: the first involves whether the government decides to issue national debts (to offset deficit) and how many debts are issued (to control the scale of national debts); the second relates to operations concerning the way, to whom, of what type and conditions new national debts will be issued as well as those already issued; and the third level covers the selling and buying of national debts by the Central Bank to implement the monetary policy. At the first level, national debts are deemed as an alternative fiscal revenue form (or a deficit financing method), so it is more likely a kind of fiscal policy. At the third level, national debts are treated merely as an operational tool of OMO for the Central Bank, so it is more likely a kind of monetary policy. Only at the second level will national debts bear the true sense of NDM.

Specifically, NDM involves: (1) design of debt category; (2) establishment of issuing conditions; (3) organization of issuing process; (4) selection of the sources of national debts acquirers; (5) supervision of the secondary market; (6) principal and interest repayment of national debts; (7) operation of national debts trading; and (8) development of debt-related systems.

NDM in this discussion is based on the above-mentioned definition.

2 NDM's effect on macroeconomic targets

NDM as a macro-control means it plays its role in economic activities by exerting a liquidity effect and interest rate effect; in other words, although NDM activities are implemented to facilitate steady growth of the national economy, a process of force conduction exists between NDM activities and their effects on national economic growth, where liquidity effect and interest rate effect are two intermediary targets used to measure and supervise how NDM activities exert effects on macroeconomic targets.

First, let's look at the liquidity effect of NDM.

Liquidity effect of NDM means the effect on the liquidity of the whole society by regulating the degree of national debts liquidity to exert an expansionary or contractionary effect on total social demand. The force conductive process can be described as: changes of liquidity of national debts → changes of social liquidity → changes of total social demand.

Therefore, the strategy aiming to change the maturities of national debts can be selected and operated as follows.

First, determine repayment terms of national debts at the appropriate time. National debts are divided into treasury bonds, treasury notes and treasury bills, depending on their liquidity. Treasury bills are most cashable and thus called "a kind of voucher only next to cash", treasury bonds are less cashable with least liquidity, and treasury notes stand in the middle. Apparently, the design of repayment terms has generated an expansionary effect or contractionary effect on total social demand. When the government decides to stimulate economic growth, it will take a policy means to increase the issuing scale and proportion of treasury bills in total national debts; on the contrary, when the government decides to tighten economic growth, it will increase the issuing scale and proportion of treasury bonds to slow down the liquidity of national debts in society.

Then, alternate between treasury bonds and bills. Differences in liquidity are not only represented in the design but also in the alternation of maturity terms. Substituting treasury bonds for treasury bills will decrease the liquidity of national debts while replacement of treasury bonds with treasury bills will increase the liquidity of national debts. According to the principle described above, alternation between terms of national debts can also be used as an effective tool for the government to exercise expansionary or contractionary economic policy.

The strategy to regulate debt repaying sources can also be selected and operated in two methods.

First, identify entities that will purchase national debts. Considering its influence on money supply, purchasers of national debts include entities in both the banking system and non-banking system. When the banking system (including commercial bank and Central Bank) purchases or holds national debts, it will increase money supply by expanding the credit scale, thus increasing monetary liquidity in society. When the non-banking system (including individuals, industrial and commercial enterprises and administrative institutions) purchases or holds national debts, it will give rise to transfer of capital use right rather than to the increment of money supply, thus giving little effect on monetary liquidity in society. For this reason, identification of national debts purchasers is also a policy means to exercise expansionary or contractionary influence on the economy. In other words, in the event of economic overheating or inflation, the liquidity of national debts in society will be reduced by borrowing money from the non-banking system and by reducing the proportion of the banking system's possession of national debts in total quantity issued; on the contrary, in the event of economic depression or deflation, the liquidity of national debts in society will be enhanced by increasing the proportion of the banking system's possession of national debts and by limiting the non-banking system's subscription of national debts.

Then, encourage targeted subscription of national debts at the appropriate time. National debts with different levels of liquidity are intended for specific investors. Commercial banks are the most liquid investors of treasury bills because they usually deal with short-term savings and loans and most of their liabilities may fall due at any time in a day or week. Other investors whose business requires less liquidity are less sensitive to selection between long-term and short-term national debts. As a result, trading of treasury bills on the secondary market will for sure affect the commercial bank's possession of national debts and the liquidity in society while trading of treasury bonds will not. Such being the case, when the government exercises expansionary economic policy, it may opt to sell the treasury bills (and buy treasury bonds simultaneously) on the secondary market to increase commercial banks' possession of national debts and increase the basis of credit expansion and the liquidity in society. When the government exercises contractionary economic policy, it may buy treasury bills (and sell treasury bonds simultaneously) on the secondary market to reduce the commercial banks' possession of national debts and narrow the basis of credit expansion and the liquidity in society.

Now let's come to the interest effect of NDM.

The interest effect of NDM means the rise and fall of interest rates on the financial market as a result of regulating the issuance of national debts or the level of actual interest rates so that total social demand will be subject to expansionary or contractionary policy. The transmission mechanism can be described as follows: the fluctuation of interest rates of national debts → fluctuation of interest rates on the financial market → fluctuation of total social demand.

First, the government may opt to regulate the interest rate of national debts, which can be achieved by determining the level of the interest rate. In the context of a modern market economy, the interest rate of national debts is a typical rate on the financial market that reflects the government's macroeconomic policy and may make a direct difference between rise and fall of interest rates on the financial market. With regard to the current situation in China, although the interest rate of national debts is contingent on the savings rate, the enterprization of specialized banks represents an irresistible trend as market orientation reform deepens. Once this requirement is satisfied, no longer will the interest rate of national debts follow the savings rate. Such being the case, the interest rate of national debts will be an effective method for the government to influence the market interest rate and then to implement its macroeconomic policy. For instance, if the expansionary economic policy is necessary, the interest rate of national debts can be lowered to bring down all interest rates on the financial market, thus stimulating consumption and investment to increase the total social demand; if it is necessary to adopt contractionary economic policy, the interest rate of national debts can be raised to improve all interest rates on the financial market, thus suppressing consumption and investment to reduce the total social demand.

Then, the government may opt to control the effective interest rate of national debts by trading national debts on the secondary market to regulate the international effective interest rate (rather than the nominal interest rate) based on the reverse change between debt price and interest rate, which is usually performed by a Central Bank or a national debts administrative department of the financial authority. Trading national debts by a Central Bank or a national debts administrative department on the secondary market may lead to a rise or fall in the prices of national debts, and further to a rise or fall of all interest rates on the financial market. Specifically, when economic growth needs to be stimulated, national debts may be bought in, which means the price of national debts will rise with the increasing demand and the effective interest rate of national debts will fall along with the decreasing market interest rate, thus generating expansionary influence on total social demand; when the economic growth needs to be suppressed, national debts may be sold out, which means the price of national debts will fall with the increasing supply and the effective interest rate of national debts will rise along with the increasing market interest rate, thus generating contractionary influence on total social demand.

If this principle is widely applied, buying and selling of national debts may influence the regulation of the structure of the market interest rate. For instance, buying treasury bills and selling treasury bonds on the secondary market will inevitably lead to inverse changes in supply and demand of these two kinds of national debts. Obviously, as the demand of treasury bills exceeds its supply and the supply of treasury bonds exceeds its demand, the price of treasury bills tends to rise (as its effective interest rate decreases) and the price of treasury bonds tends to fall (as its effective interest rate increases). In addition, the decreasing the interest rate of treasury bills will lead to a synchronically decreasing short-term interest rate while the increasing interest rate of treasury bonds will lead to an increasing long-term interest rate. Similarly, buying treasury bonds and selling treasury bills on the secondary market will lead to an increasing price of the treasury bonds (as its effective interest rate decreases) and a decreasing price of treasury bills (as its effective interest rate increases), and further to a decreasing long-term interest rate and an increasing short-term market rate. In fact, the process of fluctuating effective interest rates of both treasury bills and treasury bonds as well as fluctuating long-term and short-term interest rates indicates that the government's regulatory role in interest rates on the financial market is transferring from macro to micro control. As a result, both the total interest rate on the financial market and the term structure of the interest rate on the financial market will be subject to influence of NDM, thus leading to the fact that financial activities such as enterprise stock, enterprise debt and bank loans as well as interest rates on the financial market may possibly become objects of direct or indirect operations of NDM. In this case, it is self-evident that the government expands and strengthens its ability to regulate the financial market.

3 Coordination between NDM and other macroeconomic regulation means

Now that NDM an important means for macroeconomic regulation, its coordination with other means needs to be highly considered, especially with fiscal policy and monetary policy, two levers of economic regulation commonly employed by the state government under modern economic conditions. It is therefore necessary to define the relationship between NDM and both fiscal and monetary policy.

First, the relationship between NDM and fiscal policy:

This issue was already mentioned in foregoing paragraphs. In general, fiscal policy involves tax policy, expenditure policy and deficit-covering policy. When it comes to the basic conditions for implementation of fiscal policy, adjustment of tax policy (tax increase or decrease) and application of expenditure policy (expenditure increase or decrease) are closely related to fiscal balance. In case of fiscal deficit, there will be an issue concerning how to cover it or how to raise necessary funds. Despite several direct methods of covering fiscal deficit such as exercising fiscal overdraft, enlarging the scope of taxation and increasing tax rate, the borrowing of national debts may be the best one in terms of social and economic benefits. From a global perspective, fiscal deficits are typically cut down through issuance of national debts. In other words, national debts, as an ideal or basic method to cover fiscal deficit, can be an essential condition for the implementation of fiscal policies.

Then, the relationship between NDM and monetary policy:

As known to all, monetary policy involves the application of Open Market Operations (OMO), adjustment to discount rate and change of required reserve ratio by the Central Bank to influence the formation of the market interest rate and regulate money supply. OMO is the most powerful weapon in the hands of the Central Bank to implement monetary policy for national debts, aiming to control financial markets by trading national debts on the open market (financial market). When the Central Bank implements an expansionary monetary policy to increase money supply and ease credit creation, it will gobble up national debts on the open market and pump money into circulation; on the contrary, when the Central Bank implements a contractionary monetary policy to cut money supply and tighten credit creation, it will dump national debts and withdraw money from circulation. It is thus clear that the Central Bank's trading in national debts on OMO to regulate money supply is based largely on existence of large-scale national debts. "Huge quantity of national debts has provided the 'Federal Bank' (i.e. American Federal Reserve Bank) with opportunities to engage in large scale OMO operations . . . the existence of broad national debts market has made it possible a widespread and steady OMO market, which has therefore enhanced results of the monetary policy" (Samuelson, 1979). In this sense, NDM plays the role of a "transmission device" when the Central Bank applies monetary policy in economic regulation.

The implementation process of either fiscal policy or monetary policies is therefore correlated to NDM. The fiscal policy should have been implemented by the Ministry of Finance and the monetary policy implemented by the Central

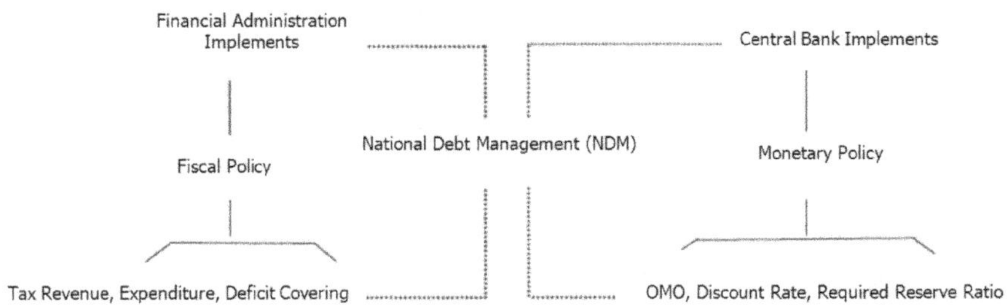

Figure 1.1 Relationship between NDM and both the FP and MP

Bank; however, they are now combined by NDM. Currently in China, NDM is regarded as a junction point or bridge between fiscal policy and monetary policy, as illustrated in Figure 1.1.

Strictly speaking, however, NDM is neither part of the fiscal policy nor part of the monetary policy, notwithstanding its indivisible correlation with both of them. After all, it is a relatively independent economic activity that operates on its own rules. For instance, NDM can't directly change the scale of fiscal expenditure or tax revenue or relevant flow, nor can it directly change the money supply. What it can influence is the fixed-size national debts, including new debts to be issued but not yet sold and old debts issued but not yet repaid (national debts already issued). For the fixed-size debts, the NDM's action on macroeconomic regulation includes carrying out management activity to help realize objectives of macroeconomic policy; for policy objectives, the overall purpose of NDM must comply with requirements of both the fiscal policy and monetary policy, but its direct purpose contradicts objectives of the fiscal policy and monetary policy. For instance, one of the NDM's direct purposes is to minimize the cost of debts. Thus, the fiscal policy should control the issuance of national debts, for such issuance has positive correlation with the cost of debts as well as the interest rate and commission and handling charges paid to the issuing agent usually increase with the increasing number of debts issued. However, the control of the debt scale is preconditioned by decreasing or eliminating fiscal deficit, which may contradict the direct purposes of fiscal policy. In addition, if the NDM finds it necessary to issue more treasury bonds at a lower interest rate and more treasury bills at a higher interest rate in order to decrease the cost of debts, it will contradict the direct purposes of monetary policy. This is because the low interest rate usually forms during the economic downturn; in case of economic recession, issuing treasury bonds will increase the long-term interest rate to and hinder the increase in investment and the formation of long-term capital. When the high interest rate forms during high economic growth, the impact of issuing treasury bills in the case of inflation is largely similar to issuing additional currency. From the above discussion, the NDM usually operates by designing the type of national debts, regulating the issuing interest rate and selecting sources of national debts, quite different from the fiscal policy that is implemented by regulating tax revenue and making decisions about government expenditure and deficit-covering policy, and from the monetary policy that is implemented by "three weapons" – the OMO, adjustment of the discount rate and change of the required reserve rate.

It is hence concluded that there are similarities and differences between NDM and the fiscal policy and monetary policy, where the former means their coordinated and concerted actions towards the same purposes while the latter suggests their joint efforts to move towards the overall goals.

We recognize that the single means of macroeconomic regulation is easy for the operation of national debts; however, it is not easy to combine various means of macroeconomic regulation into an organic acting force to fulfill the overall purposes of steady national economic growth. This is because the single means is always based on the fact that "other conditions remain unchanged" or "other aspects remain normal" and on the fact that the operation of national debts is in the charge of a specific authority that fully understands the characteristics of the single means and the objects to be regulated; whereas, various means of macroeconomic regulation need to be coordinated among different departments when these means are mutually conditional, supplementary and interpenetrative.

However, when coordinating with other means of macroeconomic regulation, especially the fiscal policy and monetary policy, NDM needs to respect the following principles.

First, the overall purposes of NDM should comply with the basic requirements of both the fiscal and monetary policies. It needs to make clear that NDM operates within the framework specified by the fiscal policy and monetary policy and within the economic environment, that the scope of its acting force is permissible to both fiscal policy and monetary policy, and that the direction of its acting force falls in line with the purposes of two policies. In other words, the main function of NDM in macroeconomic regulation is to supplement and strengthen the effects of two policies in all periods.

Secondly, the direct purpose of NDM should vary in response to different situations. When it is consistent with the overall purpose of steady national economic growth, NDM may be operated to reach its own purpose; otherwise, NDM should first meet the overall purposes of steady national economic growth and then its direct purpose.

Finally, NDM can play active roles in macroeconomic regulation while moving towards the overall purposes of steady national economic growth.

4 Further considerations: creating conditions for NDM to play its roles

However, there are specific conditions under which NDM plays its roles. In other words, conditions must be created for NDM to play roles in macroeconomic regulation. Considering China's current situation, the urgent conditions are as follows.

First, appropriately enlarge the scale of national debts. NDM's ability to regulate the macroeconomy shows a positive correlation with the scale of national debts because NDM activities are preconditioned by a large number of national debts in society. The larger the scale of national debts is, the larger the NDM's operational objects and space will be. NDM of the western developed countries grew rapidly this way. In China, the issuance of national debts in successive years has paved the way for NDM activities; however, China's operation of NDM activities remains at a low level since the restart of national debts (internal debts only) in 1981, one of the most important reasons for which is that China's national debts scale remains insufficient for start of NDB activities. In this sense, enlarging China's scale of national debts seems quite necessary.

Secondly, diversify the types of national debts. This issue has been in discussion for many years, but it remains pending, resulting in deterioration of the purchasers' enthusiasm, imbalance between treasury funds and issuance of national debts and lack of essential conditions for NDM activities. The liquidity effect of NDM is realized by adjusting and changing the type (especially the term) of national debts. In the case of a single type of national debts and lack of treasury bills (e.g. a term of several months), this macroeconomic control method will make no sense. For this reason, diversity has become an obvious feature of national debts in various countries. Take the term structure of national debts. According to the OECD's statistics in 1983, for types of the term of national debts issued by its member countries, there were 31 in Australia, 20 in Canada, 17 in Britain, eight in Sweden, seven in Finland and Switzerland, six in Belgium and New Zealand, five in Demark and Germany and therein France (Gao Peiyong, 1989). It is therefore necessary to diversify the types of national debts in China.

Thirdly, broaden the sources of debt repayment. As discussed above, one of the NDM means is to regulate and change the structure of national debts holders based on diverse sources of debt repayment. In this respect, what we should do is to break the limitations on commercial banks and the Central Bank trading in national debts and make them become national debts holders so that government bonds occupy a considerable proportion in the asset structure of the banking system. To our pleasure, the reform plan of the financial system in China has proposed enterprization of specialized banks and diversification of investment projects, and the specialized banks have become underwriters and holders of government bonds. Whether the Central Bank will be given access to the national debts market (mainly the secondary market) remains a concern, since it may induce inflation when its purchase of national debts increases the unplanned monetary base and it shows a tendency of inflation because the sales of bank loans in China are usually confirmed in the credit program at the beginning of a year. However, this will exclude the Central Bank from purchasing national debts. The solution to this problem lies in the reform of the financial system. Therefore, as the reform of the financial system deepens, the Central Bank's purchase and possession of national debts will not only expand the OMO business but also pave the way for operation of the NDM.

Fourthly, coordinate relationships, standardize and improve the competent authorities of national debts. National debts authorities serve as the operational body of NDM activities and play a vital role in macroeconomic regulation, so they are required to operate for non-profit purposes according to the state macroeconomic policy. In recent years, however, many of these authorities' behaviors have been found to be non-standard. Some financial institutions funded by financial authorities (credit and investment or securities agencies) and some national debts service agencies established by local financial authorities act as distributors on the national debts market to earn price difference income or interest income by taking advantage of the ill-formed interest rate or forcing down the purchasing price of national debts factitiously. With non-standard administration, it makes little sense for NDM to perform its functions in macroeconomic regulation. For this reason, we need to standardize NDM's behaviors and define its responsibilities, especially its position and roles in macroeconomic regulation, and set about legislation of NDM after unifying our thoughts and summarizing our experiences.

Finally, marketize the interest rate formation mechanism. The foregoing interest rate of national debts as a means to regulate the market interest rate is based on marketization of the interest rate formation mechanism. For trading of government bonds that aims to regulate the market interest rate by regulating the effective interest rate of national debts, without marketization of the interest rate formation mechanism, it will be unlikely for the interest rate of national debts and the trading of government bonds to regulate all interest rates represented by the bank savings and loan rates. As known to all, while market regulation seems more influential on the formation of interest rates in recent years, the bank savings and loan rates are determined directly by the government's administrative order, and other direct financing interest rates are subject to direct or indirect control of administrative intervention. In this sense, it is urgent that the reform be deepened in capital commercialization and interest rate marketization.

These are the basic conditions for NDM to play its roles in China's macroeconomic regulation.

(Originally published in *Economic Theory and Business Management*, Vol.4, 1993)

Bibliography

Atkinson, A. B., et al. (1992). *Public economics (Chinese version)*. Shanghai: SDX Joint Publishing Company.

Gao Peiyong. (1989). *An introduction to economics on national debts*. Changsha: Hunan People's Publishing House.

Samuelson, P. (1979). *Economics (Chinese version)*. Beijing: The Commercial Press.

2 Empirical analysis of China's national debts since reform of the economic system in 1978

I 1959–1978: not a period without national debts

The news that the Chinese government restarted borrowing money from abroad in 1979 and especially decided to issue state national debts at home in 1981 caused a sensation in the economic circles in China because Chinese citizens had been living a life with neither internal nor external debts for two decades. However, it was in the 1950s shortly after the founding of new China in 1949 that the Chinese government had borrowed some money to overcome temporary fiscal difficulties.

With regard to the 20-year period (1959–1978) without national debts, Chinese theorists attempted to find out the answer from the political and economic environment during and after that period. For example, after the breakdown of the Sino-Soviet relationship in 1958, the Soviet Union government ceased its assistance, scrapped all contracts and withdrew its experts from China; meanwhile, the western countries represented by the US imposed an economic blockade on China. Therefore, China was not allowed to borrow money in that international political environment.

After the erroneous "leftist" thought prevailed in China in 1958, the socialist system was derisively branded to have "neither internal nor external debts" and the government's borrowing behavior was considered prejudicial to the socialist country's reputation and image. Therefore, the internal political environment also denied the government's right to leverage domestic debts.

Upon successful completion of the First Five-Year Plan (1953–1957), it was generally believed that China no longer had need to borrow money due to an optimistic outlook on the development of national economy (to catch up with the western industrialized countries in the near future) and a high expectation of fiscal revenue during and after the Second Five-Year Plan (1958–1962). Unfortunately, when the Great Chinese Famine (1960–1962) broke out and economic hardships worsened, the fiscal revenue of China saw a negative growth for two consecutive years. Despite the adjustment made in the expected fiscal revenue, the issuance of national debts could not be put on the agenda.

These are indeed the reasons for the "blank period" of national debts in China. However, one of the important reasons was overlooked, i.e. a special formation mechanism of fiscal revenue that could provide a "supernormal" level of fiscal revenue had formed in China in the First Five-Year Plan period when the socialist transformation was carried out in agriculture, handicraft industry and private capitalist industry and commerce.

In 1953, the *Order for Planned Purchase and Supply of Grain* was issued by the Government Administration Council of the Central People's Government of China, emphasizing the state monopoly on the purchase and marketing of grain throughout the whole country, the scope of which was soon extended to vegetables, oils and cotton to highlight the state monopoly on the purchase and marketing of the main agricultural and sideline products (ASPs). Under this system, farmers' surplus ASPs were sold to the government at a regulated price and then supplied by the government as planned to urban industrial sectors and residents for consumption. Purchasing these supplies at a low price enabled the government to gather large resources from agriculture and supply them to urban sectors and residents at a low price; as a result, the low price of ASPs had reduced the cost of industrial raw materials, provided urban residents with in-kind benefits and reduced the labor cost of industrial sectors in pursuit of higher profit.

In 1956, the *Wage Bracket System of the Stated-owned Enterprises (SOEs), Public Institutions and Government Organs* was issued during the second national wage system reform, featuring uniform state criteria for employees' wages and promotions as well as supervision over the preparation and implementation of the wage fund plans of the SOEs, public institutions and government organs. By this means, the government could reduce industrial labor costs directly or indirectly by depressing the wage level and minimizing the promotion intervals. Consequently, the industrial sectors could also gain higher profit.

The unified collection and allocation of fiscal revenues by the state had remained unchanged since the founding of new China in 1949. Under this system, the net income gained by SOEs (mainly industrial enterprises) was turned over to and allocated by the national finance authority, leaving a tiny portion to the discretion of enterprises; therefore, the government retrieved the industrial sectors' high profit through unified collection and achieved a "supernormal" level of fiscal revenue.

The process could be described as Figure 2.1.

This special formation mechanism of fiscal revenue had produced "supernormal" fiscal revenue for the government, which could have been achieved by borrowing large sums of money.

According to a review of the literature, during the low-price purchase of ASPs by the government, about an RMB 600 billion "hidden price tax" was imposed on farmers over two decades (Financial Division of the Ministry of Agriculture, 1991); after 1956, the regular promotion system of urban employees was suspended; in the 20-year period from 1957 to 1977, there was only a small increase of employees' wages in 1959, 1963 and 1971, and only 2% in 1959; in this period, enterprises retained a very small portion of profits, with the smallest being 3.7% in 1978, and the retained portion of profits of industrial enterprises was as small as 1.7% (Ma Hong, 1982). In the 26-year period from 1952 to 1978, urban employees' annual average wage increased only 170 yuan, with an annual average growth

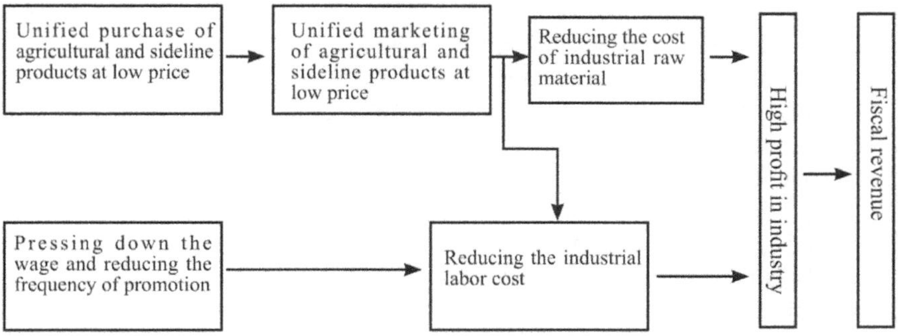

Figure 2.1 Special formation mechanism of fiscal revenue

rate of 1.3%, and decreased in 13 of the 26 years. As for farmers' income, the annual net income per capita of a rural family amounted only to RMB 133.57 in 1978 (Yuan Zhenyu, 1991). Therefore, the income of both urban employees and rural farmers mismatched national economic development in this period.

The fact that China's fiscal revenue accounted for over 30% of national income (37.2% in 1978) in a long period deserves serious consideration and means that the Chinese government has not borrowed any money during the two decades from 1959 to 1978; however, the national debts that should have been borne by the government were probably absorbed by the masses through the government's low-price purchase of ASPs and low-level wages.

II Background for re-issuance of national debts in China

As known to all, China began its economic system reform with the reform of its distribution system, aimed at reducing the share of fiscal revenue in the national income-distribution structure and stimulated enthusiasm in all sectors by "repaying debts" with fiscal revenue so as to vitalize the national economy that was dampened as a result of the traditional economic system. "Repayment of debts" with fiscal revenue meant "reducing tax and allowing enterprises to retain more profits" (National Bureau of Statistics of China, 1994).

This measure was first put into practice in rural areas. In 1979, as the household contract responsibility system linking remuneration to output was implemented, the purchase price of ASPs was raised by the government, with the purchase price index rising by 48.1% over the previous year. In 1980, the index increased 18.9% as against that in 1979. The rise in purchase price of ASPs resulted in an increasing cost of industrial raw material and living cost of urban residents, and further gave rise to an increase in the labor cost of industrial products. Therefore, the government's fiscal revenue gained from the low-price purchase of ASPs, with the profit being transferred from industrial sector to agricultural sector.

Then, the measure extended towards urban areas. Based on the SOEs' enterprise fund system implemented in 1978, the pilot profit retention system came into practice nationwide in July 1979. Enterprises involved in such pilot work were allowed to retain a required part of profits to set up the production development fund, welfare fund and bonus fund for their employees. The next January, the full-amount profit retention system was changed to base profit retention plus growth profit retention, and further enhanced the SOEs' financial rights. While implementing the profit retention system, the government also piloted the transformation of profit delivery into income tax in some SOEs. With these reform measures being issued, both the amount and rate of enterprises retaining profit increased greatly from RMB 2.75 billion and 3.7% in 1978 to RMB 14.4 billion and 21.5% in 1980 respectively. In addition, the government eased the urban employees' wage management; increased the wage income of employees in SOEs, public institutions and other organizations of different ownerships; and recovered the bonus system that had been suspended for years. In 1979 and 1980, the index of total wages of urban employees increased 10.5 and 19.4 percentage points respectively over the previous year. The increase in profit retained by enterprises resulted in the fact that the industrial sectors' profit would no longer be handed over to the state treasury through the government's unified purchase. With the increasing purchase price of ASPs and the easing of urban employees' wage management, the industrial sectors' profit was lowered by the increasing cost of industrial raw materials and labor. As a result, China's fiscal revenue arising from urban industrial sectors declined accordingly.

The effects of the aforesaid measures for reducing tax and allowing enterprises to retain profits could be analyzed from different perspectives. This paper addresses one of the effects that could not be neglected: the breakup of the traditional formation mechanism of fiscal revenue that was based on "low selling price of ASPs and low wage system" to provide "supernormal" fiscal revenue, resulting in the declining percentage of fiscal revenue (excluding debt revenue) in national income from 37.2% in 1978 to 31.9% in 1979 and further to 28.3% in 1980.

In addition, the fiscal expenditure failed to decrease with the decreasing fiscal revenue; instead, it increased due to aforesaid measures for reducing tax and allowing enterprises to retain more profits. For instance, when the purchase price of ASPs went up, the selling price was forced to remain almost unchanged so as to eliminate the social unrest arising therefrom; meanwhile, the purchase and sale price differentials and the increasing running expenses were covered by fiscal subsidy. In 1979 and 1980, the fiscal expenditures of price subsidy increased by 6.1 and 10.6 times respectively over the year of 1980. Another example: for enterprises, the increasing amount of urban employees' wages and bonuses was offset by increasing their labor cost and reducing corporate profit and fiscal revenue; for public institutions, however, the staff's increasing wages and bonuses were largely dependent on special fiscal appropriation. The increasing fiscal expenditure seemed unavoidable; the administrative cost, for example, increased by 36.1 percentage points in 1980 over 1978.

The fiscal deficit occurred as a result, amounting to RMB 17.067 billion in 1979 and RMB 12.750 billion in 1980. These deficits led to the fiscal authority's bank overdraft and further to widespread price rises. What was worse, the fiscal budget showed a negative again in 1981 when the reform deepened in reducing tax and allowing enterprises to retain more profits.

Due to serious fiscal difficulty, the Chinese government faced an unprecedented dilemma. Could the fiscal deficit be totally offset by bank overdraft? This is a solution but not the best one because it may trigger inflation based on rising prices. Once rising prices go out of control, they will deny all reform achievements.

Theoretically, the fiscal deficit can also be offset by cutting down on fiscal expenditure. However, as the vested interest and rigid fiscal expenditure may be hardly changed, there is less space to cut down on fiscal expenditure. Besides, some of the fiscal expenditure items, such as price subsidies, should not be reduced but should be increased at the early stage of reform.

Thus, a way out must be found for increasing fiscal revenue. After the breakup of the traditional formation mechanism of fiscal revenue, recovering it would go against the main reform thought son decentralization of power and transfer of profits. Also, increasing fiscal revenue through bank overdraft or money pump may do harm to economic development. Then, the last choice was to borrow money.

The Chinese government in fact recovered by borrowing money from abroad in 1979, but the borrowing had been interrupted for 20 years. In 1979 and 1980, China borrowed RMB 3.531 billion and 4.301 billion respectively from foreign countries. However, the borrowing of domestic money was not put on the agenda due to leftist restrictions in China. In 1981 when the severe fiscal difficulty forced people to face the real situation, the leftist restrictions were totally eliminated. On January 18, 1981, the *National Regulations of the People's Republic of China on National Debts*, and on January 26, the *Decision on Balancing the Financial Revenue and Expenditure and Strengthening the Fiscal Management* was approved and released by the State Council to issue national debts. The amount of national debts issued that year was RMB 4.866 billion (the planned amount was RMB 4 billion).

It was in this historical environment that China restarted the issuance of national debts.

III Dramatic changes in borrowing practice

Strictly speaking, national debts issued in 1981 were generally used as an expedient to satisfy temporary demand. China had no intention to issue treasury bonds, and its original intention was to "centralize some of the money that had been decentralized" (Gao Jian, 1993). In other words, China was not aware that the traditional formation mechanism of fiscal revenue had gone and whether it was necessary to issue national debts at that time. This was reflected by the facts that the purchasers were enterprises and public institutions, whose economic interest was less considered (i.e. the annual interest rate was only 4%, much lower than 6.84% annual interest rate of five-year bank savings), and that the traditional political mobilization and administrative apportion were used as the way to issue national debts. In addition, all the national debts issued were of little liquidity since they could neither be traded on the secondary market nor discounted or mortgaged at banks. In the long run, national debts couldn't be issued this way.

Since 1982, however, dramatic changes occurred amidst the increasingly severe financial difficulties.

As the reform deepened, the Chinese government began raising the prices of ASPs more frequently. From 1978 to 1993, the general purchase price index of ASPs rose by 2.74 times, where the purchase price index of grains rose by 3.31 times and industrial crops by 1.74 times. In the same period, the national income generated by agricultural sector grew by 5.4 times from RMB 98.6 billion to RMB 631.7 billion, but the proportion of agricultural sector's fiscal revenue in the national income fell from 3.2% to 2.59% in 1992 (though up to 3.7% in 1993) (National Bureau of Statistics of China, 1994).

After the focus of reform was transferred from rural to urban areas, the Chinese government enacted a series of measures to adjust the SOEs' profit distribution system. In December 1981, the Ministry of Finance and the State Economic Commission of the People's Republic of China proposed the multiform profit retention plan and the profit-loss responsibility plan based on the original profit retention system. In January 1983 and September 1984, the State Council approved the first and second phases of tax-for-profit reform in SOEs throughout the country. In late 1986 and early 1987, the State Council affirmed and started the nationwide exercise of the contracted managerial responsibility system for enterprises. At the First Session of the Seventh National People's Congress, the profit-tax separation idea was adopted for the reform; later on, it was geared towards the profit-tax separation, after-tax amortization and after-tax contracting system following pilot projects. In January 1994, the Chinese government carried out comprehensive reforms of the profit distribution system in SOEs while implementing the *Accounting Standards for Business Enterprises (ASBE)*, *Financial Standards for Business Enterprises (FSBE)* and tax reform. Regardless of different contents and forms, every round of reform was focused on tax cuts and profit retention to increase enterprises' disposable income. From 1978 to 1991, the amount of enterprises' retained profit in China increased over 20 times from RMB 2.75 billion to RMB 55.54 billion (RMB 70.06 billion in 1988), with an average annual growth rate of 33.5%, and the rate of the retained profit increased almost 17 times from 3.7% to 65.3% (86.7% in 1988), with an average annual growth rate of 34.5%. In the period from 1978 to 1993, the national income generated by industrial sector increased 7.65 times from RMB 184.7 billion to RMB 1.2862 trillion while the proportion of industrial sector's fiscal revenue in national income decreased 60.2 percentage points from 75.4% to 15.2% (Comprehensive Planning Division of the Ministry of Finance, 1992; National Bureau of Statistics of China, 1994).

The tax policy and system were changing constantly in the process of reform and need for further improvement. With an imperfect legal institution, backward tax-levying means and low level of tax collectors, serious problems occurred quite often in the rapid development of foreign-funded, private and individual enterprises, such as evasion, dodge, fraud and arrears of tax, which caused heavy losses of national tax revenue. According to an authoritative source, the loss of tax revenue caused by these problems throughout the country amounted to more than RMB 10 billion every year since the reform (Chu Xinhua & Xie Chun, 1993).

Delegating power to enterprises and local governments in effect meant a process to unleash the "external regulation" imposed on enterprises and local governments, but the self-regulation or self-constraint mechanism was not established at the same time. As a result, some enterprises and local governments with less external regulation failed to learn self-reliance and repeated the mistakes they had made, just like uncontrollable kids. For example, some enterprises randomly enlarged the scope of cost and expenses, perversely diluted or squeezed cost and greedily embezzled corporate profit and fiscal revenue; some local governments arbitrarily issued numerous items of preferential tax policy, disregarding the national tax decree, resulting in continuous losses of tax revenue due to unauthorized tax relief and drawback.

It was under these conditions that the proportion of fiscal revenue (excluding debt revenue) in national income continued falling (down to 28.3% in 1980, 24.4% in 1982, 20.4% in 1990 and 18.2% in 1993). Meanwhile, as the fiscal expenditure was paving the way for issuance of various reform measures (e.g. the rising purchase price of ASPs and the increase of urban employees' wages and bonuses as mentioned above required increasing fiscal expenditure), it was put under greater pressure (the fiscal expenditure in 1982 grew by 3.3% over the previous year, and by 12.1% in 1983 as against 1980. From 1978 to 1993, its average annual growth rate was 11.0% (National Bureau of Statistics of China, 1994).

Inevitably this resulted in the increase of the fiscal deficit in 1982 (from RMB 9.859 billion in 1981 to RMB 11.240 billion in 1982). Ever since then, the fiscal deficit tended to grow year after year.

The reality made people realize that China's finance must seek support from national debts and that issuing national debts would be a long-term economic activity instead of an expedient economic instrument.

This foresight resulted in remarkable achievements in the issuance of national debts:

1. The issuing scale of national debts expanded rapidly from RMB 4 billion (1981–1984) to 6 billion (1985–1986), 16 billion (1987), 25 billion (1988), 27.5 billion (1989), 38 billion (1992) and 37 billion (1993). In 1994, the figure jumped to RMB 115 billion, more than 20 times that in the early 1980s.
2. The type of national debts expanded from single government bond (1981–1986) to state major construction bond (1987), fiscal bond (1988), state construction bond (1988), special bond (1989), indexed bond (1989) and rollover bond (1991). The term of national debts evolved from single 10-year term (1981–1984) to five-year term (1985), three-year term (1988) as well

as half-year term, one-year term and two-year term (1994). In 1992, the non-physical bonds were also issued nationwide.

3 The purchaser of national debts was transferred from organizations to individuals. In 1981, the national debts were mostly purchased by enterprises, public institutions, government agencies and rich rural communes, excluding resident individuals. From 1982, however, resident individuals became leading purchasers of national debts. In 1983, the quantity of national debts purchased was evenly shared by individuals and organizations, and in 1985, the individuals' quantity outnumbered the organizations'. In 1989, other types of national debts than fiscal bond and special bond were purchased by individuals. Ever since then, individual residents (including individual businesses) had been the main force of national debts purchasers for many years.
4 The mode of issuance of national debts tended to be determined by the market. From 1981 to 1989, all national debts issued were mostly purchased pursuant to state quotas. In 1990, part of national debts was issued pursuant to market rules. In 1991, the tentative underwriting of the national debts was carried out. In 1992, national debts were issued through competitive bidding. In 1993, the primary dealer system of national debts was put into practice. In 1994, almost all of the national debts were issued pursuant to market rules.
5 Conditions of issuance of national debts were inclined towards the purchaser's preference. From 1981 to 1984, all national debts featured a long repayment term, poor liquidity and low interest rate, even lower than the bank savings rate in the same period. In 1985, the issuing conditions of national debts were improved as required by purchasers: the maturity term was shortened from original 10 years to five years, three years and further to two years, one year and half a year; and holders were allowed to discount or mortgage their national debts halfway. In 1988, the secondary market was opened so that the trading of national debts became possible; the interest rate was raised, even a bit higher than the bank savings rate in the same period; in addition, the custody service was launched so that holders could entrust the Industrial and Commercial Bank of China (ICBC) with management of their national debts.
6 The NDM's work scope widened. From 1981 to 1985, the NDM's work was limited to selling national debts. In 1986, the principal and investment repayment system was put on the agenda. In 1988, the secondary market of national debts was opened. As a result, the NDM activities incorporated all aspects of national debts, including issuance, repayment, circulation and transfer.

IV Snowballing scale of national debts during repayment peak

Both the principal and interest of national debts are considered a special debt spending item under national fiscal expenditure and need to be repaid eventually.

In 1986, repaying the principal and interest of national debts was put on the agenda. The initial repayment task seemed not so tough as expected because there were only 20% of the principal and interest of national debts issued in 1981 that needed to be repaid, i.e. RMB 0.798 billion. With the expanding scale of national debts, the debt spending grew sharply when the debt repayment peak arrived in 1990, e.g. RMB 2.318 billion in 1987, almost three times that in 1986. In 1990, the amount jumped to RMB 37.5 billion, occupying as high as 10.5% of the fiscal expenditure in the current year. During 1991 and 1992, the amount reached up to RMB 42.8 billion and 41.6 billion respectively (Zhang Jialun et al., 1992).

The expenditure of repaying the principal and interest of national debts, which amounted to several ten billions, would deteriorate China's fiscal conditions that had already suffered extreme difficulties. What the government could do at this moment was issue new debts to repay the old ones.

In fact, as early as in May 1988 and prior to the arrival of the repayment peak, the NDM Division of the Ministry of Finance (China) proposed extension of the repayment period to address the repayment peak in its report, *National Internal Debts and Repayment of the Principal and Interest*. It was envisaged that, rather than repayment of the principal and interest, all matured bonds held by organizations would be exchanged for new convertible bonds pursuant to the amount of the principal and interest payable, and all matured bonds held by individuals would be exchanged for new bonds to be issued according to the amount of the principal and interest payable (Zhang Jialun et al., 1992).

This proposal was initially put into practice during repayment of the national debts which matured in 1990, amounting to about RMB 37.5 billion almost equally split between organizations and individuals. On June 14, 1990, the Ministry of Finance and the People's Bank of China jointly promulgated the *Notice on Suspending Repayment of Organizations' National Debts Matured in 1990*, which decided on delayed repayment of all national debts (matured in 1990) held by enterprises, public institutions, government agencies and organizations as well as military units and financial institutions, and on repayment of individuals' national debts matured on July 1, 1990 by increasing the issuance of new bonds.

The national debts which matured in 1991 had been repaid pursuant to the plan made in 1988, where the matured bonds held by organizations were exchanged for convertible bonds in a more normative manner of issuing roll-over debts. In January 1991, the State Council promulgated the *Notice on Issuing Roll-Over Debts in 1991*, which decided on the conversion of matured national debts held by enterprises, public institutions and organizations as well as military units in to equivalent new five-year debts with an annual interest rate of 8%, and on repayment as scheduled of matured national debts held by individuals in a manner of borrowing new debts.

Based on successful practice in 1990 and 1991, the Chinese government seemed to have found solutions for the repayment of matured national debts. Against the real background of fiscal difficulties, repayment of old debts through issuance of new debts (which also applied to roll-over debts held by organizations) had become an inevitable choice for the Chinese government to address matured national debts. Since 1992, it was in this way that the Chinese government tried to get through the peak period of debt repayment totaling several ten billions.

Apparently, issuing new debts as a funding source for national debts expenditure consisting of both the principal and interest on national debts led to a "vicious circle" of snowballing scale of national debts, though it secured on-time repayment of matured national debts. Besides, converting matured bonds held by organizations through issuing roll-over debts would do harm to the reputation of national debts. Nevertheless, pros and cons arising therefrom has become a complex problem that requires serious consideration, analysis of which will not be detailed in this paper. However, please be noted: it was the repayment of old debts through issuing new debts that caused the expanding scale of issuance of national debts in China since 1990.

V Conclusion

In this paper, a general analysis was conducted for reasons of the rapid expansion of China's national debts since the economic system reform in 1978. As this topic involves almost all aspects of the economic system reform, some details may be overlooked in the process of analysis, but the analytic process is basically right.

According to analysis results, the rapid expansion of China's national debts occurred during the economic system reform, but it was not a product of the reform. The difference was that the economic system reform's effect on national debts had become increasingly significant.

The expanding scale of China's national debts since the economic system reform was basically caused by the decrease of regular revenues delivered by industrial and commercial taxes and SOEs after the breakup of the traditional fiscal revenue mechanism based on the "low selling price of ASPs and low wage system" to provide "supernormal" fiscal revenue, where, the national debts, as an auxiliary or supplementary source of fiscal revenue, were repeatedly used to fill the gap left over by the decreasing regular fiscal revenues. In addition, the expanding scale of national debts could also be attributed to the "repaying the old debts by borrowing new ones" circle at the arrival of the repayment peak.

The effect of the expanding scale of fiscal expenditure on the expanding scale of national debts in the same period could be traced back to the fact that the expanding scale of fiscal expenditure consisted of the expanding debt expenditure and price subsidy expenditure. The expanding debt expenditure was the expanding scale of national debts caused by the decreasing regular fiscal revenues while the root reason for the expanding price subsidy expenditure was the rising purchase price of ASPs at the cost of relatively decreasing regular revenues. In fact, the price subsidy expenditure in China had been used to supplement fiscal revenues before 1985; in other words, both the expanding debt expenditure and the price subsidy expenditure could be attributed to the decreasing regular fiscal revenues. Therefore, the expanding debt expenditure seemed not to be the root reason for the expanding scale of China's national debts in this period.

The extensional meaning of the above inference: in today's China, repairing loopholes in the decreasing fiscal revenues may be an effective method to discontinue the expanding scale of national debts, help China's national debts out of the "vicious circle" and realize growth of both the regular fiscal revenue and the national economy. This does not mean that cutting fiscal expenditure is effective for reducing the issuing scale of national debts, but it seems less effective for curbing the decreasing regular fiscal revenue at least in the recent period.

(Originally published in *Finance & Trade Economics*, Vol.4, 1995)

Bibliography

Lai Ruihua (1991). *Agricultural fund research of China*. Beijing: China Renmin University Press.

National Bureau of Statistics (1994). *China statistic yearbook (1994)*. Beijing: Statistical Press of China.

Chu Xinghua, & Xie Chun. (1993, October 20). Why are there so many tax loopholes? *Economic Daily*.

Integrated Planning Division, MOF. *Finance yearbook of China (1950–1991)*. (1992). Beijing: Science Press.

GaoJian. (1993). *The problem of national debts in China*. Beijing: China Financial & Economic Publishing House.

Ma Hong. (1982). *Economic encyclopedia of China*. Beijing: China Social Sciences Publishing House.

Yuan Zhenyu. (1991). *Research on financial deficit*. Beijing: China Financial & Economic Publishing House.

Zhang Jialun, et al. (1992). *Analysis of national debts in New China*. Beijing: China Financial & Economic Publishing House.

3 Empirical analysis of the influence of China's national debts on total social demand

The control of social purchasing power (especially compression of private purchasing power) has been treated by China's economic theorists as one of the roles of borrowing national debts. Dramatically, however, the expanding scale of national debts always concurred with the rising general price level. In 1994 when the national debts rose over RMB 100 billion, the price rise rate exceeded 20% for the first time since the economic system reform in 1978. Then there arises a question: is the influence of national debts on total social demand contractionary or expansionary in China?

In this paper, an empirical analysis is conducted of the influence of national debts on total social demand since the economic system reform in China. The analysis will address the national debts' effects on households, enterprises, governments, residents' consumption, enterprise investment, fiscal expenditure and total social demand.

Here are two points worthy of much attention. First, all households, enterprises and governments are defined with real conditions in China. Governments mean social and public service institutions such as legislature, administration, national defense, science and technology, education, culture and sports. Enterprises include SOEs, collective enterprises, Sino-foreign joint venture and rural collective economic organizations. Households refer to residents, including individual workers. Then, changes that have taken place in resident's consumption, enterprise investment and fiscal expenditure since the economic system reform are the result of joint action by various factors including national debts. In the current statistical system of China, there are no relatively accurate data corresponding to a certain factor; therefore, alternatives are adopted to get closer to the reality. In this regard, a general trend will be provided by the empirical analysis in this paper.

I Disposable income and interest rate: two factors that led to changes in household and enterprise behaviors

1 Disposable income

The influence of national debts on household and enterprise disposable incomes in China was derived from the re-issuance and expanding scale of national debts. The author pointed out in the *Empirical Analysis of China's National Debts since the Economic System Reform*[1] that the expanding scale of national debts since the economic system reform could be attributed to the fiscal policy of reducing tax and allowing enterprises to retain more profits by continuously issuing national debts for consecutive years. In other words, the fiscal policy of reducing tax and allowing enterprises to retain more profits was reflected by comparative decline of the non-repayable fiscal revenue, and the fiscal expenditure gap caused thereby would be "filled" by issuing national debts. To some extent, national debts was one of the important reasons for the government to reduce tax on households and enterprises and keep national finance in operation during the huge loss of tax and massive conversion of on-budget revenue into estimated revenue since 1978. It was during the relative decline of the non-repayable fiscal revenue that China's government debt, as an auxiliary or supplementary source of fiscal revenue, play its roles in fiscal practice.

Then, the relative decline in non-repayable fiscal revenue led directly to the increase in household and enterprise disposable incomes, and the consequent issuance of national debts would not influence the increase of households' and enterprises' disposable incomes unless purchased by state quotas, because it was classified as outgoings (rather than deduction from total income) of the household and enterprise disposable incomes and an alternative means of savings or investment of the household and enterprise disposable incomes. In addition, even though purchased by state quotas, the national debts would have less offset effect on the increase in household and enterprise disposable incomes because of repayment of the principal and interest at maturity.

The above statement is supported by statistical data. With the expanding issuance of national debts for more than a decade, both the total amount and share of the household and enterprise incomes kept rising.

From 1978 to 1992, the total amount of household and enterprise incomes grew by 7.7 times from RMB 188.888 billion to 1636.163 billion. In the same period, the national income increased by 5.6 times from RMB 301 billion to RMB 11,984.5 billion, and the non-repayable fiscal revenue excluding debt revenue increased by 2.1 times from RMB 112.112 billion to RMB 348.347 billion. The growth rate of household and enterprise incomes was obviously higher than that of national income and non-repayable fiscal revenue. It was thus an easy job to imagine the tendency towards which different growth levels would direct the national income distribution structure.

The household and enterprise incomes accounted for 62.8% of the gross national income, but the figure grew by 19.1 percentage points to 81.9% in 1992; meanwhile, the non-repayable fiscal revenue decreased from 37.2% in 1978 to 19.1% in 1992. It was not hard to understand the changing tendency of household and enterprise incomes and the government's non-repayable fiscal revenue.

It is certainly less convincing to attribute the increase in household and enterprise disposable income to the national debts' substitution of the non-repayable fiscal revenue than to say that the former is an important reason for the latter.

Based on the above facts, we can justify that in this period there was at least a considerable amount of disposable income equivalent to total debt borrowed by the government flowing into households and enterprises when the non-repayable fiscal revenue was substituted for national debts.

2 Change of interest rate

The interest rate on China's national debts is currently contingent on the bank savings rate, i.e. the administrative interest rate. At this point, it seems hard to determine how the successive issuance of national debts influences the interest rate level; however, it is not hard to find the inherent link between them from the following two phenomena.

After 1985, the issuing rate of national debts in China remained about 2 percentage points higher than the bank savings rate in the same period and kept pace with the Central Bank's adjustments of the bank interest rate. A typical example occurred in 1993 when the bank savings rate was up-regulated twice by the Central Bank to implement microeconomic policy, and the interest rate of two types of treasury bonds issued that year was also up-regulated twice, with the interest rate of three-year treasury bonds up-regulated from 10% to 12.52% and further to 13.96% and the interest rate of five-year treasury bonds up-regulated from 11% to 14.06% and further to 15.86%, still higher by 1.72 and 2 percentage points than the bank savings rates respectively in the same period. This seemed necessary to protect the interests of national debts purchasers, but in fact it implied the fiscal authority's motivation to compete with banks for urban and rural residents' savings funds. However, it was undoubted that such competition for urban and rural residents' savings funds based on a higher level of interest rate had constituted an important reason for the increase in bank rates and other interest rates. In addition, the rising interest rates would influence the Central Bank's decision on the interest rate level.

In recent years, fiscal authority required control of the fund-raising interest rate because the fund-raising activities at a higher interest rate through enterprise bonds, investment bonds and various funds had a serious impact on the issuance of national debts. From February to April 1993, the State Council published several documents stating that the interest rate of other bonds should not exceed the interest rate of treasury bonds for the same period, that no bonds or stocks should be issued until the issuance of treasury bonds and that all stock exchanges were prohibited to launch other bonds on market. These measures were essential for the issuance of treasury bonds and the smooth operation of national finance. However, when much attention was drawn to the competition between the fund-raising activities at a higher interest rate and the issuance of national debts, another problem arising therefrom was that the booming issuance of national debts also contributed a lot to the fund-raising activities at a higher interest rate. In fact, the amount of national debts issued occupied a majority of various debts (including stock) issued nationwide in recent years, and the economic entities referred largely to the interest rate of national debts (not the interest bank savings rate) when determining their financing rate. To some extent, it was the higher interest rate of national debts that contributed to the rising interest rate of all fund-raising activities.

From this phenomena, the successive issuance of national debts in China has contributed to the rising interest rate, but such contribution came in an indirect or invisible manner under the current interest rate management system. In the 1980s, all the interest rates including the bank savings rate were on the rise, to which the issuance of national debts had contributed a lot.

II Household and enterprise behaviors during the borrowing of national debts

As discussed, the successive issuance of national debts since the economic system reform in 1978 has caused two significant changes: (1) the increase in households' and enterprises' disposable incomes and (2) the rising interest rate including the interest rates of bank savings and loans. Then, how are household and enterprise behaviors adjusted when significant changes have taken place in above two factors?

1 Business sector – the so-called "transient god of wealth"

The increasing disposable income of households and enterprises is first justified by the increase of enterprises' disposable revenue. According to statistics, the amount of the retained profit and its rate by enterprises has greatly increased due to tax cuts for more than a decade; for instance, the retained profit increased from RMB 2.75 billion in 1978 to RMB 55.54 billion in 1991, and the retention rate went up from 3.7% in 1978 to 65.3% in 1991. These figures indicate that the business sector has become the number one "God of Wealth" of all sectors in China. In fact, however, the business sector is merely a "transient god of wealth".

The reason is that most of the wealth gained by enterprises from tax cuts flew into the hands of residents (households). According to the national regulation on the use of retained profits by SOEs, part of the after-tax profits should be split at 6:2:2, i.e. 60% used for enterprise development fund, 20% for the staff's bonus fund and the remaining 20% for the staff's welfare fund. According to typical surveys, however, the amount of retained profits for the two funds far surpassed those used for the enterprise development fund. In reality, the distribution of retained profits was prioritized for the staff's bonus and welfare, then for repayment of various unproductive expenditure items and finally for the enterprises' production and development.

Moreover, according to statistics on the final distribution of national income in China, during 1980–1990, the income of the government sector decreased by 7.69 percentage points from 21.72% to 14.03% and that of the business sector decreased by 13.39 percentage points from 30.73% to 17.34% while the income of households increased rapidly by 21.08 percentage points from 47.55% to 68.63%.

In effect, enterprises as the main objects of tax cuts and profit retention acted as a medium to transfer the national income from government to households; in other words, the only "winner" during the change of national income distribution was households that took away part of both the government and enterprises' incomes. It is thus very appropriate to describe business sector as the "transient god of wealth".

The reasons may vary, but there is only one result: an increasing amount of disposable income flowing into resident households in various forms has triggered the expansion of consumer demand.

2 Increase in residents' disposable income and expansion of consumer demand

According to existing statistics, the residents' disposable income has increased unprecedentedly since the 1970s. During 1978–1991, urban and rural residents' disposable income grew 6.5 times at an average annual growth rate of 17%, where the average per capita monetary income of urban residents increased 2.6 times at an average annual growth rate 10.4% and that of rural residents grew 4.3 times at an average annual growth rate of 14.3%.

Inevitably, the rapid increase in residents' disposable income led to the expansion of consumer demand. What was worse, this rising trend had persisted rather than been curbed under the conditions specified below: (1) people who had been living in the era of the "iron bowl" (free of worry about unemployment) and the "big-pot system" (equalitarian treatment of enterprises and individuals regardless of their performances) for several decades would place higher expectations on future income during the rapid increase in disposable incomes; (2) with narrower channels for individuals' investment, the residents' disposable income would mostly flow into the consumer sector; and (3) the reform of individual income distribution system in China allowed individuals to receive a one-yuan subsidy (monetary income) for one yuan retained (welfare) by themselves. Welfare made it possible that a considerable part of residents' consumer goods was not purchased by their monetary incomes from the market but provided by the government or enterprises free of charge or at low price. While the residents' monetary income increased, they still felt that their income was insufficient due to narrow expenditure items and unsmooth consumption channels.

Table 3.1 gives the changes in the distribution structure of residents' disposable incomes during 1978–1991. With the rapid growth of their disposable income, residents' marginal consumption rate declined, which further led to a decrease in average consumption rate. The marginal consumption rate maintained at about 80%, except for a few years (1989 and 1990) when it was below 50%. This means that about 80% of residents' disposable incomes that increased yearly were transferred to consumer demand.

If it is acknowledged that the increase in residents' disposable income was promoted by successive issuance of national debts, there would be a logical relation as described below: the issuance of national debts in support of tax cuts and profit retention brought down the government's non-repayable fiscal revenue; as a result, an increasing amount of national income flew into resident households through the business sector; and residents spent most of their increased disposable income on consumer goods, leading to the expanding consumer demand of residents.

Table 3.1 Distribution structure of residents' disposable incomes (1978–1991) (Units: RMB 100 million, %)

Year	*Total amount of residents' disposable income*	*Average consumption rate*	*Average saving rate*	*Average annual increase in residents' disposable income*	*Marginal consumption rate*	*Marginal saving rate*
1978	1622	98.2	1.8	178	96.4	3.6
1979	1927	96.4	3.6	305	96.6	13.4
1980	2333	95	5	406	88.6	11.4
1981	2550	95.2	4.8	217	98.7	1.3
1982	2800	94.6	5.4	250	89.4	10.6
1983	3178	93.2	6.8	378	83	17
1984	4027	92.2	7.8	849	88.9	11.1
1985	5243	92.3	7.7	1216	82.3	7.7
1986	6293	89.5	10.5	1050	63.8	36.2
1987	6872	88	12	579	80.5	19.5
1988	8837	91.8	8.2	1965	105.6	–5.4
1989	10031	86.6	13.4	1194	48.4	51.6
1990	10989	82.8	17.2	958	40.8	59.2
1991	12198	83	17	1209	84.4	15.6

Source: Quoted from Xie Pin's *Analysis of Individuals' Saving Behaviors in China, Journal of Financial Research*, 1993.

3 Rise in interest rates and expansion of enterprises' investment demand

On the one hand, enterprises encountered limited additional funds for production and development as their retained profits "leaked" into resident households in various forms. On the other hand, the investment cost increased due to increasing interest rates, especially the bank savings and loan rates. Under such circumstances, it seemed more logical for the enterprises' investment demand to be depressed than to be expanded; however, such expansion had occurred and would be likely to persist for long.

From Table 3.2 below, (1) the enterprises' total investment increased 5–6 times from 1979 to 1988. If the depreciation factor was not excluded, the net increase in enterprise investment grew 20 times from 1979 to 1988; even if the price rise factors were excluded, the increase remained high, and (2) in 1979, the total government investment and net government investment were far beyond the total investment and net investment of enterprises. In 1988, however, both the total investment and net investment of enterprises ranked first nationwide.

Why did this peculiar phenomenon happen? It could be analyzed from the following two perspectives.

Perspective 1: Elasticity of investment to interest rate. As mentioned above, enterprises were regarded as the "transient god of wealth" under the then system because they placed more emphasis on consumption (immediate interests) than on accumulation (long-term interests). This does not mean that they had no desire to

Table 3.2 Total investment and net investment of all institutional sectors (1979–1988) (Units: RMB 100 million)

Items \ Year	1979	1980	1981	1982	1983	1984	1985	1986	1987	1988
Total investment of government	592	504	434	430	517	643	715	876	858	866
Where: depreciation	60	69	75	87	106	121	143	171	202	258
Net investment	532	435	359	343	411	522	572	705	656	608
Total investment of enterprises	477	587	598	637	660	989	1659	1653	1987	2704
Where: depreciation	431	471	517	583	669	769	899	1087	1352	1783
Net investment	46	116	81	54	–9	220	760	566	635	921
Total investment of resident households	212	267	240	272	410	520	692	831	943	1253
Where: depreciation	87	114	134	156	192	239	309	346	419	621
Net investment	125	153	106	116	218	281	383	485	524	632

Source: Quoted from the *Distribution and Use of GNP in China* by GuoShuqing et al, Beijing: China Renmin University Press, 1991.

promote profit growth by means of investment, nor does it mean that they could not increase their investment by use of external funds.

Since the economic system reform in 1978, in fact, all previous adjustments of the profit distribution between government and enterprises had not depressed enterprises' desire to make investment; instead, enterprises' investment was increasingly motivated by immediate interests due to the close connection between their retained profit and total profit. Moreover, as internal financing may hinder enterprises' immediate profit, enterprises tended to seek fund support from outside.

However, funds sourced from outside, whether borrowing bank loans or issuing bonds, would be repaid with interest. The interest cost depended directly on the interest rate. So, the rising interest rate would certainly constitute restriction on enterprises' investment demand.

The elasticity of investment to interest rate was greatly weakened for the following reasons: (1) after more than a decade's reform, Chinese enterprises (mainly SOEs) had not become economic entities in a real sense due to the "parent-child" relation between government and enterprises; consequently, while the rising interest rate may increase the cost of enterprises' investment cost, they could transfer their interest burden to the government through reducing or putting off delivery of profits; even if enterprises could not afford repayment of the principal and interest, they were not allowed to declare bankruptcy, so their loss would be borne by the government; for this reason, enterprises may overlook restriction on interest cost when applying for loans; (2) the Central Bank's control of the type and size of interest rates disqualified local commercial banks' right to regulate interest rates where necessary. The rigid management system of interest rates that had resulted in disconnection between the interest rate level and the actual demand and supply of capital could hardly perform its function of interest rate adjustment; (3) under the system of repayment loans before tax, enterprises could repay loans and interests with money that should be delivered to the Treasury, so the interest cost would only influence enterprises' investment returns rather than their investment activities; and (4) seeking profit was not the only motivation of enterprises to make investment under the then financial system; the rising interest rate could only have restricted the profit-motivated investment activities.

Perspective 2: Elasticity of household savings to interest rate. When the elasticity of enterprises' investment to interest rate was weak or insufficient, the elasticity of household savings to interest rate would become more flexible. In the 1980s, especially after 1989, the urban and rural residents' marginal saving rate and the average saving rate had increased significantly, where the former increased from 3.6% in 1978 to 15.6% in 1991 (51.6% and 59.2% in 1989 and 1991 respectively), and the latter increased from 1.8% in 1978 to 17% in 1991. The decisive reason may be the high bank savings rate for the same period, notwithstanding other reasons such as the increase of residents' disposable income and the rapid expansion of savings outlets.

In recent years, the interest rate (especially the effective interest rate) has substantially stimulated the increase in household savings in China. Here is a typical example: numerous purchasers used to queue up for national debts, corporate bonds or financial bonds issued at an interest rate 1–2 percentage points higher than the bank savings interest rate for the same period. What's more, when bank deposit rate went up or when residents' savings increased, the interest income of residents came to take up a considerable proportion of their disposable income (e.g. residents' interest income in 1992 accounted for 7% of total residents' disposable income in 1991). This in turn increased the amount of residents' savings and resulted in a positive cycle: rise of interest rate → increase of household savings → increase of residents' interest incomes → acceleration of household savings.

It was in this cycle that China's urban and rural savings witnessed a dramatic increase. During 1978–1995, the average annual growth rate of urban and rural saving savings was 36%. By the end of 1995, the total amount of urban and rural savings throughout the country reached up to RMB 2.5 trillion, increasing 117 times from RMB 21.06 billion in 1978.

The rapid growth in household saving savings gave rise to great changes in the total savings structure of China. Since 1985, the proportion of household savings took up more than half of the total saving savings nationwide, and became the main source of investment funds. The major saving entities were transferred from government and enterprises (both accounting for 68.66% of total savings in 1980) to residents (accounting for 70.51% of total savings in 1991). This transfer means that the elasticity of total saving savings to interest rate had become increasingly sensitive.

Clearly, when the bank deposit rate rose, the enterprise investment increased (not decreased) because it is less elastic to bank rate than the resident's savings. The former enabled the rising interest rate to have little restriction on enterprise investment while the latter allowed enterprise investment to easily find external capital. Then, the direction to which the enterprise investment would move became quite clear.

Based on the above-mentioned fact and the rising interest rate due to successive issuance of national debts, we concluded: the issuance of national debts in China raised the interest rate; under the transitional system, the rising interest rate failed to restrict enterprises' investment demand; instead, it provided external capital for the demand by stimulating the rapid increase in residents' savings; as a result, enterprises' investment demand was expanded rather than depressed.

III Government behaviors during issuance of national debts

1 Issuance of national debts and expansion of fiscal expenditure

According to the national fiscal revenue and expenditure indices during 1979–1994 in Table 3.3, (1) the fiscal revenue and expenditure increased synchronically

Table 3.3 National fiscal revenue and expenditure indices (1979–1994)

Item / Year	*Total Revenue*	*Where*		*Total Expenditure*	*Where*	
		Non-repayable income	*Debt income*①		*Nonproductive expenditure*	*Transfer expenditure*②
1979	98.4	95.3	–	114.7	114.5	122.2
1980	96.8	93	121.8	109.2	106.5	270.2
1981	97.2	91	207	100.4	94.3	467.7
1982	100.3	92.8	237.5	103.8	98.5	425.4
1983	111.4	104.3	225	116.3	112.2	367.7
1984	134	127.1	219	139.2	136.6	299
1985	166.5	158.5	254.5	166.1	162.3	390.9
1986	201.6	189.3	391.5	209.8	191	1344.5
1987	211.3	196.2	480.2	220.4	186.4	2273.2
1988	234.4	210.3	766.9	243.6	207.8	2406.5
1989	263	237.7	801.4	273.7	232.8	2739.1
1990	295.5	262	1063.3	319.7	267.7	3461.8
1991	322.1	281	1306.7	343.3	286	3802.6
1992	370.4	310.7	1896.6	395.1	326	4569.7
1993	456.2	394.3	1965.0	479	442.2	3881.9
1994	570.2	465.4	3328.3	567.1	484.2	4806.8

①The debt income index is calculated taking the year 1979 as 100.

②The transfer expenditure covers price subsidy expenditure, debt repayment, and pensions and social relief expenditure. Other expenditures than those mentioned above are treated as nonproductive expenditure items. All money paid out is calculated by the current statistical caliber, with no adjustment being made.

Source: China Statistical Yearbook (1995), China Statistics Press, 1995.

in the 16 years except the three-year period from 1979 to 1981; (2) however, the growth of non-repayable fiscal income was much lower than the growth of fiscal expenditure, and the latter almost doubled the former; and (3) the debt income increased significantly. It is thus concluded that the fiscal expenditure increased during that period due to successive issuance of national debts. If the government had followed the rule "without external or external debts" established two decades ago and supported the fiscal expenditure only by using non-repayable income, the growth rate of fiscal expenditure would drop to that of non-repayable fiscal revenue. In other words, it was the successive issuance of national debts that made it possible for the fiscal expenditure to expand during the decline of in non-repayable fiscal revenue.

2 In-depth analysis: influence on the total social demand

According to Table 3.3, during 1979–1994, the growth of nonproductive expenditure failed to synchronize with the total fiscal expenditure, the former much slower than the latter, indicating that (1) during the 15 years, the proportion of nonproductive expenditure in total fiscal expenditure fell from 98.26% in 1979 to 85.57% in 1994, and (2) the proportion of transfer expenditure in total fiscal expenditure went up from 1.74% in 1979 to 14.43% in 1994.

As all forms of fiscal revenue were combined by the government, the distribution of fiscal expenditure amount arising from the issuance of national debts between nonproductive expenditure and transfer expenditure could be roughly estimated in the overall structure of the government's fiscal expenditure.

Based on the fact that only the government's nonproductive expenditure was directly added to total social demand as a new demand factor, we thus concluded that: (1) most of the nonproductive expenditure items under less budgetary restriction of the government due to the issuance of national debts were added to the original total social demand and (2) the proportion of nonproductive expenditure items in the government's fiscal expenditure under less budgetary restriction of the government due to the issuance of national debts indicated a downtrend, thus decreasing its proportion directly added to the original total social demand from 92.41% in 1981 (when the national debts were initially issued) to 85.57% in 1994.

Conclusion: Based on analysis of the household and enterprise behaviors during the issuance of national debts in previous two sections, we have concluded that the issuance of national debts for more than 10 years in China exerted expansionary influence on the total social demand, including the private consumer demand and private investment demand as well as the government consumer demand.

(Originally published in *Urban Finance Forum*, Vol.4, 1996)

Note

1 For details, please refer to *Finance & Trade Economics* in No.4, 1995.

4 On the relationship between tax and price in the market economy*

Section 1

Taxation theory studies are focused on the influence of national taxation on price changes and the difference in various taxation methods such as tax included in the calculated price and tax excluded in the calculated price. Theoretical studies usually evolve with practice. After tax system reform was initiated in 1994 and proposed that VAT be calculated and levied outside (originally within) the calculated price, rounds of heated discussions were aroused on these two taxation methods. In other words, the tax-price relationship has become a hot topic of taxation theory studies.

Opinions varied during heated discussions. For instance, some argued that tax should be included in the selling price so that taxpayers would not raise commodity prices and thus transfer tax to their consumers. If taxes are excluded as an independent element from commodity price, taxpayers and bearers would be separated. Some others argued that as tax included in price was borne by manufacturers, the changing tax rates would only cause an increase or decrease in enterprise profits; whereas, when tax excluded in price was borne by consumers, the changing tax rates would inevitably lead to fluctuation of commodity prices. It was also inferred that collecting VAT outside the calculated price was one of the main factors leading to the rising commodity prices in 1994.

Similar discussions are too numerous to mention. All of them are addressing one topic, i.e. the tax-price relationship in the market economy. It seems that a theoretical, practical, historical and realistic analysis of this relationship is of great importance to China's taxation theories and tax system reform.

Section 2

In a market economy, the market plays an essential role in allocation of social resources. As known to all, social resources are allocated by the market through price signals, i.e. the fluctuating or changing market prices to reflect the balance of power at both the supply and demand sides.

The impact of taxation on market prices is reflected by separating prices of taxable commodities at both the supply and demand sides. In other words, after tax levy by the government, prices of the taxable commodities are separated into two different prices, i.e. the price paid by consumers (or the market price) and the price actually received by the manufacturer (or the net price). In general, the price paid by consumers rises over the pre-tax price while the price received by the manufacturer falls below the pre-tax price. The price margin thereof is deemed as taxable limit. There are few cases in which either of two prices is equal to its pre-tax price.

In Figure 4.1, *D* and *S* standard respectively for the consumer's demand curve and the manufacturer's supply curve. Before tax levy by the government, *D* and *S* intersect at the *E* point to produce P^*, standing for the market equilibrium price, at which a transaction is conducted between consumer and manufacturer. If the consumer pays P^* and the manufacturer receives P^*, then the sales volume of commodities is q^*.

Before tax levy by the government, the original market equilibrium has been changed. At this time, tax is wedged into prices of both the consumer and manufacturer. The consumer's price rises from P^* to P_d while the manufacturer's price falls from P^* to P_s. The balance between P_d and P_s, *T*, is the tax levied by the government, where P_d is the tax-inclusive price paid by the consumer and P_s is the tax-exclusive price received by the manufacturer.

Specifically, if an ad valorem tax is levied outside the calculated price, and *t* represents the tax rate and *T* represents the tax amount levied by the government, then the influence of taxation on the price of taxable commodities will be:

$$P_d = (1+t)P_s, \text{ in which, } tP_d = T$$

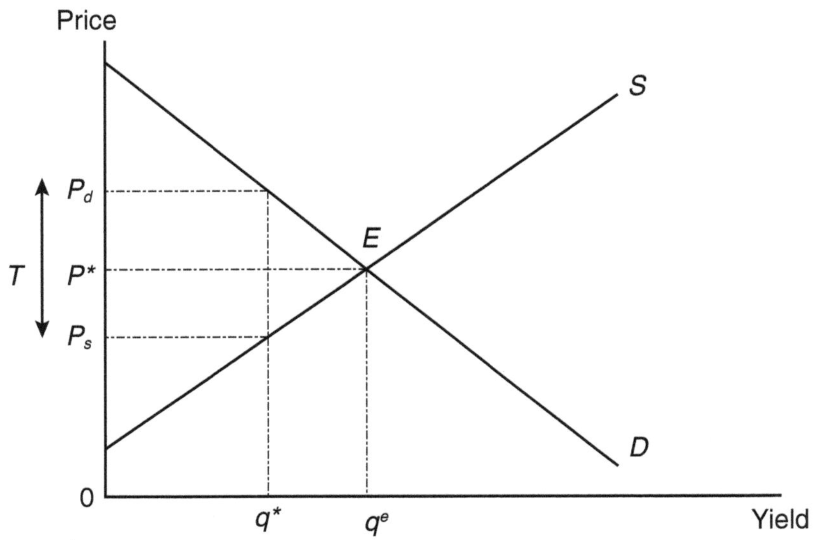

Figure 4.1 Impact of tax on market price

If an ad valorem tax is levied within the calculated price, and t' represents the tax rate and T represents the tax amount levied by the government, then the influence of taxation on the price of taxable commodities will be:

$$P_d = P_s/(1-t'), \text{ in which, } t'P_d = T$$

The sales volume of taxable commodities changes with the separation of two prices. When consumer's price rises from P^* to P_d, the demand falls from qe to q^*. When manufacturer's price declines from P^* to P_s, the demand falls from qe to q^*.

Until now it is clear that P_d paid by the consumer has increased from pre-tax P^* while P_s received by the manufacturer has decreased from pre-tax P^*. In other words, not all of the taxes payable by the manufacturer have been transferred to the consumer. The tax amount, T, collected by the government is shared by both sides, but their respective tax rate is irrelevant to the tax calculation method (tax excluded or included in price).

Then, what are the factors that determine the distribution pattern of tax burden? From Figure 4.1, if the supply-demand elasticity (i.e. the slopes of supply and demand curves) of taxable commodities is consistent, there is roughly an equal increase and decrease of P_d and P_s in relation to P^*, and the tax amount is equally split between the consumer and manufacturer.

Now let's change the demand elasticity to be greater than supply elasticity. The only difference between Figures 4.2 and 4.1 is that the slope of demand curve D is smaller than that of supply curve S, which means that the demand elasticity is greater than supply elasticity. It is thus quite clear that the tax amount T levied by the government still resembles a wedge between P_d (the price paid by consumer) and P_s (price received by manufacturer), but the increase of P_d over pre-tax P^* is less than the decrease of P_s from pre-tax P^*,

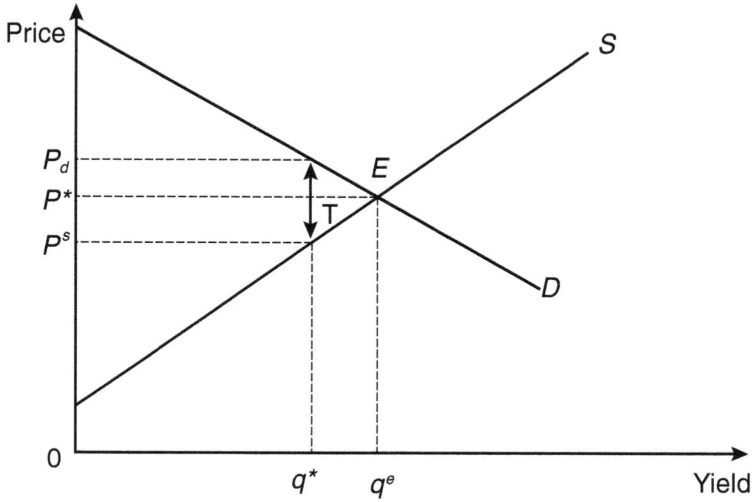

Figure 4.2 Tax-price relationship if demand elasticity is greater than supply elasticity

which means that if the demand elasticity is greater than supply elasticity, the manufacturer pays more tax than the consumer, with a tiny portion transferred to the consumer.

We can also change supply elasticity to be greater than demand elasticity in Figure 4.1. As shown in Figure 4.3, the slope of supply curve *S* is smaller than that of demand curve *D*, indicating that supply elasticity is greater than demand elasticity. After the tax amount *T* is inserted between P_d and P_s, the increase of P_d over pre-tax P^* is larger than the decrease of P_s from pre-tax P^*, which means that if demand elasticity is greater than supply elasticity, a large portion of the tax amount paid by the manufacturer is transferred to the consumer and the manufacturer pays much less than the consumer.

Based on changes in the market equilibrium of taxable commodities before and after tax levy by the government, some correlated conclusions are reached as below:

1 When tax is levied by the government for commodities, whether included in or excluded from the calculated price, the common result is that the increase in commodity price or market price paid by the consumer will decrease the commodity price or net price received by the manufacturer. The tax amount levied by the government is equal to the sum of two prices increased and decreased.
2 In a real economy, a tax is seldom borne by either the manufacturer or consumer alone; instead, it is equally split, and respective share depends on the supply and demand elasticity of taxable commodities.
3 Whether taxes are included or excluded from the calculated price, if the full tax is borne by the consumer or the manufacturer, the elasticity of either

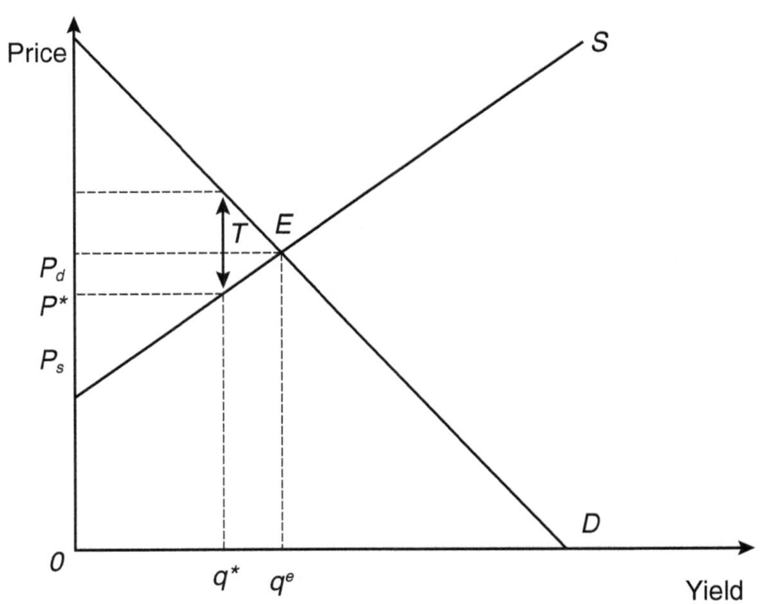

Figure 4.3 Tax-price relationship if demand elasticity is smaller than supply elasticity

the demand or supply curve will be 0 (i.e. demand curve or supply curve is vertical to the horizontal axis). But this is a theoretical hypothesis and barely exists in reality.

4 If the tax amount (or tax burden) levied by the government is not adjusted, the change in tax calculating methods (either included or excluded from the calculated price) will cause variation in taxable commodity prices.

Section 3

After a simple theoretical analysis of the relationship between tax and market price, a further discussion about various opinions on this relationship will be conducted.

It is probably caused by the special tax-price relationship developed under the traditional planned economy system.

In the planned economy, social resources were allocated by the government rather than by the market. The government did it by setting planned prices under unified management, which was steady and unchangeable with the changing supply-demand relation on the market.

Enterprises had to sell products at prices as stipulated and arrange their production activities as scheduled by the government; as a result, product profit could hardly reflect the difference between workers' subjective efforts and enterprises' business performance. Measures must be taken to eliminate the influence of price deviation from value on enterprise profitability and to adjust the product profitability. This is how the "tax included in price" system was created to match the planned price.

In the "tax included in price" system, the turnover tax became part of the planned price, calculated and levied at the tax-inclusive price. As price = cost + tax + profit and the tax rate was designed based on average profitability of different products in different sectors, taxes became a weight to balance the planned price and enterprise profit. The influence of price deviation from value would be eliminated by imposing more tax on products whose price was higher than their value. The after-tax profit earned by different enterprises would be equalized by "imposing higher taxes on higher price".

The tax-price mechanism has the following features:

1 When the planned price was set, some space was reserved for turnover tax, which was one of the components of the planned price. Tax rates for different products were also set according to their planned prices. That is to say, there was mutual restriction between commodity price and tax rate.
2 The changing taxes included in the planned price as one of its elements either synchronized with the adjustment of the planned price or just led to the fluctuation of enterprise profits. Therefore, it was unlikely for taxpayers to transfer all or part of their tax burdens by raising the prices of taxable goods.
3 It seemed that high taxes always came along with high prices, but high or low tax was not the "reasons" for high or low price, and vice versa. On the

contrary, the planned price was set out prior to arrangement of turnover tax rates, with the latter as an auxiliary tool being determined by the former. Taxation acted as a weight to regulate enterprise profitability within the range defined by the planned price.

Section 4

As to the relationship between tax and price, varying opinions may arise from the fact that the difference between the market economy and the traditional economy was overlooked.

1 The price means the market price in the market economy and the planned price in the planned economy. The former reflects comparative strengths of supply and demand fluctuating with the changing supply-demand relation on market. The latter is under unified management of the government and does not fluctuate with the changing supply-demand relation on the market.
2 In the market economy, taxation may have some effect on commodity prices; from the pricing mechanism, however, prices are determined by market supply and demand while taxation results from the government's economic policy. In the planned economy, tax on commodities keeps pace with pricing as taxation is an auxiliary pricing tool to meet requirements of the government's economic policy.
3 Transfer of tax burden is directly associated with the commodity pricing mechanism. When the interest-driven mechanism is adopted, if commodities are priced freely, i.e. market prices, there is possibility for transfer of tax burden or separation of taxpayers and bearers, whether taxes are included in or excluded from the calculated prices and whether taxpayers are the manufacturer or the consumer. If commodity prices are fixed by the government, however, there will be a different case, whatever taxation method applies or who are taxpayers or bearers. Therefore, taxes adaptive to market prices may be transferred due to elasticity of supply and demand while taxes supplementing the planned prices may not.

In summary, the tax-price relationship in market economy differs greatly from that in planned economy. In case of any confusion or overlook, paradoxes will possibly arise from discussion about how tax included in price and tax excluded from price might influence the economy. Only when value-added taxes are not included in the calculated prices in the context of market economy can we make practical comments.

(Originally published in *Taxation Research*, Vol.6, 1996)

Note

* This paper is co-authored by Prof. Yuan Zhenyu.

5 Study of the economic effect mechanism of national debts issuance

China's national debts are issued to control total social demand and transfer consumer funds to accumulation funds on the ground that: (1) as against bank overdraft, offsetting fiscal deficit by issuing national debts will not lead to expansion of money supply; (2) transferring some private purchasing power to government by issuing national debts will only result in transformation between private expenditure and government expenditure rather than an increase in monetary purchasing power; (3) government behaviors must meet the requirements of macroeconomic policy; in case of inflation, the debt income is not used as expenditure to bring down the monetary purchasing power of the whole society; and (4) a socialist country's finance is designed for production and construction, and uses debt income from consumer funds as fiscal expenditure to transfer consumer funds into accumulation funds.

Dramatically, however, China's issuance of national debts for more than a decade has kept pace with the rising prices and the GDP's utilization structure inclined to the consumer. In 1994, when the amount of national debts exceeded RMB 100 billion, the growth rate of price reached up to 20% for the first time. The problem is: what is the effect mechanism of national debts on economy?

I Ricardian Equivalence Theorem: a heuristic analytical thinking

The study of economic effect mechanism of national debts can trace back to classic economist David Ricardo. In Chapter 17 of his master work, *On the Principles of Political Economy and Taxation*, Ricardo said,

> "When, for the expenses of a year's war, twenty millions are raised by means of a loan, it is the twenty millions which are withdrawn from the productive capital of the nation. The million per annum which is raised by taxes to pay the interest of this loan, is merely transferred from those who pay it to those who receive it, from the contributor to the tax, to the national creditor. The real expense is the twenty millions, and not the interest which must be paid for it. Whether the interest be or be not paid, the country will neither be richer nor poorer. Government might at once have required the twenty

millions in the shape of taxes; in which case it would not have been necessary to raise annual taxes to the amount of a million. This, however, would not have changed the nature of the transaction."

(D. Ricardo, 1817, p 96)

This is the original text known as "Ricardian Equivalence Theorem" by modern economists.

Ricardo's key points can be concluded from this excerpt (Ping Xinqiao, 1992): First, 20 million of taxes or loans will decrease 20 million of productive capital of a nation (for a year's war); second, the principal and interest repayment due to borrowing public debts means nothing but transfer of some people's income to some other people, which will not change the total wealth of a nation; and finally, borrowing debts and taxation making a nation suffer a net loss of 20 million will bring down its people's income and consumer expenditure. The same is true of the effects of public debt and taxation on consumer behavior.

It is clear that Ricardo started his research from analyzing the relationship between public debts and other forms of fiscal revenue. The Ricardian Equivalence Theorem has in fact revealed the comparative effect of debt and taxation, i.e. the government's choice of fiscal revenue forms will not cause adjustments in people's economic behaviors. In other words, whether government chooses taxation or debt or a combination of them to offset fiscal expenditure, people's economic behaviors will not be affected.

Here exists a potential theoretical judgment: fiscal expenditure is fairly "rigid" while fiscal revenue is merely a constraint condition and determined by fiscal expenditure. If the scale of fiscal expenditure is given, either national debts or other forms of fiscal revenue will increase while the other decreases.

Modern economists began paying attention to the Ricardian Equivalence Theorem when they were concerned with the influence of national debts on the macro economy. These economists did not agree with Ricardo, nor did they stay firm on the Ricardian Equivalence Theorem; however, their discussion about the economic effect mechanism of national debts had never broken away from the original ideas of Ricardo. For instance, D. Patinkin's argument that some part equivalent to $K\ (0 \leq K \leq 1)$ of the outstanding national debts, which was treated as the total wealth, would enhance the consumer tendency was based on comparison between loan effect and taxation effect (Patinkin, 1965). J. Tobin's argument on government debt income redistribution effect and the resultant adjustment in individual economic behaviors started from the replacement between loan and taxation (Tobin, 1980).

After a "blank period" of two decades, national debts were reissued in 1979 when the economic system reform was carried out throughout China. The economic system reform had a feature that every step of reform meant reducing tax and allowing enterprises to retain more profits. Fiscal deficits arising from tax cuts needed to be covered by issuance of national debts. In some sense, national debts had provided support for government to expand tax cuts on households and enterprises and to continue operating national finance during losses of tax revenue after 1979 when on-budget revenue was transferred into off-budget revenue.

Looking back to the development more than 10 years ago, we could easily find that financial tax cuts were supported (or exchanged) by successive issuance of national debts during reform in China.

The correlation between tax cuts and successive issuance of national debts implied an important message that analysis of the economic effect mechanism of national debts could begin with comparison between national debts and other forms of fiscal revenue. The implied mutual replacement between national debts and other forms of fiscal revenue could reflect the basic framework of the complex and practical operation of national debts so that we could understand the regularity of national debts' effect on the Chinese economy.

II National debts and private demand: a micro investigation

According to logical order, national debts will first influence households and enterprises through change in private demands, such as private consumption and private investment.

Changes in private consumption and private investment with the issuance of national debts can be analyzed from two agreed conditions: first, if fiscal expenditure is given, it will change with the changing forms of fiscal revenue; then, there are only two forms of fiscal revenue available to the government, i.e. taxation and national debts. Therefore, the balance condition of government budget can be expressed as below:

$$\overline{G} = T + D \tag{5.1}$$

where G stands for fiscal expenditure, T for taxation, D for national debts, and $\overline{G}$ for fixed fiscal expenditure.

In general, under constraint of given fiscal expenditure, the government's issuance of national debts means a decrease in tax revenue (Cavaco-Silva, 1977). If ΔD stands for the amount of national debts issued and $-\Delta T$ for the decrease in tax revenue, then:

$$\Delta D = |-\Delta T| \tag{5.2}$$

The idea that the issuance of national debts causes the decrease in tax revenue (or vice versa) means the following situations: (1) the issuance of national debts may decrease the existing tax revenue; for policy purposes, while debt issuance provides tax relief for micro economic entities, the fiscal deficit caused thereby needs to be covered by the issuance of national debts; (2) the tax revenue that should have increased may not increase during the issuance of national debts; under pressure from some interest groups or based on some considerations, provisional suspension of the planned proposal aiming to increase types of taxes or raise the tax rate makes it possible that the need to increase fiscal revenue will be satisfied by issuing national debts;[1] and (3) tax evasion is severe in some periods so that the government can't solve it in a short time, so tax loss has to be covered by issuing national debts.[2]

Whichever situation occurs, tax loss will result directly in the increase in micro economic entities' disposable after-tax income (Y), and further in a chain reaction: national debts (ΔD) → tax cuts (–ΔT) → increase in disposable income (ΔY). The increased amount of micro entities' disposable income is equal to the amount of national debts issued, i.e.:

$$\Delta Y = \Delta D = |-\Delta T| \quad (5.3)$$

When the equal substitution of national debts for tax revenue (ΔD)|−ΔT|) increases micro economic entities' disposable income (|−ΔT| = |ΔY|), it equally increases the demand for private savings (ΔD). At this time, when the supply of private savings can't increase with the demand, the market equilibrium interest rate will rise.

As described in Figure 5.1, the initial situation is the market equilibrium without national debts. The horizontal axis stands for amounts of savings, investment and national debts, and the vertical axis stands for interest rate. Line I (private investment) stands for demand for savings, and Line S (private savings) stands for supply of savings. Line I and Line S intersect at Point E, suggesting that the equilibrium interest rate is R.

On the one hand, the issuance of national debts increased the demand for savings (ΔD), which caused a parallel translation of the demand curve of savings towards upper right, i.e. from Line I to Line $I + \Delta D$. On the other hand, it equally increased the disposable income of micro economic entities (ΔY) and increased the savings supply (represented by $s'\Delta D$, which is the increased savings in micro economic entities' disposable income ΔY, where s' stands for marginal propensity to save), which caused a parallel translation of savings supply towards lower right, i.e. from Line S to Line $S + s'\Delta D$. $s'\Delta D = \Delta D - c'\Delta D$ ($c'\Delta D$ is the consumption part of

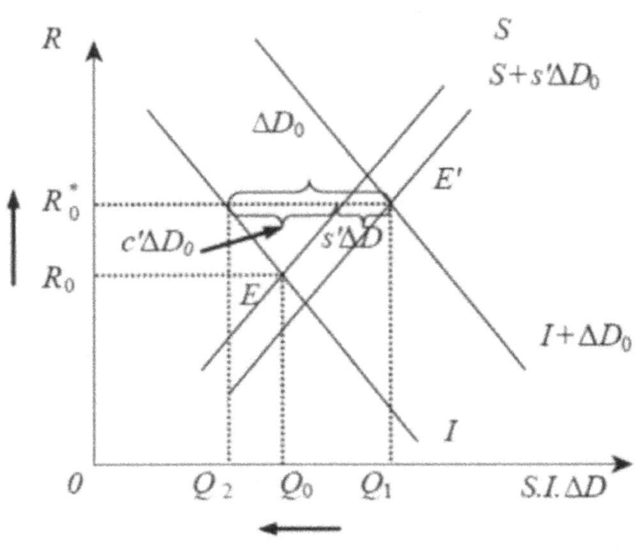

Figure 5.1 Supply of and demand for savings: determination of equilibrium interest rate

micro economic entities' increased disposable income ΔY, where c′ = – s′, and c′ stands for marginal propensity to consume). The increase of savings demand (ΔD) is higher than the increase of its supply (s′ΔD). Therefore, there forms the force to increase the market interest rate. The market equilibrium interest rate determined by Point E' at which Line $I + \Delta D$ and Line S + s′ΔD intersect is R^*:

$$R^* > R \tag{5.4}$$

Households' and enterprises' subscribing national debts and paying taxes mean transferring part of their wealth to the government, but paying taxes is a compulsory transfer of their wealth deductible from their total income while subscribing national debts is a voluntary behavior of savings or investment from their disposable income, which will not change their total wealth. Even though national debts are purchased by state quotas, it is considered as a kind of savings or investment, because both the principal and interest must be repaid eventually.

This idea enlightens the topic discussed in this paper because it means if the disposable incomes (ΔY) are increased due to issuing national debts (ΔD) and decreasing tax revenue (–ΔT), the micro economic entities will certainly spend part of them on immediate consumption. (It is determined by marginal propensity to consume c′. In general, the marginal propensity to consume will in any case be greater than 0.) Even if they need to purchase more national debts in the future, trading one kind of assets (cash or savings) for another kind (national debts) will not change their total wealth. It is unlikely for a rational and economic man to ignore the increase in his disposable income or put them into the bank as savings.

Conclusion 1: Issuance of national debts will certainly increase private consumption. If ΔC stands for increased amount of private consumption, the formula below will work:

$$\Delta C = c'\Delta Y = c'\Delta D = c'(|-\Delta T|) \tag{5.5}$$

As to private investment, on the one hand, it is a function of the interest rate and has a negative correlation with interest rate, which means $I = I(R)$, $dI/dR < 0$. On the other hand, it also stands for the demand for private savings. The market interest rate is determined by comparison between supply of and demand for private savings, so, if the rise in market interest arises from issuance of national debts, private investment's behavior will depend on comparison between its interest rate elasticity and private savings. This can be summarized in three situations below.

Situation 1: The private investment (I) is inelastic to interest rate, but the private savings (S) is elastic to interest rate. When the market interest rate rises, micro economic entities' investment expenditure remains unchanged, but the supply of their savings increases accordingly; as a result, the market interest rate increases with the increasing private savings until it reaches a certain point. In this situation, the increasing equilibrium interest rate due to issuance of national debts will not bring down the private investment, i.e. ΔI = 0.

Situation 2: The private investment (*I*) is elastic to interest rate, but the private savings (*S*) is inelastic to interest rate. When the market interest rate rises, micro economic entities' supply of savings keeps unchanged, but their investment expenditure decreases accordingly; as a result, the market interest rate increases with decreasing private investment until it reaches a certain point. In this situation, the increasing equilibrium interest rate due to issuance of national debts will bring down the private investment, and the decreased amount equals that of private consumption, i.e. $|-\Delta I| = \Delta C\ (= c'\Delta Y)$.

Situation 3: Both the private investment (*I*) and the private savings (*S*) are elastic to interest rate. When market interest rate rises, both the micro economic entities' supply of savings and their investment expenditure will be adjusted accordingly, and both will move towards opposite directions; as a result, the market interest rate increases with the decreasing private investment and increasing private savings until the amount of private savings to increase the amount of national debts is equal to private savings. In this situation, the increasing equilibrium interest rate due to issuance of national debts will bring down the private investment, and the decreased amount of private investment will be less than the increased amount of private consumption, i.e. $|-\Delta I| < \Delta C\ (= c'\Delta Y)$.

Let's look back to Figure 5.1. Line *I* and Line *S* incline towards the lower right and left respectively. At the initial equilibrium, the interest rate is R0; both the private investment and the savings are Q0. When national debts ΔD are issued, the curve of savings demand translates in a parallel manner towards upper right from Line *I* to Line $I + \Delta D$ while the curve of the savings supply translates parallel, towards the lower right from Line *S* to Line $S + s'\Delta D$. Then, a new equilibrium is formed at Point *E'*, where Line I + ΔD and Line S + s'ΔD intersect. The new equilibrium interest rate is R, and R0* > R0; the private investment is Q2, and the balance between Q1 and Q2 is the amount of national debts issued ΔD0.

Clearly, only in the second situation does $|-\Delta I| = \Delta C$ appear. Strictly speaking, however, the first two situations are theoretical hypotheses that hardly happen in practice, and the third is real economic life.

Conclusion 2: The issuance of national debts will increase private consumption and decrease private investment by increasing the equilibrium interest rate. Relatively, the decreased private investment is less than the increased private consumption, so the comprehensive effect is that the private demand (*P*) expands, which is expressed by the following formula (2–6):

$$\Delta P = -\Delta I + \Delta C > 0 \tag{5.6}$$

III National debts and government expenditure: a macro investigation

The issuance of national debts has more direct effect on government than on households and enterprises, seen in the change in government expenditure.

After issuance, the interest on all national debts must be paid on time before maturity pursuant to agreed terms, except the treasury bills (which are usually issued at a discount, with interest withheld). Whatever methods the government adopts to pay the interest, whether installments or bullet repayment, and whatever source of such payment, either increasing tax or issuing new debt, repayment of the interest on national debts certainly constitutes an item under government expenditure, i.e. interest expenditure on national debts.

When national debts become mature, their principal should be repaid as agreed. Similarly, whatever methods the government adopts to pay the principal, whether installments or bullet repayment, and whatever source of such payment, either financing new debt, increasing tax or budget surplus, repayment of the principal of national debts constitutes an item under government expenditure, i.e. capital expenditure on national debts.

Whether to repay the interest or capital, such repayment is an "additional expenditure" in some sense, which means that debt expenditure including interest and capital has resulted from the issuance of national debts.

Besides, debt expenditure has a positive correlation with the scale of national debts, i.e. the greater the scale of national debts is and the greater the pressure to raise market interest rate is, the greater the interest expenditure and capital expenditure for national debts will be.

After analysis of the fiscal expenditure tendency based on political behaviors of government agencies and officers, J. M. Buchanan's Public Choice conducted that the government seeking the greatest power over public institutions instinctively tended to expand fiscal expenditure (Buchanan, 1992).

However, the government's intention to expand fiscal expenditure doesn't mean increasing fiscal expenditure without any limitation. In real economic life, there are factors that may limit the scale of fiscal expenditure. The elasticity of fiscal revenue is a main constraint condition (Liao Le, 1992, p. 164). If the fiscal revenue is constant, it will strongly constrain the government's control of fiscal expenditure, and the government's willingness to enlarge fiscal expenditure will also weaken. On the contrary, if the fiscal revenue is flexible, it will not constrain the government's willingness to expand fiscal expenditure, and its willingness to enlarge fiscal expenditure will strengthen. If the government's fiscal revenue comes only from taxation and national debts are not accepted by micro entities or are forbidden by law, the fiscal revenue will remain relatively constant.[3] In this case, there is a rigid constraint on government's control of fiscal expenditure caused by fiscal revenue. Due to the "coerciveness" and "gratuitousness" of taxation, micro entities' "tolerant" tax level is relatively stable (Atkins & Stiglitz, 1992, p. 412). Generally, there will be resistance against government's intention to increase tax (tax rate or types). Whether it is political or economic resistance, open or implied, it is one factor that constrains the government's intention to "artificially" increase tax revenue. In addition, the "fixed" nature of taxes determines that the tax objects and their proportion or quantity must be confirmed in advance by law. Unless the tax law changes, the government should obey the confirmed standard that can't be changed at will. This is another factor constraining the government's intention to "artificially" increase tax revenue. It is thus apparent that so long as the government's intention to "artificially" increase fiscal revenue[4] is restricted, the government's intention to enlarge fiscal expenditure has to be weakened.

In addition to tax revenue, when the government decides to finance revenue by issuing national debts, increasing tax can be replaced by the issuance of national debts to reach its purpose. Now, fiscal revenue is not relatively constant but tends to increase. In this case, the constraint on government's control of fiscal expenditure caused by fiscal revenue may be flexible because national debts have three natures (voluntariness, reimbursement and flexibility) different from tax. The "voluntariness" and "reimbursement" of national debts mean that micro entities may purchase national debt as a form of their savings or investment. In general, the government's increasing fiscal revenue by issuing national debts will not dissatisfy micro entities. The "flexibility" of national debts means that the issuance of national debts may be adjusted contingent on government financial conditions so as to determine when, how and how many national debts can be issued. The discussion above indicates that it is possible to increase fiscal revenue "artificially".

Obviously, the government's intention to enlarge fiscal expenditure will strengthen as long as fiscal revenue is increased "artificially".

More importantly, if the government's fiscal expenditure is enlarged due to issuance of national debts, the "rigid" nature of fiscal expenditure may lead to a yearly increase in the issuance of national debts so that national debts may be transferred from "temporary revenue" to "recurrent revenue", resulting in further expansion of fiscal expenditure. On the one hand, it seems easier to increase than decrease fiscal expenditure, because increasing fiscal expenditure will provide some direct or indirect interests for micro entities while decreasing fiscal expenditure will be resisted or opposed by vested interests. National debts should be issued on a yearly basis to maintain fixed fiscal expenditure, the scale of which should be increased to ensure that net revenue financed by national debts will not decrease after deducting the debt expenditure or increase over the previous year. Obviously, increasing the issuance of national debts helps increase the fiscal expenditure. On the other hand, as discussed above, the debt expenditure caused by national debts and the increasing debt expenditure caused by increasing the scale of debts are two factors for enlargement of fiscal expenditure.

The analysis above can be verified by literature review. One of the most important reasons why national debts appeared later than taxation is that tax can't satisfy the demand of the increasing fiscal expenditure due to expansion of government functions. If the fiscal expenditure is restrained by the government's capability to keep taxation and budgeted revenue and expenditure in balance, national debts as a method to break or weaken this "restraint" will be favored by government of all countries.

For this reason, economists' explanation of the increasing fiscal expenditure will not work without the rising fiscal revenue (Peacock & Wiseman, 1967). To control fiscal expenditure, the way to restrict the source of fiscal revenue should be found. Buchanan (1992) argued that the decreasing the financial sources was the only way to control the government expenditure.

Conclusion 3: The issuance of national debts to incur government debt expenditure and weaken government budgeted constraint will expand the scale of the government fiscal expenditure.

IV National debts and total social demand: aggregate effect

From a macro perspective, total social demand consists of private consumption, private investment and government expenditure. By investigating the influence of national debts on these factors, we can analyze the overall trend of total social demand.

Analysis above indicates that the influence of national debts on the scale of fiscal expenditure has first incurred the debt expenditure and then weakened the government's budget constraint.

This instructive phenomenon reminds us that the expansionary fiscal expenditure due to the issuance of national debts may influence the total social demand in different ways.

The fiscal expenditure covers different items and is classified by economists for different purposes. It is typically classified into exhaustive expenditure and transfer expenditure according to economic features of the fiscal expenditure, which is an economic analysis method (Chen Gong, 1991), as detailed below:

1 Exhaustive expenditure is directly presented as government actions such as purchasing goods or labor, including expenses for purchasing goods or labor to maintain daily administrative actions or to carry out national investment. The former covers government administrative fees, and the latter includes government capital appropriation. Despite different purposes, there is one similarity: that the government spends money on goods or labor, and then utilizes these goods and labor to perform various government functions. This means that the government makes deals with equivalent exchange as other economic entities usually do.
2 Transfer expenditure is directly presented as gratuitous and unilateral transfer of capital, including expenditure on annuity, subsidiary and dole as well as repayment of principal and interest of debts. The purposes are certainly different, but there is one similarity: that the government gains little after paying the capital. In this process, no exchange has ever occurred.
3 Exhaustive expenditure leads to the fact that some capital controlled by the government is used to trade for goods or labor provided by micro economic entities. In this process, the government is the purchaser of goods or labor in the market to occupy social economic resources under the control of government rather than of households or enterprises. So, the government's exhaustive expenditure is part of total social demand.
4 Transfer expenditure leads to the fact that some capital controlled by the government is invested gratuitously and unilaterally in households or enterprises to create disposable income for micro economic entities. This just means a transfer of capital and doesn't reflect the government's intention to occupy social economic

resources. On the contrary, transfer merely means reallocation of resources among social members, where the government acts as an intermediary. The final destination of the capital is determined by the transfer expenditure's objects (i.e. households and enterprises) and their marginal propensity to consume and expectation of the return on investment. In other words, the government cannot determine whether the capital is used to purchase goods or labor and what proportion is utilized. Therefore, although transfer expenditure has significant influence on total social demand, it is not part of total social demand.

From differences concluded above, it is commonly recognized that fiscal expenditure due to the issuance of national debts influences total social demand in two different ways: first, the government expenditure is added into total social demand as a new demand, such as government exhaustive expenditure; second, it is inserted into total social demand by transferring the usage of the capital, such as government transfer expenditure. The former will cause the expansion of total social demand while the latter simply changes the structure of total social demand but does not increase its aggregate.

Obviously, the debt expenditure due to the issuance of national debts is a part of government transfer expenditure, and can't be or will not be added to total social demand. The only fiscal expenditure that can be "superimposed" onto total social demand is the expansionary fiscal expenditure caused by weakening the government budget constraint arising from the issuance of national debts.

The expansionary fiscal expenditure caused by weakening government budget constraints can be further classified into exhaustive expenditure and transfer expenditure so that not all of them can be superimposed onto total social demand. How much the total social demand increases will be determined by the proportion of exhaustive expenditure to expansionary fiscal expenditure.

As all types of fiscal revenues are combined for use in practice, we have to infer the distribution of fiscal expenditure between exhaustive expenditure and transfer expenditure according to the total structure of fiscal expenditure. The problem is that the proportions of exhaustive expenditure and transfer expenditure are different in different countries. Even in one country, these proportions are different in different periods.

Nevertheless, common sense tells us that whatever total structure of fiscal expenditure or however economic development influences it, the exhaustive expenditure must be part of fiscal expenditure so that some part of expansionary fiscal expenditure caused by weakening government budget constraint due to the issuance of national debts will be directly superimposed onto total social demand.

This is not the end. The macro fiscal theory (Eckstein, 1979) indicates that any increase in government exhaustive expenditure will cause total social demand to multiply through a "fiscal multiplier".

As illustrated in Figure 5.2, $C + I + G$ stands for total social demand, ΔG^* stands for the increase in government exhaustive expenditure, and $C + I + G + \Delta G^*$ stands for total social demand after government exhaustive expenditure increases. Clearly, in the case of the increase of government exhaustive expenditure ΔG^*, the balance

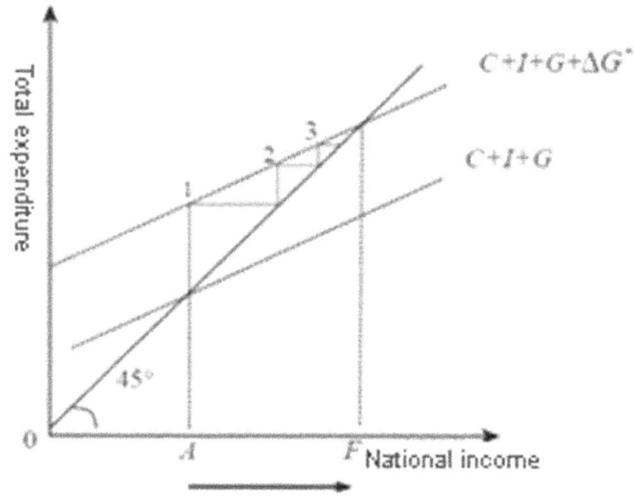

Figure 5.2 Multiplier process due to the increasing exhaustive expenditure

of national income increases from *OA* to *OF*, and *AF* is several times ΔG^*. This means that the increase in government exhaustive expenditure due to the issuance of national debts has an expansionary "multiplier effect" on total social demand.

Conclusion 4: In the view of the aggregate, the issuance of national debts has an expansionary effect on total social demand including private consumption, private investment and government exhaustive expenditure.

V National debts and total social demand: structural effect

The influence of the issuance of national debts on total social demand involves two issues, First, what are the capital sources used by micro economic entities to purchase national debts? Are they savings, investment or consumption? Second, for what are the funds raised by issuing national debts used? Is it exhaustive expenditure or transfer expenditure, or recurrent expenditure of exhaustive expenditure or investment expenditure (construction expenditure in China) of exhaustive expenditure?

For the sake of simple analysis, it is hypothesized that all the "output" savings are transferred to "input" investment in the circulation process, i.e. $S = I$. If we know the division ratio of consumption and savings of households' disposable income, then the investment will flow into consumption expenditure and investment expenditure, as detailed below:

1 After analysis of the influences of national debts on private demand, we find that national debts are taken as substitution for tax revenue. Tax revenue will decrease and micro economic entities' disposable income will increase

if national debts are issued. The issuance synchronizes with the increase in micro economic entities' disposable income, so does the issuance scale; apparently, however, not all the micro economic entities' capital used to purchase national debts is disposable income; some of it may be the increased disposable income. So, entities' disposable income and the ratio of consumption and savings will be less than the circulating amount of national debts. As the purchase of national debts is the micro economic entities' behavior of savings or investment, their capital used to purchase national debts are mainly savings. The savings from disposable income and from the increased disposable income will be the first source used to purchase national debts. Only if these capitals can't satisfy purchase of national debts will micro economic entities consider purchasing national debts with their consumer funds.

2 According to Keynes' absolute income theory (1963), as disposable income increases, people's marginal propensity to consume and marginal propensity to save will change in opposite direction: the former tends to decrease and the latter to increase. Besides, the decrease in marginal propensity to consume will cause the decrease in its average propensity to consume, and the increase in marginal propensity to save will also cause the increase in its average propensity to save. This means that the increase in micro economic entities' disposable income due to the issuance of national debts may lead to a decrease in its average propensity to consume and an increase in average propensity to save. In this process, the share of savings of micro economic entities' disposable income will increase while the share of consumption will decrease. According to inference that micro economic entities will purchase national debts first with their savings, the "influence" of the issuance of national debts on consumer funds will further weaken.

3 The micro economic entities always purchase national debts with cash or bank savings. While bank savings are not treated as savings funds, it is right that most bank savings are not pertaining to micro economic entities' immediate consumer funds but can be transferred to investment funds through a bank intermediary. In addition, micro economic entities can also sell other securities or real assets in order to purchase national debts. Apparently, these securities or real assets are micro economic entities' accumulation funds or stocks transferred from savings funds or investment funds. This means that consumer funds are not the main portion of micro economic entities' financial sources used to purchase national debts.

4 The analysis above indicates that the economic influence of national debts on households and enterprises is expressed as the increase in private consumption and decrease in private investment.

According to the views mentioned above, savings funds or investment funds are the main sources micro economic entities used to purchase national debts. Only part of it involves consumer funds or money intended for consumption expenditure. Comparatively, it seems that the amount of savings funds or investment funds is greater than that of the consumer funds or money intended for consumption expenditure.

For the foregoing reasons, the usage of various forms of fiscal revenue is always bundled together in practice, so we can infer the usage of capital financed by national debts according to the general structure of fiscal expenditure. See details below:

1. The literature review indicates that the proportions of exhaustive expenditure and transfer expenditure to total fiscal expenditure are 45.2% and 41.0% respectively in developed countries, almost half, but 61.5% and 22.5% respectively in developing countries. The former is almost three times the latter.
2. In China, during market-oriented reform, the fiscal expenditure structure shifted from preference for exhaustive expenditure to preference for transfer expenditure. In 1978, exhaustive expenditure and transfer expenditure[5] occupied 98.3% and 1.7% of total fiscal expenditure respectively. By the end of 1994, the former fell to 77.67% and the latter went up to 22.33%.

As to the current fiscal expenditure structure in China, transfer expenditure accounts for about 25% and exhaustive expenditure accounts for 75% of the capital financed by issuing national debts. In other words, the ratio of exhaustive expenditure and transfer expenditure is about 3:1 in expansionary fiscal expenditure due to the issuance of national debts. As to the development tendency of the fiscal expenditure structure in China, the ratio of these two kinds of expenditure is likely to reach the level in developing countries, i.e. 6:4.

In addition, the transfer expenditure that comes from and will go back to private sectors will not generate direct demand for social goods or labor, which neither increases the aggregate nor influences the structure of total social demand.[6] So, our analysis will concentrate on exhaustive expenditure that generates direct demand for social goods or labor. See details below:

1. Segmentation of exhaustive expenditure between recurrent expenditure and investment expenditure is highly similar in both the developed and developing countries. This means a higher proportion of recurrent expenditure than investment expenditure. If exhaustive expenditure is taken as 100%, then the proportion of recurrent expenditure is 77.2% and investment expenditure 22.8% in developed countries, and recurrent expenditure 81.4% and investment expenditure 18.6% in developing countries. In short, the ratio between recurrent expenditure and investment expenditure stays at about 8:2.
2. Over the years, the proportion of basic construction expenditure (including productive construction and non-productive construction) to the financial exhaustive expenditure in China has dropped dramatically from 41.4% in 1978 to 11.9% in 1994. Even by the current calculating caliber of construction expenditure, including productive capital construction expenditure, innovation expenditure and agriculture support expenditure, the proportion of construction budget expenditure in the whole yearly budget in 1994 was just 25.16%.

Apparently, the main part of exhaustive expenditure financed by issuing national debts is presented as recurrent expenditure, and only a small part is presented as investment expenditure. The recurrent expenditure consists largely of exhaustive expenditure, so it is also possible that the main usage of revenue financed by issuance of national debts is exhaustive expenditure rather than transfer expenditure.

Let's now analyze the capital sources used to purchase national debts and the usage of revenue financed by issuance of national debts. The issuance of national debts means an action that transfers some capital from households and enterprises to government. Savings or investment funds are the main part of micro economic entities' capital sources to purchase national debts while recurrent (exhaustive) expenditure is the main part of exhaustive expenditure financed by issuance of national debts, so this process might be: the total social consumption expenditure composed of private consumption expenditure and direct government consumption expenditure tends to increase while the total social investment expenditure comprising private investment expenditure and direct government investment expenditure tends to decrease.[7]

Conclusion 5: From the structure of national debts, the issuance of national debts has caused the total social consumption investment structure to move towards a preference for total social consumption.

VI Conclusion

In this paper, the influence of the issuance of national debts on total social demand is analyzed according to the demand aggregate and structure, the result of which indicates that the issuance of national debts has an expansionary influence on the aggregate of total social demand, where the influence on the total social demand structure is reflected by increasing total social consumption and decreasing total social investment.

The conclusion above is beyond expectation because it is absolutely different from economists' views on the functions of national debts in China, though it basically matches the process of national debts issuance since the reform. This can be confirmed through empirical analysis of the relationship between national debts and total social demand in China (Gao Peiyong, 1996).

Now, the reason why the issuance of national debts is generally treated as a force to control total social demand and transfer consumer funds to accumulative funds is that the following facts are overlooked.

Fact 1: The fiscal expenditure is "rigid" while national debts have a substitution relation with other forms of fiscal revenue. Only if the scale of fiscal expenditure is fixed and can't be adjusted or cut artificially will the issuance of national debts and tax revenue increase or decrease in opposite directions, thus leading to an increase in micro economic entities' disposable income. Inevitably, the increasing disposable income of micro economic entities will cause private consumption to increase. While private investment tends to decrease, it can't be compared with the increasing tendency of private consumption. Therefore, the influence of the issuance of national debts on households and enterprises means the increase rather than the decrease of private demand and private consumption.

Fact 2: The revenue financed by issuing national debts is used in combination with other revenues. The issuance of national debts will not happen until revenue can't cover expenditure. The revenue financed by debts will be spent; so, if the revenue financed by issuing national debts is transferred to expenditure, fiscal expenditure will expand inevitably; if fiscal expenditure expands, some part of it will be superimposed onto total social demand; if the government ties up various forms of fiscal revenue, it seems uncertain that the revenue financed by issuing national debts will be transferred to investment expenditure; if revenue financed by debts involves total fiscal expenditure, including transfer expenditure and exhaustive expenditure, it is inevitable that the revenue financed by debts will be transferred to the government's recurrent expenditure. Therefore, the influence of the issuance of national debts on total social demand will be reflected by the increase rather than by the decrease of its aggregated amount. The same is true of total social consumption.

Fact 3: The fiscal expenditure structure in China has been transferred from productive construction finance to public finance since the economic reform in 1978. Construction expenditure is no longer the main body of fiscal expenditure in China, and its structure tends to incline towards recurrent expenditure that takes up the largest proportion in the aggregate of fiscal expenditure, and most revenue financed by the issuance of national debts will be spent on recurrent expenditure. If debt revenue from private savings funds or investment funds is used as recurrent expenditure under the fiscal expenditure, the total social consumption expenditure comprising private consumption expenditure and government consumption expenditure will tend to increase.

Fact 4, the most important one: In 1994, the Chinese government carried out an important measure to offset financial deficit by issuing national debts instead of bank overdraft. While the measure to cover financial deficit is transferred from a "dual-track approach" (both bank overdraft and issuance of national debts) to a "one-way approach" (only issuance of national debts), it is not significant in practice to issue national debts in order to reduce or avoid expansion of money supply caused by overdraft.

The extended sense of the above conclusion is that things might reverse when the economy is threatened by inflation. It was thus expected to ease the excessive social purchasing power by the issuance of national debts and to transfer some part of consumer funds to accumulation funds so that the market balance would be maintained between supply and demand.

(Originally published in *Economic Research Journal*, Vol.9, 1996)

Notes

1 China's situation in 1991 was a typical example. Since the measure to increase tax revenue of 7 billion by raising 2 percent of retail business tax rate had not been issued on

time, in order to cover the budget difficulty caused by it, the Council State decided to issue RMB 10 billion of national debts (Ma Hong & Sun Shangqing, 1992, pp. 149–150).

2 These three situations have co-existed since the economic reform in China.

3 The actual situation is not so simple. However, if other financial revenues such as profits and fees delivered SOEs by are analyzed, the result will not change fundamentally but the process will be more complex. So, it takes tax as a typical form of financial revenues discussed above.

4 The meaning of "artificially" increasing financial revenue is used as against "naturally" increasing financial revenue which is the result of economic growth.

5 The calculating caliber of transfer expenditure is the expenditure on price subsidiary, debt, pension and social reliefs. All items under expenditure are exhaustive expenditure.

6 It did not take into consideration the influence of tax revenue deriving from progressive tax that was transferred to transfer expenditure; instead, it just considered cases where revenue from national debts was transferred to transfer expenditure.

7 The reason why they are called direct government consumption expenditure and direct government investment expenditure rather than government consumption expenditure and government investment expenditure is that the funds invested in private sectors by transfer expenditure are used by micro economic entities for consumption and investment, so it constitutes the indirect government consumption expenditure and indirect government investment expenditure.

Bibliography

David Ricardo (1817). *On the Principles of Political Economy and Taxation. London: John Murray.*

Atkins, A. B., et al. (1992). *Public economics*. Shanghai: Shanghai SDX Joint Publishing Company.

Buchanan, J. M. (1976). Barro on the Ricardian equivalence theorem. *Journal of Political Economy, 84*(2).

Buchanan, J. M. (1992). *Public finance in democratic process*. Shanghai: Shanghai SDX Joint Publishing Company.

Cavaco-Silva, A. A. (1977). *Economic effect of national debts*. New York: St. Matin's Press Inc.

Chen Gong. (1991). *Finance*. Chengdu: Sichuan People's Publishing House.

Eckstein, O. (1979). *Public finance*. Chengdu: Prentice-Hall Inc.

Gao Peiyong. (1996). Empirical analysis of the influence of national debts upon total social demand. *Urban Finance Forum*, (4).

Ma Hong,& Sun Shangqing. (1993). *Economic situation and expectation (1991–1992)*. Beijing: China Development Press.

Muller, D. (1992). *Public choice*. Beijing: The Commercial Press.

Patinkin, D. (1965). *Money, interest and prices*. New York: Harper & Row.

Peacock, A., & Wiseman, J. (1967). *The growth of public expenditure in the United States*. London: Allen & Unwin.

Ping Xinqiao. (1992). *Principles of finance and comparative finance institution*. Shanghai: Shanghai SDX Joint Publishing Company.

Ricardo, D. (1981). *The works and correspondence of David Ricardo*. Beijing: The Commercial Press.

Tobin, J. (1980). *Assert accumulation and economic activity*. Chicago: University of Chicago Press.

6 Several opinions about the scale of China's national debts

I Current major risks: higher debt dependence degree of the central fiscal expenditure

Many indices are used to measure the scale of national debts, but two of them are most frequently used in China. The first one is the proportion of accumulative amount of national debts in the GDP in the same year. The stock of national debts is used to reflect the proportional relationship between the accumulative amount of national debts and economic aggregate in the same year, so it is also called "debt-to-GDP ratio". The second is the proportion of the issuing scale of national debts in the fiscal expenditure in the same year, which looks at the issuing scale of national debts to reflect how the fiscal expenditure depends on debts in a year, so it is also called the "debt dependence degree of fiscal expenditure".

As to the first index, by the end of 1997, the unpaid aggregate of national debts amounted to RMB 592.88 billion, accounting for about 7.93% of the GDP in the same year, which seemed much lower than 52.0% in America (1992), 52.7% in Japan (1992), 25.8% in Germany (1991), 37.2% in the UK (1991), 29.6% in France (1992) and 15.1% in Thailand (1989). For this reason, it was widely argued that the scale of national debts in China was not as large as expected.

As to the second index, the issuing scale of national debts in 1997 was RMB 247.683 billion, accounting for 22.29% of national fiscal expenditure (i.e. sum of both the central government's and local government's expenditures) and for 55.76% of the central government spending. It was not low, even on the high side, as compared with the debt dependence degree of fiscal expenditure in other foreign countries. At the same time, the issuance of national debts in these years increased by 30% on a yearly basis (e.g. 58.99%, 31.87%, 26.95, and 28.71%in 1994, 1995, 1996 and 1997 respectively). For this reason, the rapidly expanding issuing scale of national debts in China became a public concern.

While the accumulative amount of national debts is not large, the issuing scale and growth rate are on the high side. The reason why these two phenomena co-existed is the short history of national debts issuance in China, only 19 years since 1979. In western developed countries, especially in the United States, the accumulative amount of national debts has reached the high level today because it has accumulated for hundreds of years. The problem is: if the issuing scale of national debts in China continues with the weak trend like this, the accumulative amount of national debts will be hard to control or even catch up with the aggregate in western developed countries that had hundreds of years' experience in issuance of national debts.

Moreover, the proportions of national debts in national fiscal expenditure and the central government's expenditure are calculated by two different calibers, such as the "debt dependence degree of national fiscal expenditure" and the "debt dependence degree of the central fiscal expenditure". In fact, national debts in China are issued as fiscal revenue financed by the Central Government, which is included in the central budget, scheduled and used by the Central Government. The local government is not allowed to issue debts, so local fiscal revenue has nothing to do with debts, nor does local fiscal expenditure. In other words, the amount of national debts issued, which is used as a numerator in the formula to calculate debt dependence degree, is the amount of debt revenue of the central finance. Therefore, it is the debt dependence degree of the central fiscal expenditure that can demonstrate the issuance exactly. It is very important to understand this point when considering the risk of national debts in current China. The debt dependence degree of national fiscal expenditure exceeds the internationally accepted threshold (15–20%), but it is accepted in China; however, when the debt dependence degree of the central fiscal expenditure reaches up to 55.76%, it is on the high side from any perspective. The central fiscal expenditure is used to "satisfy social public demand", and more than half of its capital sources arise from the issuance of national debts, which can hardly match the essence of government activity itself, nor can it sustain in a long term because there are potential risks.

With the increase of national debts, the debt dependence degree of the central fiscal expenditure tends to rise. During 1994–1997, the degrees of central fiscal expenditure's dependence on debts were 52.14%, 53.68%, 55.61% and 55.76% respectively, with an average annual growth rate of 1.21.

Therefore, risks about the scale of national debts in China include the large issuing scale of national debts (not the accumulative amount), which is reflected by the fact that the debt dependence degree of the central fiscal expenditure (not the debt dependence degree of national fiscal expenditure) is on the high side.

II High debt dependence degree of fiscal expenditure: a comprehensive reflection of various contradictions in the period of institutional transition

The high degree of fiscal expenditure's dependence is the result of the large issuing scale of national debts. Under the current economic system, facts that determine the issuing scale of national debts in China include both the current year's fiscal revenue and expenditure – fiscal deficit, and the accumulative result of the past years' fiscal revenues and expenditure – and the current year's amount used to repay the principal and interest of national debts. Take the budget in 1998 as an example. It was planned to issue RMB 280.86 billion of national debts, which was calculated by the sum of RMB 46 billion used to cover the deficit and RMB 234.86 billion used to repay the principal and interest on national debts in the same year. Therefore, in order to explore the reason why the debt dependence degree of fiscal expenditure is on the high side, we need to look into both the past and the present facts, as detailed below:

1 Institutional reform. One of the greatest features of economic system reform in more than 10 years is that every step forward of the reform almost forced finance (especially the central finance) to reduce tax and allow enterprises to retain more profits. The deficit arising from reducing tax and allowing enterprise to retain more profits was first covered by overdraft from the Central Bank (loan) and issuing national debts; then, in consideration of curbing deflation, overdraft from the Central Bank (loan) to cover the deficit was cancelled after 1994, and issuing national debts was used to achieve the same purpose. As the method to cover the deficit was transferred from a "dual-track approach" to a "single channel", the issuing scale of national debts increased from several billions in 1980s to dozens of billions in 1990s, even exceeding 100 billion in some years.
2 During the "absence" of taxation under the traditional economic system, the national income distribution system decided to use state monopoly for purchase and marketing of ASPs and unify the national urban employees' wage system as a precondition. Therefore, the fiscal revenue structure during that period featured a combination of tax and profits, with emphasis on profits. Besides, most tax and profits were contributed by SOEs. Since the implementation of reform and the opening-up policy in 1979 and in combination with the process of marketization, the state monopolies on purchase and marketing of ASPs and the unified national urban employees wage system were broken in succession, but the former had not exited completely. However, the fiscal revenue financed by formal tax was faced with the challenge of the inertia effect of the long-term "no (apparent) tax" period. Because of psychology and behavior in adaptation, various economic entities evaded tax intentionally or unintentionally. In absence of strict control of tax collection as well as law-based tax administration, various behaviors of tax evasion were just like a "virus" spreading consistently and causing great loss of national tax revenue. Since the tax reform in 1994, this contradiction has been eased, but the problem hasn't been solved yet. As to the "rigidity" of fiscal expenditure, the "absence" of tax revenue that might be the "top player" in fiscal revenue system led to increasing dependence on non-recurrent fiscal revenue national debts, and went beyond the scope of national debts.
3 Impact of non-normative government revenue. Since the implementation of reform and the opening-up policy in China in 1979, the proportion of budgeted fiscal revenue in the GDP decreased dramatically, but the non-normative revenue items such as off-budget revenue and revenue outside the system expanded sharply. It was thus estimated that the ratio of non-normative

government revenue and budgetary revenue was about 3:2. On the one hand, it was a wide concern that governments at all levels established charges collectable by themselves and conducted self-controlled revenue and expenditure to earn off-budget gains. On the other hand, it was noticeable that the growth in non-normative government revenue was conditioned on "squeezing out" normative budgetary revenue. Without the transfer from budgetary revenue to off-budget revenue and revenue outside the system, the non-normative government revenue could not expand so quickly. The problem is that the result caused by the impact of non-normative government revenue on budgetary revenue was directly performed as the decreasing proportion of fiscal revenue in the GDP. The proportion of fiscal expenditure in the GDP did not decrease with the deceasing fiscal revenue (e.g. in 1995, the proportions of fiscal expenditure and fiscal revenue in the GDP were 13.3% and 10.7% respectively), and the gap between these two data only could be filled up by non-recurrent fiscal revenue (i.e. issuing national debts).

4 Borrowing new debts to repay the old ones. The principal and interest on national debts have to be repaid. In case of fiscal difficulty, especially of central fiscal difficulties, when the peak of debt repayments arrives, the government is forced to borrow new debts to repay the old ones in order to deal with the exchange of matured national debts. Not only the capital expenditure of national debts but also the interest expenditure depend heavily on the issuance of new debts. In addition, since 1994, the repayment of the principal and interest on national debts was transferred out of the budget to form the "third budget" – the debt budget, which paralleled the recurrent budget and construction budget but was not reflected in the complete budgetary expenditure. For instance, RMB 191.683 billion of 247.683 billion (77.39%) of the revenue financed by debts in 1997 were used to repay the principal and interest on matured national debts because they were not covered by national budgetary expenditure of RMB 919.706 billion. Though the peak of debt repayments totaled 100 billions or even hundreds of billions, the cost was much more than national debts.

5 Expanding financial expenditure. The relative decrease in budgetary income, especially of the recurrent revenue, did not lead to a relative decrease in fiscal expenditure. On the contrary, the government's spending increased sharply during the tide of reform and opening up. The utilization of national debts provided the government with an opportunity to break the budgetary constraint of recurrent revenue on fiscal expenditure. Besides, as the NDM system was incomplete and lacked effective constraint on national debts, the fiscal expenditure expanded again and again. From 1979 to 1997, the annual growth rate of fiscal expenditure (including debt expenditure) reached up to 15–20%, far higher than the growth rate of GDP. A chain reaction thus occurred: fiscal expenditure expanded → fiscal deficit increased → the issuing scale of national debts increased → fiscal expenditure expanded even faster → the issuing scale of national debts increased further.

III A currently urgent thing: bring down the higher debt dependence degree of the fiscal expenditure

Though the successive issuance of national debts for more than 10 years had a positive effect on economic and social development in China, it also placed some risk on national finance through enlarging the issuing scale of national debts and raising the debt dependence degree of the central fiscal expenditure. In order to reduce or even avoid this risk and help operation of national debts go the right way, we must try our best to make a macro arrangement to decrease the higher debt dependence degree of the fiscal expenditure.

But, what are the solutions to bringing down the high dependence degree?

1 Further improving the tax system to collect all the tax collectable. With the constraint on the existing scale of fiscal expenditure, there exists a substitutional relationship between recurrent fiscal revenue and national debts. As the "cross line" of national debts is the result of the "absence" of tax, the "homing" of tax that is the lead player of fiscal revenue system should be used as a key step to decrease the debt dependence degree of the fiscal expenditure. We should build a faith to ensure that the issuance of national debts will decline by one percentage point if the national tax revenue increases by one percentage point, and that the debt dependence degree of the fiscal expenditure will decrease naturally if the tax dependence degree tends to rise. Therefore, we should achieve the main purpose of "collecting all the tax collectable" and carry out legal tax construction by improving the tax system. We should build a new tax revenue relationship between tax levy and payment in the future, by which tax sectors collect tax according to law and taxpayers deliver taxes and fees according to law consciously. Loopholes in taxation must be closed to minimize the loss of national tax revenue.

2 Screening various expenses and fees to standardize the government revenue mechanism. In the market economy, whatever the form of revenue, fiscal funds are the essence of the revenue financed by the government. Therefore, transfer of non-normative government revenue dispersed to different sectors and areas to normative government revenue can be scheduled by financial sectors to enlarge the aggregate of recurrent revenue. This will have fundamental significance for decreasing the debt dependence degree of the fiscal expenditure.

Considering the complicated non-normative government revenues and extensive range of stakeholders, it is suggested that these revenues be regulated by first screening them out and then incorporating them into the state budget. First, we should screen out all government fees to determine whether they are reasonable and unreasonable, and eliminate all unreasonable or arbitrary fees. Second, we should regulate reasonable fees in different ways. Any fees featuring tax (nominal name is "fee" but is "tax" in nature) should be managed as tax. Any fees that can be turned into tax by expanding the tax base should be collected in a unified manner. In addition, we should set up new tax categories and collect them in a new manner. For "fees" that are included in the tax system improperly, we should regulate the notation and extension strictly according to the specified charge rates in the market economy, classify them into "fees for registration" or "charges for use" and manage them with administrative measures. Finally, for government revenue that is included in the management system of taxes by "tax-for-fee" reform or is covered by fees for registration and charges for use through "regulating fees", we should adopt the transit method to make a separate budget or incorporate them into the government budget at a stroke.

3 Financial sectors and banks should work together to decrease the cost of issuing national debts. At present, it includes two items: interest expenditure and handling expense of promotion and exchange. Undoubtedly, these two kinds of expenditure are the necessary cost of issuing national debts and will not be avoided. However, the cost and standard of such expenditure are worth investigation. If expenditures are too much, it will be deemed as unnecessary cost because this will not only increase the national financial burden but also increase the issuing scale of national debts in the case of the current arrangement about the sources of repayment for principal and interest of national debts.

It must be noted that with the advancement of national debts' credit and its liquidity, the masses have developed the mindset to purchase national debts, so its issuing interest rate can be a little lower than other financial tools for the same period; however, the rate should not follow the bank savings interest rate, nor can it be higher than bank savings interest rate for the same period. Meanwhile, the enthusiasm of national debts operators needn't be driven by a high handling charge as before; instead, the handling charges to promote or exchange national debts should be reduced. The key is that whether the interest expenditure of national debts or the expenditure on the handling charges is used to promote or exchange national debts, no changes can be controlled by financial sector or bank alone. This purpose can be achieved if the financial sector and bank work together and proper arrangements are made during macroeconomic system reform, though there may be great difficulties. As the cost of issuing national debts has great influence on national fiscal difficulty and on the issuing scale of national debts, and as the steady macro economy depends heavily on the debt dependence degree of the central fiscal expenditure, this task has to be fulfilled and put onto the agenda as soon as possible.

4 Expenditure on repayment of the principal and interest should be "divided"; in other words, the interest should be included in the recurrent budget, and the new debts should be limited to expenditure on repayment of the principal capital. Considering different natures, the principal and interest expenditure of national debts should be treated in different ways. The capital expenditure of national debts can be retained in a "debt budget", and can be covered by new debts so that it will form a real permanent balance. The interest expenditure of national debts should be listed under the "recurrent budget" so that it should treat the recurrent revenue (mainly the tax) rather than the debt as the source of repayment. If the interest expenditure is confused with the capital expenditure of national debts (both are repaid by new debts during the circulation of

borrowing for repaying), the capital of national debts will not change as the time elapses and the interest expenditure of national debts will increase day by day. In fact, during the circulation of national debts in China, the interest expenditure of national debts will increase the scale of national debts.

By the way, inclusion of interest expenditure, especially the recurrent budget of national debts, into the budget is internationally accepted. In China, the interest expenditure of national debts is excluded from the state budget in order to reduce the deficit. Take the situation in 1996 as an example. If the interest expenditure of national debts was not covered by the budget, the central budget deficit amounted to RMB 61 billion; if it was, however, the central budget deficit that year would reach RMB 93.86 billion (if the interest expenditure of national debts was one-fourth of the total principal and interest expenditures of national debts totaling RMB 13.143 billion). Take a look at the situation in America in the same year, the federal budget deficit was \$107 billion and the interest expenditure of national debts listed in budget was \$203 billion. In 1996, if it were calculated by the caliber in China when the interest expenditure of national debts was excluded out of budget, neither budget deficit nor financial surplus totaling \$150 billion would be there for American federal government. The problem is that the damage caused by purposefully underestimated fiscal deficit is a formal deficit. Be noted that all social sectors may have underestimated the national fiscal difficulty (especially the central fiscal difficulty) due to purposefully underestimated fiscal deficit, which may confuse the government decision on fiscal issues.

After the interest expenditure of national debts is included in the budget, some implied fiscal deficit is transferred into the public fiscal deficit, and the fiscal deficit is presented completely. So, asking the government to reduce fiscal deficit and cut down the issuing scale of national debts may help create a good social environment.

5 Transfer of the measure to verify the issuing scale of national debts at the beginning of the year to an internationally accepted measure to control the year-end accumulative amount of national debts. At present, the Chinese government has control over the scale of national debts by verifying the planned issuing scale at the beginning of the year, which was already submitted to the People's Congress for approval. It is different from the internationally accepted measure to control the year-end accumulative amount of national debts. National debt is a kind of fiscal revenue, so it is proper to control the year-end accumulative amount. Due to its outstanding nature of "reimbursement" and "flexibility", national debt differs from recurrent revenue, including tax. It is payable, so operation of revenue financed by debts must consider its time cost. If debts are issued but unused, the "squeezing effect" suffered by non-government sectors will make no sense, and the government sector will lose interest expenses. As national debts are flexible, there is space for government to increase or decrease the issuing scale according to the real situation. Therefore, the issuing scale of national debts can be determined by social demand, and it can avoid idle or wasted fiscal capital to the maximum.

If the issuing scale of national debts is confirmed at the beginning of the year and the issuance is organized as planned, the revenue financed by debts will become a fixed amount. However, this fixed amount is probably far away from the real fiscal operation. As thus, national debts may become less flexible, so may the relatively fixed recurrent revenue. In addition, all or part of the revenue financed by debts with less flexibility may be left idle, but the payable cost still exists. The issuance of national debts in 1996 was a typical example in China. On the one hand, the change of foreign exchanges reduced the principal and interest expenditure at home and aboard, and the central budget deficit could be slightly lowered. On the other hand, the issuance of national debts was organized as planned at the beginning of the year, so it was not adjusted according to the real situation and the national debts that would have been managed flexibly became a "rigid" demand. As a result, the surplus revenue financed by debts in 1996 amounted to RMB 4.312 billion, which had to be carried forward to the next year.

Such being the case, we would better follow the internationally accepted practice that it is unnecessary to confirm the detailed issuing scale of national debts at the beginning of the year and that the People's Congress only needs to adopt the aggregate regulation to control the year-end aggregate. The Ministry of Finance once made a discretionary decision to confirm the issuing scale, issuing type and issuing date of national debts according to real fiscal revenue and expenditure in the budgetary year. In fact, even the control of the scale of national debts alone will not weaken the power of the People's Congress to control it.

6 Try to reduce expenditure. Reduction of fiscal expenditure seems always difficult but not impossible. The key is that all sectors need to work together. If they can think of the function of finance again under the market economic system, and if they can consider the whole society's capital allocation to advance the efficiency of capital utilization, the current fiscal functions in China will be simplified. If all sectors can consider it from a macro perspective of lowering the debt dependence degree of the fiscal expenditure and tackling the dilemma of national fiscal difficulty, and if they put aside some vested interest or individual interest, China's fiscal expenditure will be reduced significantly.

(Originally published in *Public Finance Research*, Vol.3, 1998)

Bibliography

International Monetary Fund. (1995). *International capital market – prospect and policy (Chinese version)*. Beijing: China Financial Publishing House.

Liu Zhongli. (1997, March 19). Report on the operation of central and local budgets in 1997 and the draft of central and local budgets in 1998. *People's Daily*.

National Bureau of Statistics. (1997). *China statistical yearbook (1997)*. Beijing: China Statistic Press.

7 Macro views on taxation

Analysis of several current major taxation issues

In recent years, I pondered and wrote some papers about many tax issues, especially those in China. When looking back at these papers, I find that I analyzed tax issues from macro views. In addition, each of my papers addresses one special issue or one aspect of the issue in a particular context. It occurs to me that there is still an unfinished and urgent task: is it possible for me to establish a complete theoretical framework based on the existing papers? If so, how can I use this framework to analyze the current major tax issues and make some instructive judgments or draw some inspirations?

The consideration above runs through this paper.

Section 1

1.1 Macro view on taxation means to "define" taxation properly according to the correlation and interaction between tax and other facts so that taxation can play its due roles in the course of economic and social development. In other words, taxation should be put in its place and perform its functions and responsibilities. It can't be "absent", i.e. negligent in the performance of its duties, nor can it "cross the line", i.e. do what it should not do.

1.2 It is necessary to study the tax issues not only from a micro view but also from a macro view, as proved by both the history and reality. Many problems look fuzzy from a micro view but crystal clear from a macro view. In addition, many schemes that appear reasonable and effective in a micro view may not in a macro view. In some cases, there are many difficulties and doubts about partial equilibrium analysis of certain tax issues from the view of taxation authority; but when changing the mind to do general equilibrium analysis in a macro view, we may find that it is just like Columbus' discovery of the New Land or like seeing a light in darkness or like awaking from a dream.

Therefore, careful attention needs to be paid to macro analysis of tax issues. It is a world full of multivariate functions by which we live, so a multivariate – not only one variate of tax – should be taken into consideration during tax research; moreover, researchers should consider the whole process of the operation of tax rather than some part of it. Only by such analysis can we make conclusions closer to reality.

Section 2

2.1 After all, taxation is one form of state revenues to be financed by the government. In the government's revenue and expenditure system, taxation stays at the side of state revenue. In case of the modern market economic system, there are kinds of revenues the government can gain, including taxes, debts and fees; however, tax is relatively an optimized kind of government revenue.

2.2 Tax revenue has three features. First, there is coerciveness, which means tax is mandatorily levied by the government according to law. Once there is assessable income or taxable action, taxpayers must pay taxes in full. Then, the government revenue from taxation is reliable in amount. Second, freedom from payment, which means the government needn't repay it after levying or it costs government nothing. Then, the government revenue from taxation always has "no scrupulosity". Third, stability, which means the government levies taxes of a confirmed amount according to law. Unless the tax law changes, the government revenue from taxation can't be regulated casually at a certain economic development level.

National debts are characterized by voluntariness, repayment and flexibility. Voluntariness means that the issuance of national debts is based on voluntary subscription. Whether subscribing or not and how much to purchase is at the purchasers' will. Therefore, the government revenue from issuing national debts is not so reliable in amount. Repayment means that once national debts are issued, the government has to repay the principal and interest according to agreed terms. Therefore, the government revenue financed by issuing national debts always has "worries behind". Flexibility means that the circulation of national debts is not confirmed by law in advance, but is decided discretionarily according to the government revenue and expenditure. Therefore, the government revenue so financed can be regulated flexibly.

Government fee is a form of revenue financed by the government through exchanging or providing direct services. In general, there are two kinds of normative government fees: fee for registration and fee for use. Fee for registration includes the cost of production and handing charge when the government provides certain services or administration for residents. This fee must be limited in the fields where the government provides certain services or administration. In addition, it must be limited to the cost of production and handing charges, not used to make profits. Fee for use must be charged for the use of public facilities according to certain standard. It must depend on the public facilities provided by government, excluding public goods or services. It should also reflect the revenue principle that only the user pays. Fee for registration should be managed as a fund that can be only used to maintain and construct public facilities, with the rates not higher than average unit cost of a public facility. Therefore, the revenue gained either by fee for registration or by fee for use will not be big and the usage of it should be restricted.

2.3 Government revenue is used to cover government expenditure. The nature of government expenditure determines and constrains the nature of government revenue.

In the process of marketed-oriented reform, the aim of fiscal reform and development in China is confirmed by public finance. One basic feature of public finance is to satisfy public demand. For any item that does not belong to or can't be included into the field of public demand, government finance will not get involved. For any item that belongs to or can be included in the field of public demand, government finance must get involved. Government expenditure is used to provide public goods and services, regulate income distribution and implement macro control policy. One common character of these items of expenditure is to have no return on investment. In other words, the money the government spends on satisfying public demand has almost "no return".

2.4 Considering the features and characters of revenue and expenditure, it is not hard to make a conclusion that taxation is the only lifeline of government operation. Taxation must play a leading role in the government revenue system while other forms of revenue, such as national debts and fees, will only supplement.

This reveals that if the concept of "tax dependence" (the proportion of tax in government expenditure) is created in relation to the "degree of dependence on national debts" (the proportion of revenue from national debts in government expenditure), we should try to advance the tax dependence degree in order to regulate the government revenue system in the market economy.

2.5 If we look back at the current pattern of China's government revenue, we will find that the proportion of tax revenue of the normative budgetary revenue is very high (93.3% in 2000); however, based on the GFS system (government finance statistics) adopted by the IMF, including off-budget revenue, governmental fund revenue and social security funds, the proportion of tax revenue of the government revenue seems not so high. According to Chen Xiaopin (2001), it is estimated that China's government revenue in 2000 amounted to RMB 2631.487 billion, 1.97 times the budgetary revenue. Therefore, the proportion of tax revenue of the government revenue was only 47.9%.

What's more, the revenue calculated by the IMF's method is not the whole revenue of the Chinese government. Together with non-normative revenues such as fees, collected money and penalties, the proportion of tax revenue of the government revenue is much lower.

Conclusion: China's taxation must return to its original functions, i.e. advancing the "tax dependence degree" to make tax become an essential source of government revenue.

Section 3

3.1 Tax on households, national economy and people's livelihood is treated as the core of tax system, so it always attracts extra attention.

In general, the proportion of tax revenue in the current GDP, i.e. tax revenue/GDP, is used to measure the tax burden borne by enterprises and residents. This reveals a country's tax burden in total rather than one enterprise's or resident's tax burden, so it can be called macro tax burden.

3.2 As to general tax burden, China's tax revenue amounted to RMB 1.266 trillion in 2000, and the GDP of that year was RMB 8.941512 trillion, of which tax accounted for 14.16%. The figure was not high as compared with global average level.[1] However, there will be a different case if it goes deeper.

The problem lies in the "numerator" rather than in "denominator". The calculated tax revenue is just the government revenue collected by tax sectors according to the tax system. In China, there are other government revenues. The normative budgetary revenue includes enterprise revenue, education surcharges and sundry income, which can be calculated correctly but is not covered by budgets such as off-budget revenue, governmental funds and social security funds. This revenue is gained out of system and can't be calculated correctly, including various fees, penalty and accumulation funds; they are charged by sectors and governments at all levels. If all the four kinds of revenue above are put together, the aggregate of China's government revenue will double the tax revenue.

According to Chen Xiaopin's data in 2000, the first three kinds of government revenues amounted to RMB 2.631487 trillion, accounting for 29.43% of the GDP. The fourth form of government revenue (gained out of system) occupied 5% of GDP,[2] and the proportion of total government revenue including revenue gained out of system was 34.43% of GDP, 2.43 times the pure tax burden.

3.3 From the perspective of social resource distribution or from the view of residents, however, the classification of government revenue and the difference between tax burden and non-tax burden are nothing but the government's inner issues. How much does the government get from GDP? How much do enterprises and residents pay to the government? Or, what is the final distribution of GDP?

If the total government revenue is used to measure China's current "total tax burden", the result is much higher than the general tax burden.

Conclusion 2: China's current tax burden should be measured by both the "general tax burden" and the "total tax burden".

3.4 The general tax burden is not high, but the total tax burden is heavy. The basic reason for this complex situation is that China's current action on government revenue and its mechanism is not normative. Whether or not the first two forms of government revenue are covered by the budget, they are normative, but the other two are not. Considering the co-existence of normative and non-normative government revenue, with the latter being higher in amount than the former, Premier Zhu Rongji described the pattern of government revenue at that time as "fee higher than tax" and started "fee-to-tax" conversion in 1998.

In fact, the "fee-to-tax" conversion was not intended to transfer the entire "fee" to "tax" but to standardize government revenue action and its mechanism. Only the items with the nature of tax or those that are named "fee" but are really "tax" can be listed under tax. Any items that belong to fee and those that are named "fee" and are real "fees" must be standardized. Items that are charged arbitrarily must be cancelled.

Complex problems persist. The initial reason why non-normative government revenue appeared and spread was not because people preferred "fee" to "tax", but because the collection of normative tax didn't go well. Against a background where much tax could not be collected and the gap in government expenditure was getting bigger and bigger, a natural choice was to set up new items of charges, i.e. charging fees by non-normative administrative means. There was a saying that "shortage of tax can be supplemented by fee". However, this failed to solve the problem of tax collection, and drew much attention to charging more fees. As long as the normative and non-normative revenues were stable and reliable, many government sectors would prefer "fee" to "tax". Therefore, there appeared a "tax squeezed out by fee" phenomenon, i.e. expanding the items of charge to impact the tax base, retaining central tax by taking the liberty to make conditions for tax cuts and encouraging enterprise to evade tax. The phenomena "preferring fee to tax" and "tax squeezed out by fee" continued and created the pattern of government revenue that "fee is more important than tax".

3.5 Apart from the reason of "fee-to-tax" and the history of "tax" and "fee", let's look back at the progress to strengthen tax collection and "fee-to-tax" conversion. It is not hard to understand the economic effect from a macro view.

The enhancement of tax collection led to rapid growth of tax revenue. After the government tried hard to realize the purpose of the increment of RMB 100 billion in 1998, it seemed that tax revenue had been rising since 1999. In 1999, the increment of tax was about RMB 150 billion at a growth rate of 16.2%. This was the first year that the tax revenue exceeded RMB 1000 billion. In 2000, the increment reached up to RMB 234.8 billion at a growth rate of 22.8%. In 2001, this figure jumped to RMB 251.1 billion, with the growth rate of 19.8%. Therefore, tax revenue marched towards an amount of RMB 1.5172 trillion.

There is no essential progress in "fee-to-tax" conversion. As a vital part of "fee-to-tax" conversion, the scheme of transferring road tolls to fuel taxes remains at its demonstration stage; the rural reform of tax and fee is still implemented as a pilot project in minority provinces like Anhui. One breakthrough is that the "purchase cost of vehicle" has been transferred to "vehicle purchase tax" since 2001.

One develops rapidly but the other develops slowly, so there is an imbalance between them. Since non-normative government revenue can't decrease with the increase of normative government revenue, it is not hard to estimate the direction to which the "total tax burden" borne by enterprises and residents and the distribution of GDP will evolve.

Conclusion 3: With the rapid growth of tax revenue and low progress of "fee-to-tax" conversion, the current "total tax burden" borne by Chinese enterprises and residents is getting heavier and heavier, and the distribution of GDP shows preference for the government.

3.6 In any situation and at any time, the existing scale of tax revenue is taken as the starting point in the design of the overall tax system and during the arrangement of one tax category. As the real rate of tax will not reach 100% in practice, whether to select the tax base or the tax rate, the design of tax system will follow the principle of "wide coverage and narrow usage", i.e. considering the real rate of tax collection that makes the tax rate wider and higher. The product of tax base, tax rate and real rate of collection is the tax revenue gained from one tax category or the whole tax system, so the product of tax base and tax rate is just the theoretical or nominal tax burden. The real tax burden should consider the real rate of collection, where any change of any factor will change the real tax burden. This means that even if there is no measure to increase theoretical or nominal tax burdens, such as expanding the tax base or raising the tax rate, with the improvement of tax collection, the real tax burden will increase accordingly.

The new tax system implemented since 1994 was verified by the real rate of collection at that time. Ever since then, especially after 1998, the collection of tax has been greatly improved. If the real rate of collection at that time could reach the present level, the current tax system, especially the tax base and tax rate, would be quite different.

Conclusion 4: According to the "general tax burden", China's current real tax burden is improved significantly as compared with 1994.

Section 4

4.1 As a basic source of government revenue, tax revenue is the permanent topic for discussion. What idea should it keep when the scale of tax revenue is confirmed, and what scale of tax revenue should it be? These two questions should be answered first.

4.2 As one kind of government revenue, taxation aims to cover government expenditure. The scale of tax revenue involves the relationship between government revenue and expenditure. In all ages, there are two ideas used to handle the relationship between government revenue and expenditure: "expenditure based on revenue" and "revenue based on expenditure" (Gao Peiyong, 2001). "Expenditure based on revenue" means confirmation of the scale of government expenditure according to the scale of government revenue. "Revenue based on expenditure" means confirmation of the scale of government revenue according to the scale of government expenditure.

Apparently, they are just two sides of a coin. However, different ideas may lead to totally different results.

4.3 In the planned economy, there is indeed space for the idea of "expenditure based on revenue". With the support of economic and social systems (such as state monopoly on the purchase and marketing of ASPs, eight-grade wage system, planned price for industrial products and unified fiscal revenue and expenditure system), both the government and enterprises can centralize almost all social resources. The government sector has the right to arrange social resources; as a part of it, government revenue and expenditure can be conducted following the principle of "expenditure based on revenue".

However, in the new environment of the market economy where the market performs its functions in resource distribution, the "expenditure based on revenue" can't match real life or carry out "expenditure based on revenue" activities.

For instance, once government cannot control all the social resources, and the proportion of fiscal revenue in the GDP decreases, the government expenditure will be reduced so that it can match the revenue according to the idea of "expenditure based on revenue". In this case, however, it will be hard for the government to operate the state apparatus and perform its functions, and it will be impossible to stop the increase in expenditure in the case of decreasing revenue. Therefore, the government is forced to gain revenue based on the demand of expenditure and to advance the proportion of fiscal revenue in the GDP.

For instance, according to "expenditure based on revenue", there mustn't be a subjective arrangement on deficit spending. In fact, the macroeconomic policy (such as proactive fiscal policy) needs support of deficit spending, and the impulse to increase the scale of government expenditure forces state finance to make arrangements for expenditure to exceed revenue. This is not the result of "expenditure based on revenue" (it doesn't reach balanced finance or surplus finance, but gets the opposite result), but the result of fiscal deficit.

For instance, one of the basic intentions of "expenditure based on revenue" is to constrain expenditure by revenue. However, this leads to another fact that the government should try best to finance revenue and plan expenditure based on revenue. Government likes spending more and it has the power to do so. Over these years, revenue hasn't constrained government expenditure but incentivizes the government to increase revenue by political power in order to satisfy the demand of expanding expenditure. Against such a background, the government tried to "make more extra money" by various means, even including non-normative means, but the fact is that the proportion of normative revenue in the GDP decreased and the proportion of non-normative revenue in the GDP increased continuously. This is why a rare pattern of government revenue that "fee is higher than tax" has formed.

4.4 It seems necessary to replace the "expenditure based on revenue" with "revenue based on expenditure" in order to handle the relationship between government revenue and expenditure under the market economic system.

Seeking the source of the "revenue based on expenditure", we can find that government expenditure is the cost of government action, which can be considered as the cost to perform government functions. Under the market economic system, the reason why government action is needed or government is required to perform its functions is the public demand that is not satisfied by market. To satisfy public demand, the government needs to provide public goods and services. To provide public goods and services, the government needs to spend. If the government wants to spend money, it needs first to collect money from social members who consume public goods or services. Obviously, public service means the connection between revenue and expenditure, and the amount of revenue and expenditure must be used to satisfy public demand.

For this reason, we will find the relationship: market economy → public demand → government function → government expenditure → government revenue. It means that under the market economy, the government must define its functions according to public services. Once the government function is defined, the scale of government expenditure used to support the government action will be defined. Once the scale of government expenditure is confirmed, the scale of revenue used to cover expenditure will be confirmed. Questions to be raised should be "how much does the government need" and "how much can the government finance".

Organizing government revenue and expenditure by such thought is adaptable to the market economic system, which can also satisfy the demand that the government performs its functions and will not go beyond the enterprises' and residents' tolerance.

Conclusion 5: With the transition from a planned economy to a market economy, the government should follow the idea of "revenue based on expenditure" rather than "expenditure based on revenue" when confirming the scale of government revenues, including tax revenue.

4.5 The scale of government revenue must be confirmed according to expenditure. Tax revenue, as one of the basic sources or primary part of government revenue, should follow this idea. The scale of tax revenue must be confirmed based on the confirmed government revenue according to its "orientation" in the whole revenue pattern and its connection and cooperation with other forms of revenue. In other words, confirmation of the scale of tax revenue can't be separated from other forms of revenues. Tax revenue, government fees and other forms of government revenue must be covered by government revenue and allocated according to the assigned tasks.

4.6 There are many sources for the Chinese government to finance its revenue. Revenues financed in different places are managed by different government sectors rather than by financial sectors engaged in the management of government revenue and expenditure. There are various management methods of government revenue, and co-existence of normative and non-normative revenue is natural because the entire scale of government revenue lacks a unified consideration or complete organization. Forms of government revenue without the control of aggregated scale are usually designed for special tasks or purposes. Acting as one pleases is the basic situation of China's government revenue in recent years. The problem is that if it goes on like this, is there any limitation on government revenue? Or, is there any limitation on enterprises' and residents' tax burden?

Conclusion 6: The design of the tax system and the definition of tax revenue must consider the whole pattern of government revenue. Tax reform must be connected to "fee-to-tax" conversion, which should be organized as a whole based on the consideration of the scale of government revenue.

Section 5

5.1 Tax revenue is not merely a form of government revenue. It also regulates income distribution and promotes continuous and steady economic development. The differences are that financing revenue is the basic function of tax revenue, and regulating income distribution and promoting continuous and steady economic development are a derived function.

5.2 The function to regulate income distribution means tax revenue can regulate income distribution among residents.

5.3 Regulating income distribution is a new function of China's tax revenue under the market economic system. In the planned economy, tax revenue also involves regulation, though it focuses only on profit distribution among enterprises. Moreover, as to regulation of profit distribution among enterprises, tax revenue just played a supporting role at that time when the product price was determined by the planned sector rather than by the market. Despite different prices and values, the price system needed support from taxation, i.e. products whose prices were higher than their value would be taxed much, and products whose prices were lower than their value would be taxed less or even exempted, thus eliminating the influence of the difference between price and value on enterprise profits to enable all enterprises to start from the same starting line. "High price with high tax and low price with low tax" is the informed conclusion on how tax regulated enterprise profit distribution at that time. The regulation of income distribution among residents was carried out by the state monopoly for the purchase and marketing of ASPs and the eight-grade wage system (Gao Peiyong, 2002). In case of state monopoly on the purchase and marketing of ASPs, the only place to get monetary income for farmers was to sell their ASPs to state-owned commercial sectors. The price and place of ASPs were controlled by the government, so government determined how much farmers could get and how much they could retain. As to the eight-grade wage system, the only place to get income for urban employees was through wages. As government controlled the wage standard and had the power to adjust it, the government also determined how much urban employees could get and how much they could retain. With support of these two basic economic systems, resident income distribution was naturally controlled by the government, and it was unnecessary for tax revenue to perform the function of income distribution regulation.

After market reform broke the state monopoly on the purchase and marketing of ASPs and the eight-grade wage system, there was no base or measure for government to directly regulate resident income distribution. As the old regulation mechanism was eliminated and the traditional planned economic measures remained immature, a new regulation mechanism needed to be established to replace the traditional mechanism and regulate income distribution. At this time, there was an environment for tax revenue to transfer the "potential function" of income distribution regulation to the "real function".

5.4 In the frame of the market economy, tax has the natural advantages to regulate income distribution. Almost all types of taxation can regulate resident income distribution. The differences lie in the way to perform this function and in the transmission mechanism of the function.

By collecting direct tax and progressive tax, including income tax and property tax, the government can centralize the high-income group's income and allocate it to the low-income group and the vulnerable group by transfer payment. Therefore, for these two kinds of taxation, especially the individual income tax, both the economic books and government economic documents take them as the first choice of redistribution. As to indirect tax and regressive tax such as turnover tax, though they are deemed equal for everyone, the high-income group consumes more goods and services than the low-income group; thus the amount of turnover tax paid by the high-income group is higher than that paid by the low-income group. For the revenue centralized by these tax categories, whether used to provide public goods or services or used to provide transfer payments to the low-income group or vulnerable group, it has performed the function of redistribution. The difference is that its function is not as obvious or pertinent as that of direct tax.

Conclusion 7: Tax revenue is the most important measure in the distribution of GDP in the market economy. No other methods or tools can rival it.

5.5 Applying the tax function of income distribution regulation to the pattern of China's current resident income distribution needs some special skills. This is because China's current resident income distribution gap appears against a special background which seems impossible in other countries. See details below.

First, the appearance and advancement of China's current resident income distribution are led by government distribution policy. From the early stage of reform to the end of the 1990s, all government policies on income distribution were based on the tone of "laissez faire" and "tolerance", which first "allows some people to become rich first and then the richer bring along the poorer" and then "gives priority to efficiency with due consideration to fairness". The basic starting point is to exchange income distribution for rapid economic growth; then the economic growth is required to ease the income distribution inequality automatically (Wang Shaoguang, 2001). During the past 20 years, governments at all levels did little to regulate income distribution. They watched the gap getting more and more serious, but they were afraid to go back to the old idea of equalitarianism. So, the appearance and advancement of China's current resident income distribution is the designed result.

Second, China's current resident income distribution gap appears and widens when the government role is distorted. In the planned economy, government can play the role of government and enterprises to centralize almost all social resources and organize resource allocation as a whole. However, while the old pattern of resource allocation is broken, and the new one based on the market has formed, especially during the downtrend in the proportion of fiscal revenue in the GDP, few government sectors considered the overall situation from a macro view, and most of them shifted their attention to their own interests. What's more, few government sectors were transferred from public interest providers to a mixed body pursuing both public and private interests. As the government "role" is distorted, the government finds it hard to consider the phenomena that the resident income distribution gap appears and widens and to put the regulation of the resident income distribution gap on the agenda. Effective measures that may damage their vested interests are not adopted.

Finally, China's current resident income distribution gap appears and widens in the period of institutional transition with a "system vacuum". As mentioned above, in the planned economic system, there was an effective system to regulate resident income distribution, but it was weakened and even disappeared with the development of market-oriented reform. At the same time, the new regulatory system hadn't been established yet, so there was a "system vacuum" that caused the income distribution to go out of control. Since there was no institutional norm or order about income distribution, it is not a surprise that the income gap appeared between urban and rural areas, between high-income and low-income groups, and among regions, industries and forms of ownership.

5.6 Against such a background, taxation, as the government's most important tool to regulate income distribution, should perform its functions in a new manner and in a combination of theory and practice. At present, a proper choice is to solve the problem of income distribution by standardizing government behaviors in three fields: 1) adjusting policy, i.e. changing the "laissez faire" or "tolerance" attitude to get involved positively in resident income distribution; 2) correcting orientation, i.e. following the principle that the public interest is the only intention of government; and 3) simplifying systems, i.e. establishing and improving the income distribution system in the market economy. Therefore, the government should specify the regulating functions of taxation and put them into practice. In fact, based on normative government behavior and cooperation with other regulatory measures, there is space for taxation to perform its regulating functions on income distribution.

In order to solve the problems concerning income distribution in China, the government must take various measures for income redistribution including tax, but it can't totally rely on the redistribution mechanism. In current China, it is important to build a fair base for primary distribution, and it is urgent to solve the problem of "unfair primary distribution". Unless the problem of "unfair primary distribution" is solved, various regulations on redistribution will not work well, and the situation of the "great income distribution gap" will not be eased.

Conclusion 8: Taxation should aim at the regulation of resident income distribution, but it is not inclusive, i.e. not all the problems of income distribution in current China can be solved by it.

Section 6

6.1 Taxation's function to promote continuous, steady economic development is also called the macro regulation function, which means that tax can promote continuous, steady economic development.

6.2 According to macroeconomics, the relationship between taxation and continuous, steady economic development is concluded as two "stabilizers". The first one is an "automatic stabilizer", which means that tax can offset the economic fluctuation automatically by a smart arrangement of the tax system. For instance, as to income tax in different periods of economic depression and economic prosperity, its amount will be decreased or increased automatically to slow economic downturns or depress inflation. The second is a "manual stabilizer", which means tax can be a kind of economic power to maintain general balance between demand and supply so as to promote steady macroeconomic development by proper decisions on tax policy made in different periods, such as reducing tax during economic depression and increasing tax during economic prosperity.

During historical economic development, both stabilizers performed quite well. Income tax with the feature of automatic change was included in every country's tax system and played a role in supporting steady economic development. It is still amazing that the tax cut policy carried out by the Reagan government more than 20 years ago and the tide of tax cuts driven by it made a great contribution to economic growth in America and the world. In China, despite the short period of carrying out tax policy to regulate total social demand, tax policy helped promote China's rapid economic growth. In the era of planned economy, though there was no concept about total demand and supply or macro economy, and tax was not like tax in modern times, tax was still adopted to regulate the economy. Moreover, tax regulation did influence the total demand and supply or macroeconomic balance. Therefore, China's theorists and government sectors are very familiar with the macro-control function of tax policy and its mechanism.

6.3 The problem arises from the judgment about current situation. Since 1998, when government took a proactive fiscal policy to deal with deflation, there were different opinions about tax cuts. At the annual economic working conference, whether the government should carry out tax cuts or not was frequently discussed. Especially in the recent two years, under the background of tightening collection and rapid growth of tax revenue, discussions about tax cuts are prevailing.

6.4 Tax cuts involve many complex factors that should be screened.

Pure tax cuts won't be fully accepted because tax is the cost of government action after all. Enterprises have to reduce cost, which means reducing the cost of government action, though tax is good for anyone at any time. The only restricted condition is that government can perform its functions as usual. Therefore, tax cuts should be used to balance income and expenditure. Discussions about tax cuts must also be correlated with government revenue and expenditure or government functions. This is the first point.

There is a special implication in tax cuts. A normative government action aims to reduce tax by regulating or improving the existing tax system, such as reducing tax categories, narrowing the tax base and decreasing the tax rate. Letting tax evasion slide or ignoring the existing tax system in providing tax relief for enterprises and residents is not what tax cuts are meant to do. Therefore, we should understand tax cuts with the normalized idea against the background of the market economy, and should not take it as a non-normative action determined by a leader or Party and government department. This is the second point.

In the frame of the existing tax system, the tax sector naturally takes the responsibility to collect tax according to law. Moreover, this is an objective which the tax sector must try to pursue. Therefore, complaining about tightening collection and advancing collection efficiency or complaining about that the tax sector follows a rigid program to impose a heavy tax burden on enterprises and residents is no doubt one-sided and improper. On the contrary, the tax sector must take all necessary actions to collect tax according to law. This is the third point.

However it is described, the purpose of tax cuts is to "reduce burden", i.e. reduce the burden borne by enterprises and residents and promote high economic growth. Therefore, any measure that helps reduce the burden borne by enterprises and residents can realize the intention of tax cuts, and it can be seen as a "substitutional" measure of tax cuts. This is the fourth point.

With the knowledge above, it is easy to reach an agreement about tax cuts.

6.5 As the purpose of tax is to finance revenue for government action, its scale depends directly on the scale of government expenditure. If it cannot adjust government functions, the scale of government expenditure can't be reduced as expected; if tax cuts cannot satisfy the adjustment of government functions, the result must be one of the following: the government is forced to increase the scale of national debts to fill the gap caused by tax cuts, or it is forced to change tax policy.

When the government tries to reduce the scale of government expenditure based on real government functions, we are depressed to find that situation mentioned above seems highly likely in China. On the one hand, the adjustment of government functions in the period of institutional transition is very slow. In the existing legal framework, no effective restraint mechanism could restrict the expansion of government expenditure. The financial sector is not able to reduce the scale of expenditure. On the other hand, since the reform, the difficulty of fiscal revenue and expenditure in China has never eased the fact that the deficit continues year by year and the scale of national debts increases year after year. So there is little space to adjust the scale of expenditure. If government expenditure can't be reduced, in case of financial difficulty, tax cuts will get worse.

Therefore, the implementation of tax cuts must follow the idea of "revenue based on expenditure" as described in 4.4, i.e. the government should carry out tax cuts while standardizing government functions and decreasing government expenditure. Moreover, it is more urgent and important to regulate functions and reduce expenditure.

6.6 As tax cuts are a kind of institutional arrangement, it should be realized by normative actions such as adjusting or improving the tax system. We should look at it from along-sighted view. If the design of the tax system is combined with periodic economic fluctuation, the tax system should be adjusted with the change in economic situation so that it can meet the government demand of economic intervention because taxation is more a steady measure than a good policy. SOEs should be supported by state finance, but it is improper to support it by tax cuts. To solve deflation, tax policy and expenditure policy should focus on different aspects. The short-term projects can be supported by fiscal expenditure policy while the long-term institutional innovation must be supported by tax policy.

Therefore, tax cuts should be a long-term strategic institutional innovation. The short-term measure, especially the emergency measure, should not affect the long-term aim to adjust the institutional structure.

6.7 The current tax system was established in 1994. Since then, the pattern of the tax system hasn't been adjusted, nor has the tax policy. The government has not increased tax categories (except transferring the vehicle purchase fee to vehicle purchase tax which is covered by "fee-to-tax" and re-collecting interest income tax which belongs to individual income tax), or widened the tax base or raised the tax rate. There have been no measures regarding tax increases in recent years. The tax system and policy remain the same. The recent rapid growth of tax revenue can be analyzed from the perspective of economic growth to tighten tax collection and adjust the one-off policy, including "fee-to-tax" conversion.

It is common sense that tax revenue naturally increases with economic growth, and will increase under a one-off regulatory policy. Pursuing the increase in tax revenue by tightening collection and advancing collection efficiency is the bound duty for tax sectors. Therefore, the current tax policy can't be analyzed according to a tax increase, and the situation of tax revenue can't be described as deviating from tax cuts.

6.8 According to the analysis in 3.5 and 3.6, the "total tax burden" and "general tax burden" borne by enterprises and residents has become heavier in recent years. From macro view of promoting continuous, steady economic development, it is necessary and possible to reduce tax burdens on enterprises and residents.

In order to reduce "total tax burden", we should standardize government revenue action and its mechanism. For taxation or other forms of government revenue, the important point is to determine if it is a normative mechanism. The purpose of tightening collection and starting "fee-to-tax" is to establish a normative mechanism. If government can finance revenue at will, the burden borne by enterprises and residents will not be relieved. The reason why people hate government fees is the non-normative mechanism. Therefore, if the heavy tax burden borne by enterprises and residents is caused by asynchrony between tightening collection and "fee-to-tax", and if the slow process of "fee-to-tax" is caused by the small operating "space" left by normative government revenue, it is urgent to speed up "fee-to-tax" conversion when rapid growth of tax revenue weakens the dependence on non-normative government revenue. Moreover, the "fee-to-tax" conversion should be combined with adjustment of the tax system to consider the scale of government revenue and tax burden borne by enterprises and residents as a whole from a macro view of standardizing government revenue action and its mechanism (Gao Peiyong, 1999a). Once the government revenue action and its mechanism are standardized, the tax burden borne by enterprises and residents will decrease automatically. In other words, the purpose of tax cuts can be realized by standardizing government revenue action and its mechanism in China.

In order to reduce "general tax burden", the government should do two things. First, it can review the pattern of tax system confirmed in 1994 according to the fact that tax collection was improved. If possible, it should adjust the current tax system. For instance, according to the analysis in 3.6, the real rate of tax collection has increased and the production of the tax base, tax rate and real rate of tax collection has also increased. As to value-added tax, the wide productive tax base and high tax rate of 17% seem unnecessary. Narrowing the tax base and decreasing the tax rate accordingly are optional actions, so it is necessary to re-plan the whole pattern of the tax system. Second, based on the fact that the shortage economy has gone and inflation has been replaced by deflation, the government should review the policy tendency of the current tax system and take this opportunity to correct the tax system arrangements that hinder economic development, e.g. transferring the productive value-added tax to consumptive value-added tax to advance enterprises' ability to upgrade and expand investment, transferring the business tax levied by the sale of real estate and the construction and installation industry to added-value tax to reduce enterprises' comparative heavy investment cost, and reducing some products' consumption tax properly to stimulate consumption demand. China's tax system may stride forward to help the development of the market economy and steady economic growth by clearing up the laws, regulations and policies about taxation as well as the stipulations made by economic sectors and governments at all levels.

6.9 It is very important to be aware of what we can do and what we can't do by discussing tax cuts from a macro view, which may help avoid making specious decisions.

Conclusion 9: Tax cutting is a systematic program and its implementation requires support from other sectors.

Conclusion 10: According to the market economy, proper choices for tax policy against the background of current national conditions include "reducing burden", reviewing the scale of government revenue and re-constructing the pattern of government revenue by standardizing government revenue action and its mechanism.

Section 7

7.1 The slogan of "law-based tax administration" has been chanted for many years. Building a law-based social environment for tax administration is also an aim pursued for many years. However, once we look back at the road of law-based tax administration and review the real tax environment in China, we will find that all this is confusing and hinders the process of law-based tax administration in China. But why?

7.2 In the author's opinion, the deepest problem about law-based tax administration is: properly defining taxation and regulating relevant authorities' behaviors (Gao Peiyong, 1999b). In short, this involves the concept and operating rules of taxation.

This issue seems simple but is complex in fact because it contains political and economic ideas, obeys a rule in certain economic system and relates to the layout of the whole operation mechanism of taxation. It is a compound product of superstructure and economic foundation.

7.3 In the era of planned economy, the government was the representative of the public-owned economy. Government revenue and expenditure were operated within the range of the public-owned economy, especially the stated-owned economy. Government revenue was mainly financed through public-owned economic units while government expenditure mainly flew into public-owned economic units. As the revenue was financed by these units and the expenditure flew into these units, how to arrange the operation was determined on their own. Based on this idea, taxation at that time was considered as "essential deduction" within public ownership by political power. The civilians were the objects and the government was the subject of "essential deduction", so taxation was just a nominal concept whose essence was "essential deduction". As "essential deduction", how to deduct it or how to confirm its amount seemed unnecessary.

From the planned economy to the market economy, the economic system environment has changed, and the explanation about taxation has also been corrected. But why should it be corrected and how to correct it? The answers remain unclear. The chronic measure to replace "essential deduction" with "due obligation" became acceptable to theorists and government at that time. Although it was far-fetched to make tax payment a glorious obligation for every citizen, this measure was getting closer to the market economy as compared with the "essential deduction".

However, "due obligation" was proposed based on "essential deduction", so it was still characterized by a planned economy. With advancement of market economic consciousness, it was hard for taxpayers to accept an idea that placed more emphasis on obligation than on right; moreover, this idea also puzzled government about taxation, the result of which was not worth all efforts devoted to law-based tax administration.

Conclusion 11: Taxation and its operation rules should keep pace with the times, i.e. it should be adjusted pursuant to the changing economic environment.[3]

7.4 It is encouraging that the proposal and construction of the public finance frame provides a good platform for law-based tax administration. It can be said that, for China's financial operation mechanism, replacing "national finance" with "public finance" is not only the adjustment of expenditure but also a complete and fundamental reform because it covers all revenue, expenditure, management and relevant ideas and rules.

In the frame of public finance, the only reason why government exits or operates is to provide public goods or services for all social members. Government revenue and expenditure depend on producing or providing public goods or services generally. Government revenue is financed to produce or provide public goods or services. Government expenditure is also used to provide public goods or services to benefit all social members. Government revenue and expenditure are deemed as "doing its own business by its own property" in the planned economy but as "doing public business by public property" in the market economy.

7.5 Once law-based tax administration is put under the frame of public finance, many issues which were confusing will become clear at once.

In the market economy, the essence of government is just a special industrial sector that produces or provides public goods or services while enterprises and residents are consumers of public goods or services. Terms usually used to describe private goods or services include production and consumption as well as purchase and sale of public goods or services. Enterprises and residents have to pay tax to exchange it for consumption rights in public goods or services. The government collects taxes to provide public goods or services.

Once taxpayers pay tax by law, they can enjoy the rights to ask government to provide public goods or services; once government collects tax by law, it has to undertake its obligation to provide public goods or services. Public goods or services consumed by taxpayers originate from the public goods or services provided by government sectors, and the funds used to provide public goods or services originate from taxes paid by taxpayers. So there is symmetry between the obligation to pay tax and the right to consume public goods or services, and between the power to collect taxes and the obligation to provide public goods or services. Tax relationships among different main bodies are expressed as a symmetry between power (right) and obligation.

Conclusion 12: Taxation in the market economy can be concluded as the "symmetry between power (right) and obligation".

7.6 Government's behaviors in taxation are distinguished from the tax sector's taxation behaviors in that the tax sector collects tax to finance public goods or services for government and that the government uses tax revenue financed by tax sectors to provide public goods or services. So, the tax sector is called "tax levier" and the government "tax user".[4] In practice, the essential relations of taxation among behavior subjects is "trinitarian", i.e. enterprises and residents "pay money", the tax sector "collects money" and government "spends money". Governments at all levels and enterprises and residents stay at two poles, and the tax sector serves as the bridge to link these two poles.

It is necessary to distinguish government sectors from tax-related behaviors and name them differently. There are government officials who don't know the funds are financed by tax revenue, so some of them spend money wastefully. There are government officials who don't know their wages originate from tax revenue, so some of them think of performing government functions as a gift to the public. There also are government officials who pay no attention to tax work or even obstruct tax work. However, from the chain of "enterprises and residents → tax sector → government sectors", we can see the key position and decisive function of governments at all levels for law-based tax administration; whether the taxpayer can pay tax based on law and whether the tax levier can collect tax based on law are determined by whether the tax user can use tax efficiently to some extent. If the taxpayer finds that tax revenue paid by them is used improperly or ineffectively, the behaviors about tax payment will be in disorder. Tax collection will also be affected.

Conclusion 13: Tax users' ideas and behaviors about taxation not only influence taxpayers but also tax leviers' ideas and behaviors about taxation. So the emphasis on law-based tax administration should be shifted onto tax users.

7.7 Once the symmetry among taxpayer, tax levier and tax user is considered, we can make the conclusions below: in current China, the advancement of law-based tax administration and construction of social environment for law-based tax administration depend on confirmation of the ideas of the taxpayer, tax levier and tax user, and on standardization of their behaviors.

Enterprises and residents should have "tax payment consciousness", i.e. the money paid to the tax sector is tax revenue. Tax is a necessary cost to provide enterprises and residents with public goods or services. Just like paying bills after consuming at restaurants or stores, paying tax for public goods or services is legally required; any behaviors related to tax evasion is just like theft; correspondingly, tax evasion means reducing the quantity of public goods or serviced enjoyed by other members. Therefore, the appearance and spread of tax evasion concerns everyone's major interest. Every taxpayer has the right to stop or correct tax evasion; the operating funds of government are paid by taxpayers and should be used to provide public goods or services for all social members. Taxpayers have the right to supervise the usage of tax revenue.

Conclusion 14: As taxpayers, enterprises and residents are obligated to pay taxes, and they also have the right to consume public goods and services.

The government sector should have "tax user consciousness", i.e. the money they spend comes from tax revenue. Tax revenue originates from enterprises' and residents' income, which is hard-earned money; enterprises and residents should pay taxes because the government provides public goods or services for them. The government must use every cent carefully to provide public goods or services for all taxpayers and accept supervision from "taxpayers". When using tax revenue, the government must be supervised by the people's congresses at all levels and the masses, since tax revenue is the base and lifeline of the operation of government sectors. Without tax revenue or if collection of tax is hindered, the government will not produce or provide public goods or services. Governments at all levels must take good care of law-based tax administration as they care about their "provisions" – fund sources.

Conclusion 15: As the tax user, the government sector must not only perform their obligations to produce or provide public goods or services but also operate the power to maintain the authority of tax law and ensure proper use of tax revenue.

The tax sector should have "tax levier consciousness", i.e. the money they collect from enterprises and residents is tax revenue. Tax revenue is the funding source to produce or provide public goods or services. Tax revenue is collected as required in time to perform government functions, operate the state apparatus and steady social and economic development. Tax is the necessary cost of public goods and services paid by consumers. The tax payer is not only the payer of tax but also the beneficiary of public goods or services; strict enforcement and law-based tax administration involve all social members' major interests. The role of tax levier is just like a ticket seller: it collects tax from the taxpayer (passenger) according to law and uses it to finance public goods or services; it also punishes the tax evader (ticket evader) according to law, to forbid free-riding.

Conclusion 16: As the tax levier, the tax sector must not only perform their obligations to stop tax evasion but also operate the power of tax collection to ensure fairness and seriousness during law enforcement.

The confirmation of the idea of "symmetric power (right) and obligation" and the standardization of taxpayers, tax leviers and tax users' behaviors will create and promote a new environment for law-based tax administration.

(Originally published in *Taxation Research* in Vols.2 and 3, 2000)

Notes

1 Yang Zhiqing's research (1997) indicated that the macro tax burden of most developed countries is about 35%, and the index of developing countries ranges between 20% and 30%.

2 Typical survey data in 1996, higher than that in 2000.

3 The detailed discussion about the evolution of China's tax conception can be seen in the writer's monograph named *Discussion about Upgrading Tax Conception* published by Taxation Research, Vol.3, 1999.

4 The writer's suggestion about tax users first appeared at the Beijing Kuangou Tax Work Forum hosted by director Jin Renqingin August 1998. Since that time, it has been accepted and appears in various literature frequently. Systematic discussions about tax-payers, tax leviers and tax users can be seen in the monograph *Tax Payer, Tax Levier and Tax User* published by *Guangming Daily* on September 26, 2000.

Bibliography

Chen Xiaopin. (2001). Research on the reasonable scale of government finance in China. *Information and Data on Chinese Finance and Economics, 22.*

Gao Peiyong. (1999a). Discussing upgrading concept about tax. *Taxation Research, 3.*

Gao Peiyong. (1999b, January 25). Fee-to-tax: The essence to standardize the government revenue mechanism. *Economic Daily.*

Gao Peiyong. (2001). Discussion about the "expenditure based on revenue" and "revenue based on expenditure" on condition of current growth trend about fiscal revenue. *Finance & Trade Economics, 3.*

Gao Peiyong. (2002). Standardizing government behavior: The key to solve the current problem about current income distribution in China. *Finance & Trade Economics, 1.*

Wang Shaoguang. (2001). Political influence of income inequality. *Inside Information on Economic Reform, 18.*

Yang Zhiqing. (1997). International macro tax burden. *Taxation Research, 6.*

8 Four basic judgments on tax cuts

Since implementation of the proactive fiscal policy in 1998, the topic of tax cuts has been discussed for four years. In general, the understanding about tax cuts has become deeper and wider, and conclusions have become more realistic as well. Now, it is the time to summarize these discussions and make judgments accordingly.

Judgment 1: tax cuts are always right

This is because tax is the cost of government actions. Just like enterprises that have to reduce business costs and advance productivity, the government, as a special industrial sector, needs to cut down taxes paid by enterprises and residents for public goods or services, provided that the quality and quantity of their public goods or services do not hence worsen or decrease. In that case, the cost and efficiency of government actions will be reduced and improved respectively, and even the resource allocation and welfare of the whole society will be bettered. It is good for anyone at any time. Therefore, any suggestions or solutions about tax cuts are worth encouraging. Moreover, tax cuts should be an aim for the government to pursue constantly and industriously.

Judgment 2: the purpose of tax cuts is to ease burden

The purpose of tax cuts, especially in the current situation, is to ease the burden on enterprises and residents caused by government, by which it expects to boost domestic demand to achieve high economic growth. So, any income gained from enterprises and residents by government can be taken into consideration as burden alleviation. However, tax cuts are not the only way to ease burden.

According to the general pattern of current government revenue in China, tax is just one kind of burden caused by the government. Besides, there are other ways to gain revenue for government, where normative budgetary revenue includes enterprise revenue, education surcharge and sundry income; the revenue that can be calculated correctly but is not covered by the budget includes off-budget revenue, governmental funds and social security funds; and the revenue gained outside of the system that can't be calculated correctly includes various fees, penalties and collective funds, which are charged by government sectors and governments at all levels. If the four kinds of revenue above are put together, the total amount of China's government revenue will at least double tax revenue.

According to a preliminary estimate, in 2000, the aggregate of tax revenue totaled RMB 1266 billion, accounting for 14.16% of GDP that year. If the second and third forms of government revenue are put together, the figure would be RMB 2631.487 billion, accounting for 29.43% of GDP. Then, if the fourth form is added, i.e. revenue gained out of system, it would be 5% of GDP (typical survey data in 1996, higher than that in 2000), and the proportion of total government revenue including revenue out-of-system in the GDP was 34.43%.

Whether covered by the budget or not, the former two are normative government revenue and the latter two are non-normative government revenue. Due to the co-existence of normative and non-normative government revenue, the amount of the last one is higher than the former one; in 1998, Premier Zhu Rongji described the pattern of government revenue as "fee is higher than tax" and started "fee-to-tax" conversion. Therefore, following the view that China's government revenue action and its mechanism need to be standardized, the government would reduce non-normative government revenue rather than reduce normative government revenue, and reduce government fee rather than reduce tax.

In fact, whether tax or government fees or other forms of government revenue, what matters is whether a normative mechanism exists or not. If government can gain revenue at will, the burden borne by enterprises and residents will not be eased. The reason people hate government fees lies in the non-normative mechanism.

What's more, one of the most important reasons why the burden borne by enterprises and residents becomes heavier is the asynchrony between tightening collection and "fee-to-tax" conversion. On the one hand, tightening tax causes the real rate of collection to increase and support the rapid growth of tax revenue. On the other hand, the process of "fee-to-tax" conversion is so slow that there has been no essential progress till now. As one develops rapidly but the other slowly, imbalance occurs between them. The non-normative government revenue can't decrease with the increase in normative government revenue. Therefore, when the rapid growth of tax revenue weakens the dependence on non-normative government revenue, it is urgent to speed up "fee-to-tax" conversion. Moreover, the "fee-to-tax" conversion should be combined with adjustment of the tax system in order to regulate the scale of government revenue and the burden borne by enterprises and residents from the macro view of standardizing government revenue action and its mechanism. Once government revenue action and its mechanism are normative, the burden borne by enterprises and residents will decrease automatically. In other words, tax cuts can be realized by standardizing government revenue action and its mechanism in China, and its policy effect may not be second to tax cuts.

Judgment 3: expenditure reduction is more important than tax cuts

As tax is collected as a fiscal source, its scale is directly determined by the scale of government expenditure. There are only two results from tax cuts if there is no adjustment in government function and no decrease in fiscal expenditure: first, the government has to increase the issuance of national debts in order to fill the revenue gap caused by tax cuts; and second, the government has to initiate another tide of charging of fees to fill this gap.

The problem is that once the government tries to reduce the scale of government expenditure according to real government functions, we are depressed to find that the occasions above are very possible in China. On the one hand, adjustment of government functions during the period of institutional transition is very slow, although it didn't cut old functions but created new functions. Under the existing legal system, there is no effective mechanism to restrict the expansion of government expenditure. The financial sector is not able to reduce the scale of expenditure. On the other hand, the government sectors that still keep the idea of federal imperial power in a planned economic system used to gain revenue from enterprises and residents by administrative methods and non-normative methods for years. The financial and tax sectors also have no ability to stop the spread of non-normative government revenue action and its mechanism.

Therefore, if the government has to cut taxes, other measures to reduce the scale of government expenditure must be issued synchronously. Moreover, comparing tax cuts with expenditure reduction, we find that the latter has priority over the former.

When government expenditure decreases but tax revenue fails to decrease, there is the second result: the surplus revenue can be used to cover the bills over the years or reduce the continual deficits and national debts. Needless to say, it is just like a timely rain for fiscal difficulty alleviation and fiscal risk prevention.

Judgment 4: tax cuts are currently possible and necessary

The existing tax system in China has been implemented since 1994. The objective economic and social environment has changed greatly ever since then. With the advancement of tax collection as well as the good systematic base established by the new tax system, the real rate of collection in China has increased. It is estimated that the rate of collection increased by at least 10%, and the increase in the real rate of collection not only installs an "accelerator" for tax revenue but also changes the real social tax burden.

Common sense tells us that in any situation at any time, the design of an entire tax system and the arrangements for one tax category are based on the existing scale of tax revenue. However, the existing revenue is not determined by the product of tax base and tax rate. The real rate of tax will not reach 100% in practice, whether tax base or the tax rate is selected, and the design of the tax system will follow the principle of "wide coverage and narrow usage", i.e. the real rate of collection makes the tax rate wider and higher. Therefore, it is different from "systematic" tax burden, i.e. it is the product of tax base and tax rate, but the "real" tax burden is the product of tax base, tax rate and real rate of collection. Any change in any factor will change the real tax burden, which means that even if there is no measure to increase systematic tax burden such as expanding the tax base or raising tax the rate, the real tax burden will rise with the improvement in tax collection.

Under the current tax system in China, both the tax base and the tax rate are confirmed according to the real rate of collection achieved in 1994. If the real rate of collection at that time could reach the level now, the tax system in China especially the tax base and tax rate would be quite different. For instance, the wide productive tax base and high tax rate of 17% are unnecessary to value-added tax. The current real tax burden in China increased as compared with that in 1994. In the real situation of the tax system, it is necessary and possible to review and adjust the real tax burden in order to reduce the tax burden borne by enterprises and residents.

So far, it is very important to be aware of what we can do and what we can't do by discussing topics such as tax cuts from a macro view, which will help avoid making specious decisions.

(Originally published in *Guangming Daily* on July 2, 2000)

9 Finance and taxation situations, policies and reforms

A review of several major finance and taxation issues in the face of the "Eleventh Five-Year Plan" period

Preface

When the "Tenth Five-Year Plan" period comes to an end and the "Eleventh Five-Year Plan" period arrives, we should work hard to make a comprehensive and systematic review of current major finance and taxation issues, and make profound and meticulous judgments on finance and taxation situations, policies and reforms in the Eleventh Five-Year Plan period. This is not just because China's finance and taxation reforms are placed in a critical position in the *CPC Central Committee's Suggestions on the Formulation of the Eleventh Five-Year Plan for National Economic and Social Development, a paper released at the Fifth Plenary Session of the Sixteenth CPC Central Committee* and will become a major battle of the crucial war during the whole Eleventh Five-Year Plan period, but also because it has already reached a very significant threshold after a decade's development since 1994. Many changes and elements in this sector now become the global focus, hot topics and difficulties concerning China's overall economic and social development. The subject of this paper is proposed in this context.

Next, what shall we do?

To review the reality is to seize the future; to look back at what've done in the last five or more years is to outline a work program for the next five or more years; but it's neither necessary nor feasible to reach deep down in every aspect, whether important or trivial. One practical and effective option is to do less for more. In other words, we should focus on major matters, loosen the control of minor matters, seize the critical points and get a global perspective from deep analysis of major issues. Under the guidance of these ideas, this paper selects six issues concerning China's finance and taxation reforms and development for discussion, such as changing the scale of fiscal revenue and expenditure, making judgment on fiscal risks, ensuring sustainable rapid growth of tax revenue, weakening the government budget constraint mechanism, defining prudent fiscal policy and initiating a new round of taxation system reform.

I Changing the scale of fiscal revenue and expenditure

1 Scale of fiscal revenue

According to Figure 9.1 below, the 12-year period from 1994 to 2005 saw a sustainable rapid growth of the scale of China's fiscal revenue, clearly quite different from what was before 1994. The national revenue was barely RMB 521.810 billion in 1994, up to RMB 1000 billion in 1999, RMB 2000 billion in 2003, and hit a record high of RMB 3162.8 billion in 2005. The ratio of fiscal revenue to GDP increased from 10.95% in 1994 to 17.35% in 2005.

For the scale of fiscal revenue, there are two points to be clarified.

First, our fiscal revenue is not absolutely equivalent to our tax revenue. There is a series of complicated calculations standing in between. Taxes of various categories are calculated as tax revenue of the previous year published by the State Administration of Taxation (SAT) every January 1, plus tariffs and agricultural taxes such as agriculture (animal husbandry) taxes, taxes on agricultural specialty products, farmland occupation taxes, deed taxes and net of export rebates. The actual fiscal revenue is computed as the taxes of various categories plus all special incomes including education surcharges, pollution discharge fees, usage charges of urban resources and net loss of business.

Second, the scale of fiscal revenue should be determined after comparisons. Usually there are two reference coefficients. If compared with the actual figure of the previous year, its scale will be "increased"; but if compared with its budget or planned figure this year, its scale will be "excessive". The increased revenue is not the excessive revenue, for both may have a great distance. Take the year of

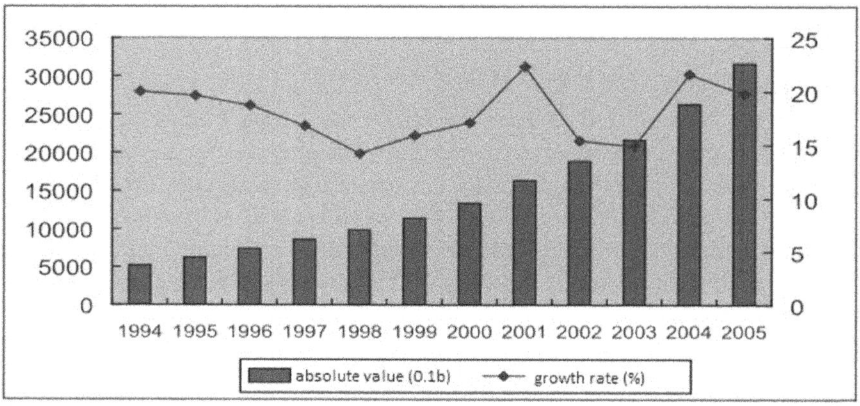

Figure 9.1 Changes in the scale of China's fiscal revenue (1994–2005)

Sources: Editorial Committee of China's Finance Year Book: *Finance Year Book of China (2004)*, *China State Finance Magazine*; Ministry of Finance: *Reports on 2004 Central and Local Budget Performance & 2005 Central and Local Budget Draft*, China's Finance, Vol.4, 2005; Jin Renqing: *Deepen the Reform, Adhere to the Scientific Development, and Compose a New Finance Epic – a Speech Delivered at the National Work Conference on Finance*, December 19, 2005

2004 for instance: the national fiscal revenue was RMB 2636.947 billion, and its increased amount was RMB 468.117 billion while its excessive amount was RMB 282.613 billion.[1]

2 Scale of fiscal expenditure

Figure 9.2 gives the changes in the scale of China's fiscal expenditure in the period from 1994 to 2005. This period witnessed a sustainable rapid growth in the scale of China's fiscal expenditure. National spending was barely RMB 579.262 billion in 1994, up to RMB 1000 billion in 1998, 2000 billion in 2002 and hit a record high of RMB 3370.8 billion[2] in 2005. The ratio of fiscal expenditure to GDP increased from 12.16% in 1994 to 18.49% in 2005.

Similarly, comparison was also used in determining the scale of fiscal expenditure. If compared with the actual figure of previous year, its scale will be "increased", but if compared with the budget or planned figure this year, its scale will be "excessive". The increased amount is equivalent to the excessive amount. Take the year of 2004 for instance: the national expenditure was RMB 2848.689 billion, and its increased amount was RMB 383.689 billion while its excessive amount was RMB 171.825 billion, 15.57 percentage points over the previous year.

3 Summary: problems to be explored

The reason why the changes in the scales of fiscal revenue and expenditure matter so much is that they reflect how the government works in resource allocation. Some problems arise from the scale changes in the last 12 years, which should

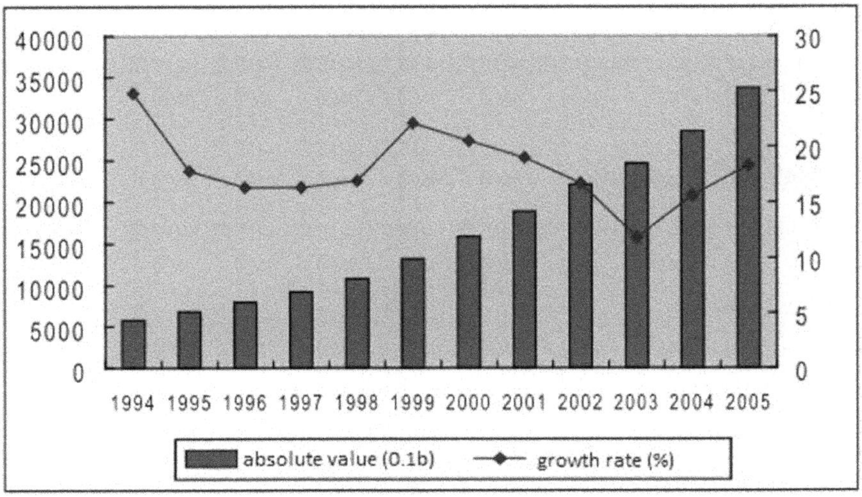

Figure 9.2 Changes in the scale of China's fiscal expenditure (1994–2005)

Source: See Figure 9.1.

be seriously considered and well solved in the Eleventh Five-Year Plan period, including:

1 Whether it's necessary to raise both ratios of fiscal revenue and expenditure to GDP after a decade of high rise. Both scales grew at high rates in those years. As a result, the GDP distribution pattern is gradually lopsided in favor of the government. If it was necessary to raise both ratios in the first few years after 1994 when finance and taxation reform as an ascending ratio was a kind of correction to some extent, how about now?
2 What's the optimal ratio of fiscal revenue to GDP? To lower the ratio was one of our goals at the beginning of the reform and opening up. It was 31.2% in 1978 and hit the new China's record of 39.3% in 1960. However, the figure kept a steady decline in 16 years from 1978 to 1993 and then turned to ascend for 12 years from 1994 to 2005. Now we need to figure out the appropriate ratio.
3 The ratios of fiscal revenue and expenditure to GDP mentioned before just reflect their budgetary scales respectively rather than the actual ones. Take 2005 for instance: if such major spending programs as debt due payment, social security, off-budget and beyond-system programs were credited into the RMB 3400 billion of fiscal expenditure of the year, the ratio in reality would have been at least 30% more and even exceeded the 1978 ratio.
4 Whether there is an end for the expanding public expenditure and under such circumstances, whether it's necessary to legitimate the constraint mechanism for both scales of fiscal revenue and expenditure. We need to know fiscal revenue and expenditure were quickly scaled up in the last 12 years on the basis and support of the rapid revenue growth; fiscal expenditure was able to expand in a quickly just because its constraints were loosened due to the rapid revenue growth. On this account, the government reveals a stronger preference for expansionary spending and is gradually losing its control. So how will it go on?

II Making judgments on fiscal risks

We usually assess the fiscal risks by two indices: fiscal deficit and national debts.

1 Fiscal deficit

Figure 9.3 shows three changes that China's fiscal deficit has experienced during the 12-year period from 1994 to 2005. To basically realize the goal of the elimination of fiscal deficit during the Ninth Five-Year Plan period, our fiscal deficit kept descending in its both absolute and relative values from 1994 to 1997. The year of 1997 saw a deficit valued at RMB 55.845 billion and the deficit-to-GDP ratio down to 0.7%, but its second half witnessed everything turned upside down by the Southeast Asian financial crisis. A proactive fiscal policy was carried out in 1998 and resulted in a booming fiscal deficit. It rose to RMB 309.6 billion and

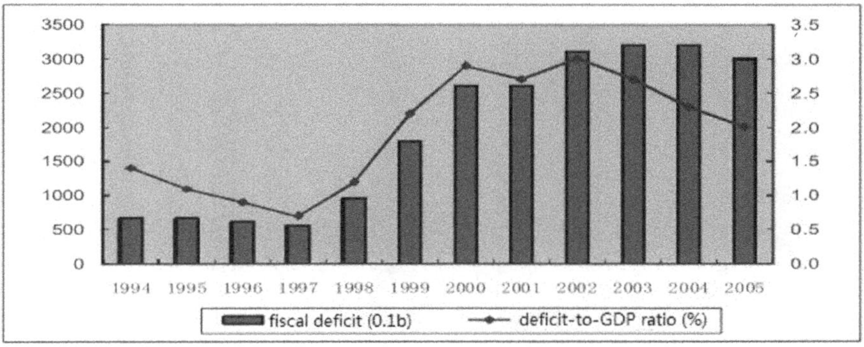

Figure 9.3 Changes in China's fiscal deficits and the deficit-to-GDP ratios (1994–2005)

Source: See Figure 9.1.

the deficit-to-GDP ratio climbed up to 3.0% until 2002. When China's economy began to expand again, the deficit started to be under control. It stayed high up at RMB 319.8 billion in 2003; nevertheless, its proportion of GDP was cut down to 2.7%. In 2005, the two figures were down further to 300 billion and 2.0% respectively.

2 *Scale of national debts*

We need to distinguish two measurable indicators before discussing the scale of national debts. One is the debt balance or the accumulated amount of debts, referred to as a stock indicator. The other is debt issuance volume, referred to as a flow indicator.

Let's review the debt balance first. Figure 9.4 describes how the debt balance and the balance-to-GDP ratio changed from 1994 to 2005. We know from Figure 9.4 that the balance had a fast year-on-year growth. It was barely RMB 283.2 billion in 1994, 6.1% of GDP; RMB 607.4 billion in 1997, 8.2% of GDP; RMB 234.33 billion in 2002, 22.4% of GDP; and up to RMB 329.33 billion in 2005, 22.33% of GDP.

When measuring the current balance of China's national debts, we need to pay more attention to two matters.

One is that China increases its debt balances per year by an amount equivalent to the sum of the current year's fiscal deficit and the long-term construction treasure debt issued by local governments, unlike other countries which increase only by the amount of their deficits of the current year. The reason is our statutory budget law stipulates that the local governments at various levels shall neither constrain deficits nor raise funds from borrowing. However, a compromise has been made since 1998 due to the implementation of a proactive fiscal policy. The additional treasury debts for construction issued by the central government per

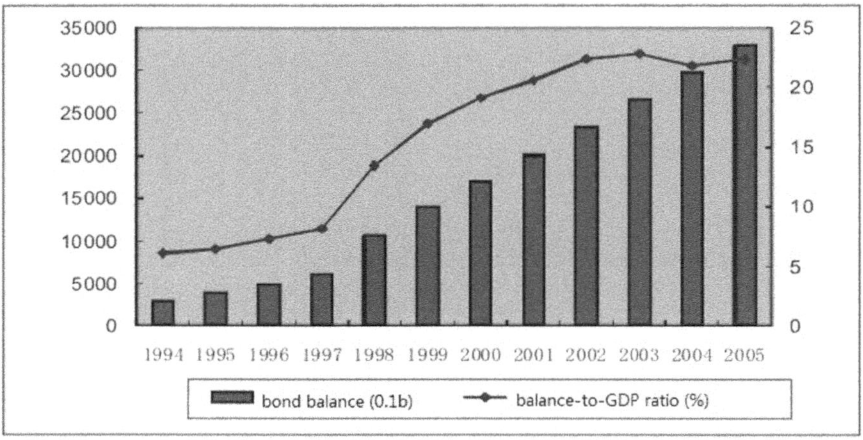

Figure 9.4 Changes in China's debt balance and the balance-to-GDP ratios (1994–2005)

Source: See Figure 9.1.

year actually contain a share nominally credited to the local governments at various levels. The problem is that this share is not included in the current statistics and has amounted to RMB 253 billion.

The other is that a special T-bond (treasury debt) of RMB 270 billion was issued to supplement the capital funds of state-owned commercial banks in 1998. This amount is usually omitted from the calculation of national debt balances due to its long maturity (30 years) and special issuance (internal transfer).

Anyway, these two debts discussed before belong to the Chinese government. We should not omit but include the construction T-bond that has been issued by the central government but credited to local finances for eight successive years and the special T-bond issued in 1998 to the national debts balance.

Then, let's move to the issuance volume. From a comprehensive perspective, the determinants that are critical to the issuance scale of national debts are payments on debt due, payments to make up for deficits and expansion-intended fiscal policies. In other words, the three factors together determine the total amount of national debts to be issued. The long-term construction T-bond is just a part of the national debts issued per year and its cut doesn't mean the issuance scale of the whole of national debts is cut down.

Figure 9.5 indicates a sharp rise and then a slowdown of the issuance scale of long-term construction T-bonds after 1998. It increased from RMB 100 billion at the very beginning to RMB 110 billion, then 150 billion for three consecutive years and then was cut down to RMB 140 billion, 110 billion and 80 billion. By the end of 2005, its accumulated issuance amount has reached RMB 990 billion and the share credited to local finances has amounted to RMB 253 billion.

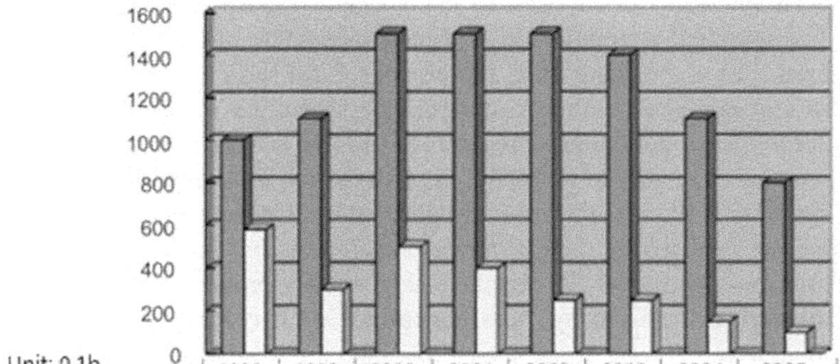

	1998	1999	2000	2001	2002	2003	2004	2005
Issuance volume	1000	1100	1500	1500	1500	1400	1100	800
credited to local	580	300	500	400	250	250	150	100

Figure 9.5 Changes in the issuance scale of China's long-term construction T-bonds (1998–2005)

Source: See Figure 9.1.

Despite the three-year cut of long-term construction T-bonds, the whole issuance scale of national debts is not accordingly reduced. For instance, the issued long-term construction T-bond was cut from RMB 110 billion in 2004 to RMB 80 billion in 2005, but the whole national debts issued was increased from RMB 702.2 billion in 2004 to RMB 702.34 billion in 2005.

3 Summary: problems to be explored

In the author's opinion, fiscal risks, among all economic risks that we have discussed and been faced with so far, are the last line we should defend. In other words, fiscal risks are the most important and austere among all economic risks. Had public finance no potential risks, or were the last defense line held, any other risks wouldn't cause real troubles, or would be under control finally even if they were major.

After reviewing how the two indicators of fiscal risk have changed in the last 12 years, we arrive at some judgments, including:

1 The correlation of fiscal deficit to the unbalanced fiscal revenue and expenditure or the fiscal difficulty is already weakened in China today. We used to believe fiscal deficit was the outcome of unbalanced fiscal revenue and expenditure all along and viewed as a fiscal difficulty unless it worked for the expansionary fiscal policy. The change in fiscal deficit tells a different story, that fiscal revenue had a rapid growth in the last 12 years. Some years,

e.g. the year of 2004, saw both fiscal deficit and excessive fiscal revenue, with the latter being much more than the former. It becomes very simple sometimes to completely wipe out fiscal deficit by employing a part of excessive revenue.

2 The so-called internationally accepted safety line or alert line doesn't even exist. For a very long time, to keep our fiscal risks under control, we have strictly complied with two control lines specified in the EU's Maastricht Treaty: fiscal deficit no more than 3% of GDP and the national debts balance no more than 60% of GDP. But in recent years, a closer survey on economic systems of EU members has enlightened us that both the 3% and the 60% are not justified by their historical experiences but outcomes of their compromises. And some EU members have already broken the two lines and are raising their levels today. Take France and Germany for instance: their deficit-to-GDP ratios were about 4% in 2003 and their ratios of the debt balance to GDP were 65.4% and 62.5% respectively in 2002. Thus, what shall we do to control our fiscal risks when both control lines don't make any sense?

3 Thorough researches on our fiscal deficit and national debts balance remind us of what we calculate and discuss now, whether the level of fiscal deficit or the debt balance is just a tip of the iceberg. In addition, a great amount of implicit and contingent deficits and debt still remains vague. When we know little about our finance, it doesn't work even we manage to keep our deficit and debt balance under the so-called safety or alert line. The real risk comes closer when we know nothing about the whereabouts and capabilities of our enemies.

4 We should strengthen our research on fiscal risks and establish a defense or precautionary system against fiscal risks suitable for Chinese situations during the Eleventh Five-Year Plan period, because now we have no effective measures to slow or stop such a possible trend that various economic risks are gathering in finance.

III Ensuring sustainable rapid growth of tax revenue

1 "Magic cube" growth track

Figure 9.6 shows a constant rapid growth of China's tax revenue after 1994. It's somewhat like a "magic cube", which even daunts those professionals familiar with taxation operation mechanisms and the prevailing taxation pattern in terms of estimates and factors of tax revenue growth.

Let's check out these specific figures. The national tax revenue was barely RMB 478.9 billion in 1994, and increased by RMB 100 billion year on year till 1997. Unexpected situations occurred in 1998. We spared no efforts to overcome many deflationary difficulties before we increased RMB 100 billion of tax revenue over the previous year. But after 1999 our tax revenue seemed to move into such a fast traffic lane that it first hit RMB 1000 billion in 1999, then RMB 1500 billion in 2001, RMB 2000 billion in 2003, RMB 2500 billion in 2004 and RMB 3000 billion in 2005.

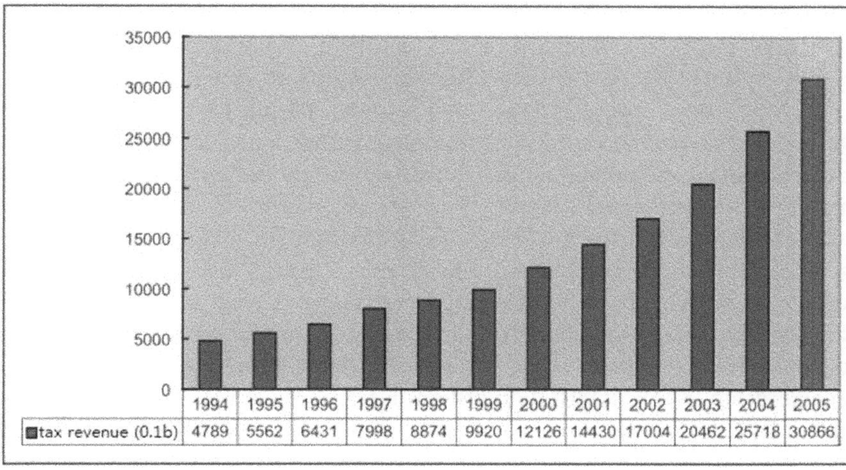

Figure 9.6 Constant rapid growth of China's tax revenue (1994–2005)

Source: See Figure 9.1.

2 Explanations on tax revenue growth

We should be aware that the rapid 12-year growth of China's tax revenue is achieved when no major adjustments are made to the taxation system. The tax revenues do have great jumps forward in its worldwide history, but they are results of their system reforms, such as new categories of taxes, or tax rate raise, or tax base extension. That's why China's story is quite interesting.

Why can China's tax revenue keep up rapid growth for a decade? We used to explain it with the theory of "three factors", which were economic growth, policy adjustment and taxation enhancement. But the increment valued up to RMB 500 billion in 2004 revealed more profound reasons behind this. Now the three-factor theory is replaced by the multi-factor one. The latter attributes our constant rapid growth to economic growth, price rise and the unbalanced structure of tax sources, unbalanced regional development, taxation enhancement and unbalanced import and export.[3]

Obviously the multi-factor theory gives us explanations more comprehensive and realistic than the three-factor theory. However, it's a miracle for China to obtain a rapid growth of tax revenue without any changes in its system for over 10 years. To examine this unusual phenomenon we have to start with China's special factors. What on earth are they?

After a closer look at the six factors, we find probably taxation enhancement is the real accountable and special one, different from other countries. The SAT study reported (Xu Shanda, 2004) China's actual tax collection rate was a little more than 50%in 1994 and rose to 70%in 2003, by 20 percentage points in the 10 years. Accordingly, the amounts of taxes evaded and tax revenue were reduced and increased respectively. Why has China's tax collection rate so much room to develop upward?

Reasons can be found after we check out the birth background of our statutory tax system. In late 1993 the Chinese government faced two urgent problems, which were severe inflation and shortage of finance. In order to curb the high inflation rate up to 20%, the government made full use of all possible maneuvers including the tax system, which was designed with a focus on inhibiting the overheated economy. Besides, in order to reverse the downward trend of the ratio of fiscal revenue to GDP, boosters for revenue increase were incorporated into the tax system. When the two aspects outweighed the other considerations and the actual tax collection rate remained at about 50%, the philosophy of budgeting liberally and spending sparingly turns out to be a logical choice for tax system design. It means we should set up a system framework capable of collecting RMB 1000 billion in taxes if we intended to obtain the goal of RMB 500 billion in tax revenue at the actual collection rate of 50%.[4] In other words, China's statutory tax system reserved much room for development at its birth. For certain the tax revenue soars over the steady rise in the actual tax collection rate. The development prospect of our statutory tax system is likely the most important support for our constant rapid growth in tax revenue in the last 12 years.

3 Summary: problems to be explored

Our constant rapid growth in tax revenue catches wide attention, because it concerns the GDP distribution among government and non-government departments and our macro issues of tax burdens. More importantly it has a significant influence on our overall economic and social development.

Now it seems we might need to ponder those conclusions drawn from the analysis of both phenomena and reasons for the 12-year rapid growth in our tax revenue.

1 Doubts have spread in recent years over whether it's normal to have tax revenue growing faster than GDP. We should know the key lies in what references we measure against, because different references come to totally opposite conclusions. For instance, if we measure against the statutory tax system, it's normal. If they abided by the regulations of the statutory tax system, the law-based tax administrations would do their jobs well in the collection of all taxes payable; if they deliberately failed to collect or under-collect the amount of taxes payable, they would fail to live up to their responsibilities. But if we change another reference, such as normal economic and social development, the final conclusion is the opposite. A tax system needs to always match up with the economic and social development of the country. Our statutory tax system was born 12 years ago and remains almost unchanged over the earthshaking changes of the last 12 years. It's like a grown-up still wearing his childhood shoes. How can the two fit? The ever-lasting tax system is

no longer appropriate when our economic and social situations have gone through 12-year changes. What's even worse is it's now impeding our economic and social development.

2 Debates have never ever stopped on the nominal and actual tax burdens since the birth of the tax system due to its design philosophy of budgeting liberally and spending sparingly. Do enterprises and residents pay too many taxes? The answer is positive and its argument is nothing but our statutory tax system. Coincidentally Forbes ranks China the last but one against the so-called Tax Misery Index. However, if we talked about the tax burden in the shoes of the government, the answer would be negative and its argument would be our ratio of annual tax revenue (taxes actually collected) to GDP. As our tax administrations enhance their taxation and the actual tax collection rate keeps ascending, the disparity between the nominal and actual burdens is getting smaller. We believe the actual burdens on enterprises and civilians were quite appropriate at the birth of our statutory tax system, but are they still suitable today, after 12 years?

3 One of the working goals of the tax administrations is to enhance taxation for more potential revenue. A good prospect in future is that we will have tax employees with better occupational qualities, updated techniques and facilities and greater efforts for tax collection and management. Consequently the nominal and the actual tax burdens will definitely get closer. It's expected that our tax revenue won't stop growing in the following five or more years unless our statutory tax system changes its pattern, or its changes catch up with the rise of our actual tax collection rate and the development process of our economy and society. Is it a possible end for this growth trend? If it is, when?

4 All problems noted earlier are ascribed to whether our statutory tax system can keep pace with our economic and social changes. In the author's view, the tax system should be more advancing with the times than any other economic system, and after months of rapid growth in tax revenue, no matter positive or negative, should be verified and solved over the up-to-date development of our tax system. In other words, the rapid growth in tax revenue over the past decade delivers us an important message that a new round of taxation system reform needs to start as soon as possible.

IV Weakening government budget constraint mechanism

The tough nut has long existed that the central budget has too loose a constraint mechanism on its spending. The reform of the budget management system itself has indeed made much breakthrough progress during our construction of public finance systems in recent years. But if we look at the macro environment that manipulates the government budget constraint mechanism, we will find it was relatively weak in the past 12 years, but has intensified recently. The two clues are the expanded scales of off-budget revenue and expenditure and the oral report of the government budget that was abolished on the NPC agenda.

1 Off-budget revenue

As noted earlier, we have to distinguish the "increased revenue" from the "excessive revenue" before we measure the growth of our fiscal revenue. Unlike the increased amount, which is measured against the actual figure of the previous year, the excessive amount is measured against the budget or planned figure for this year. It breaks the control of our current budget and is beyond our budget framework or plan.

Table 9.1 reveals the changes of our off-budget revenue in the period from 1994 to 2003. It became a regular component of our fiscal revenue and expenditure after 1994, and its scale inclined to get larger on the whole. For instance, its absolute amount was RMB 45.8 billion in 1994 but reached RMB 410.145 billion in 2004. As far as its relative amount was concerned, its share of the total revenue of the current year and that of the increased amount for the current year were 8.8% and 52.7% respectively in 1994, up to 15% and 69% respectively in 2004.

Figure 9.7 indicates the off-budget revenue rose with the fiscal revenue increase in recent years especially after 2002 and its share of both central and local revenue went up sharply, up to 8.73% and 12.81% respectively in 2004.

2 Off-budget expenditure

The next problem is where have these "excessive" funds been spent?

Similar to the measurable indicators of the excessive revenue, the amount above our expenditure budget or planned figure per year is so-called overspending. The tricky issue is our excessive revenue per year is finally completely spent

Table 9.1 Changes in China's off-budget revenue (1994–2003)

Year	*Revenue*	*Increased revenue*	*Budgetary revenue*	*Budgetary increase*	*Off-budget revenue*	*Ratio of OBR to revenue*	*Ratio of OBR to increased revenue*
1994	5218.10	869.15	4759.95	411	458.15	8.8	52.7
1995	6242.20	1024.10	5692.4	474.3	549.8	8.8	53.7
1996	7407.99	1165.79	6872.18	629.98	535.81	7.2	46.0
1997	8651.14	1243.15	8397.94	989.95	253.2	2.9	20.4
1998	9875.95	1224.81	9683.68	1032.54	192.27	1.9	15.7
1999	11444.08	1568.13	10809	933.05	635.08	5.5	40.5
2000	13395.23	1951.15	12338	893.92	1057.23	7.9	54.2
2001	16386.04	2990.81	14760.2	1364.97	1625.84	9.9	54.4
2002	18903.64	2517.60	18015	1682.96	888.64	4.7	35.3
2003	21715.25	2811.61	20501	1597.36	1214.25	5.6	43.2
Total	119239.62	17366.30	111829.35	9956.03	7410.27	6.2	42.7

Sources: National Bureau of Statistics: China Statistical Yearbook (2004); Editorial Committee of China's Finance Year Book: Finance Year Book of China (2004).

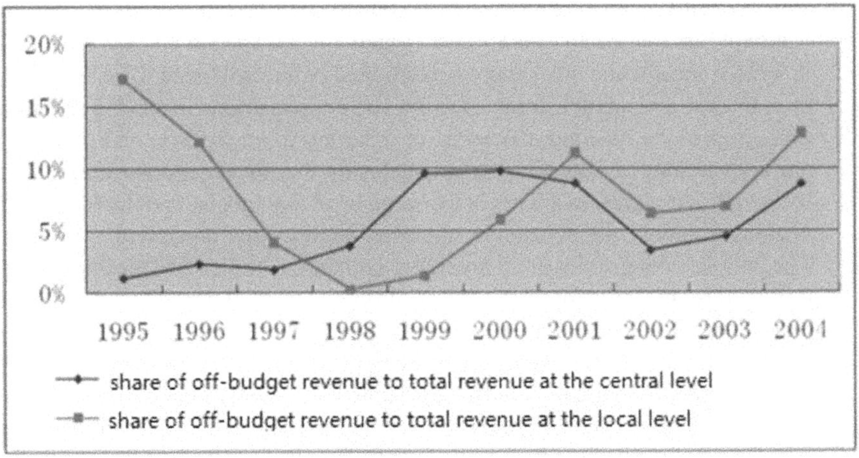

Figure 9.7 Changes in the shares of off-budget revenue to the central and to the local revenue (1994–2004)

Source: See Figure 9.1.

in the same year under our statutory budget management mechanism. Not a penny is saved. It seems like a "one-way shuttle" going from our excessive revenue to our excessive expenditure.

On account of the substantial rise in our fiscal revenue due to a great amount of excessive revenue, we kept overspending in the last few years. A typical example happened in 2004. RMB 410.145 billion of excessive funds neither made up for the current deficit nor was reserved as a budget surplus, but was directly and totally spent.

3 Abolishment of the oral report of government budget

More dramatically, in early 2005 the once-a-year national and local people's congresses at all levels decided to make an extraordinary reform, which was to abolish the oral report of the government budget but to submit only its written report. Apparently it was an agenda adjustment for the purpose of saving valuable meeting time, but from the fact we knew the essence was the reform actually weakened the constraint mechanism of the people's congresses on the government budget that was supposed to be strengthened.

1 In the previous once-a-year NPCs, Report on the Work of the Government, Report on the Plan of National Economic and Social Development, Report on the Government Budget, Report on the Work of the Standing Committee of the National People's Congress, Report on the Work of the Supreme People's Court, and Report on the Work of Supreme People's Procuratorate used to be

official agendas at the same level. Both oral and written reports were needed. But now the Report on the Government Budget and the Report on the Plan of National Economic and Social Development are required to be delivered only in written form while other reports mentioned before still need to be delivered in both oral and written form. Despite such explanations as saving meeting time, improving meeting efficiency or adhering to be realistic and practical, our conventional minds arrive at a conclusion that these reports examined at the people's congresses are not at the same level any longer, and the Report on the Government Budget is not as important as any other document.

2 The people's congresses at all levels are legislative bodies and their principal task is to review and approve a series of proposals including the government budget reports submitted by the administrative departments. The reason is the government should engage in public management activities that are intended to satisfy social public demands. Government activities, of course, should be unveiled to the public and get approval from the legislature that represents a large variety of social members as they are for the public needs and concern all social members. Nevertheless, not all government activities need to submit their official statements to the legislature as they are too diversified. It's neither impossible nor necessary to submit all. The ideal and effective way for the legislative bodies is to focus on the keynote, which reflects and covers the contents of all government activities. In fact the keynote is the fiscal revenue and expenditure.

It's easy to figure it all out. The government has to pay for things, so it needs to raise funds at first. Unavoidably, all aspects of government activities are thus involved. Fund-raising or spending activities for the purpose of public management are always the core contents of all government activities. Compared with other documents on other public management activities submitted by other administrations, the government budget submitted by the finance authorities should be the one that affects the whole and should be most important path and window for the legislature and social members to review and supervise government activities. "The governments can only fulfill all of their duties when their revenue and expenditure meet their budgets": this is a law about the operation of administrative departments. It summarizes the relation between government budgets and other official statements. That's why, among all administrative statements in reality, the government budgets over all others, consume the most time and energy of the legislative bodies of all countries during the review. No doubt the government budgets outweigh any others! It seems that we attend to the trifles but neglect the essentials if we degrade the review priority of government budgets in the core position.

3 China's public finance system has been established for seven years since 1998 when the public finance goals were officially set. The Third Plenary Session of the Sixteenth CPC Central Committee convened in October 2003 established the goal of "improving the public finance system" into the Decisions on Several Issues of Improving the Socialist Market Economy System. Unlike the finance revenue and expenditure pattern that state-owned

economy units mattered most in the planned economy, the public finance system distinguishes itself by its public orientation wherein it raises funds from and works for the whole public rather than only state-owned economy units. By "to raise funds from the whole public", it means all taxes, whatever categories of taxes, or whatever tax bases and rates, are directly or indirectly paid by all social members; by "to work for the whole public", it means all funds, whatever the scale or structure, are spent on the welfare of all social members and how they are spent concerns the vital interests of all social members. Only one thing will draw widespread attention when it's engaged with money. It closely binds the regular lives of the ordinary with the nation's politics, and arouses the enthusiasm and initiatives of all social members to the greatest extent for their participation in political affairs.

From the perspective of strengthening the construction of socialist political civilization, it's undoubtedly very important to connect the daily life of ordinary people with state politics as much as possible and set up a bridge between the two. The government budget, based on public finance, is such an indispensable bridge. It tells us that any move that weakens the government budget mechanism a little deviates from the construction goals of our public finance system and from the direction of socialist political civilization as well.

4 Our government budgets in reality do have many defects such as not covering all governmental departments; too extensive, general and opaque budgets; and a weak rule of law. These issues are always discussed and need to be corrected as soon as possible. They are supposed to be more complete, intensive, transparent, scientific and more constraining on governmental behaviors in taxation and spending after the reforms. To fulfill these goals, the people's congresses at all levels have to enhance their approval and supervision of government budgets. The improvement will be a most important and reliable push for reforms.

In that context, it's not too much but too little time that the people's representatives spent on reviewing government budgets; it's not too troublesome that they listened, read and reviewed, but too little that they listened, read and reviewed. It seems like they are doing a perfunctory job rather than a real one. If the people's congresses at all levels needed to reform their agendas on the government budget reports, they should increase rather than reduce the review time and enhance rather than relieve the review efforts. It would definitely slow down the progress of the reforms on government budget system and might even lead to negative consequences if the atmosphere of the under-serious review were to be diluted, the weak efforts made to the review were to be lessened and the countable review procedures were to be omitted.

4 Summary: problems to be explored

Debates on the weakening constraint mechanism for government budgets noted earlier tell us that we should not hold an over-expectation on the status quo of the laws of government budgets. Looking to the economic and social development pattern in the Eleventh Five-Year Plan period, we find it's urgent and necessary to well solve some issues as follows:

1 What's the scientific way to estimate revenue? It's a good thing to have "excessive revenue" in the past 10 years, especially a huge amount in the last several years. Everything has a price. The governments at all levels would be capable of good solutions to any tough challenges if they had some excessive and idle funds. However, it's also quite challenging for us to have such excessive revenue for long. Our measurement is one of the reasons that our fiscal revenue is way above its budget. We usually estimate our revenue by 2 or 3 percentage points over our estimated GDP increase. Take the year of 2005 for instance: its GDP was estimated to increase 8%, accordingly its revenue increase estimate would be 11%(8 + 3). In fact the 12-year history indicates that the increase in the actual fiscal revenue of the current year is always way above its estimate. How can the huge excessive revenues not roll in consequently? If the current estimate measurement is not scientific, how can we adjust it?
2 How can we get on the right track that suits our national conditions and effectively intensifies the constraint mechanism for government budgets? Under the current budget management mechanism, decisions and procedures about the embezzlement of off-budget revenue are usually done within the administrative system, rather than approved by the people's congresses at all levels. Those pro forma procedures are usually gone through after the embezzlement of the funds. Fiscal deficit and excessive revenue that should have been mutually conditioned go their separate ways. Take the year of 2004 for instance: its excessive revenue was RMB 410.145 billion while its fiscal deficit was RMB 319.177 billion. Generally the excessive funds cannot be embezzled unless they make up for the deficit first. In that case, the excessive revenue that could be overspent was just RMB 90.968 billion. In fact, the deficit of RMB 319.177 billion still existed while the "excessive revenue" of RMB 410.145 billion was totally spent beyond the budget. The whole spending scale was out of the control of the budget and exploded, and the government desires for financial expansion were greatly encouraged; what's even worse, fiscal deficit and the unbalanced revenue and expenditure or the fiscal difficulties were more irrelevant, government budgets were no longer intact or serious, and the people's congresses at all levels were put in an awkward position to supervise and constrain government budgets.
3 How can we get the oral reports of government budgets back to the agendas of the people's congresses at all levels and take effective measures to intensify the NPC's supervision and constraint on government budgets as soon as possible? This is an unavoidable major issue in the Eleventh Five-Year Plan period. Basically the people's deputies and people's congresses at all levels are liable to review government budget reports and supervise the use of taxes on behalf of taxpayers. When our constraint mechanism on government

budgets is quite weak, it's not a reform to abolish the oral report system and only keep the written reports on the people's congresses, or at least, it's not for the public finance system construction or the goals of socialist political civilization under market-oriented reform. We should take all necessary measures to strengthen the people's congresses' supervision over the government budget.

V Defining prudent fiscal policy

1 Material meanings of the prudent fiscal policy

The Chinese government started a prudent fiscal policy in 2005; before that it was the proactive fiscal policy accompanying us for seven years. We should say it was a major change from a proactive to a prudent policy. Now it's very necessary to figure out the material meanings behind the change.

By far the best authoritative explanation to the prudent fiscal policy has two keynotes. One is it should be appropriately tight. This is the biggest difference between the prudent and the proactive policies, as the latter emphasizes "expanding domestic demand". When the fiscal policy transfers its emphasis from "expansionary" to "appropriately tight", it makes a big move. The other keynote is to reduce the both fiscal deficit and issuance of long-term treasury debts for construction. This is the other biggest difference between the two policies, as the proactive policy is noted for the increase in the both fiscal deficit and issuance of long-term treasury debts for construction. During the adjustment of the policy orientation, this is the other big move, that "double increases" are turned into "double decreases".

Let's review fiscal revenue and expenditure against the measurable indicators of "appropriately tight" and "double decreases" of the previous three years (see Figures 9.3 and 9.5).

Although the year of 2004 saw no announcement of the exercise of a prudent fiscal policy and still saw a flying flag of the proactive policy, the absolute value of our fiscal deficit was downscaled from RMB 319.8 billion in 2003 to RMB 319.1 billion, 0.7 billion less; the relative value, the share of our deficit to GDP, was downscaled from 2.7% in 2003 to 2.3%, 0.4 percentage points less. The long-term treasury debts for construction issued were downscaled from RMB 140 billion in 2003 to RMB 110 billion in 2004, RMB 30 billion less. These figures indicate we actually aimed at and already achieved "double decreases" and were also exercising "an appropriately tight policy" in 2004. In that year we made "prudent" moves in the name of the "proactive" policy.

It was in 2005 when we officially transferred to the prudent policy. It's the first year that the prudent policy finally lived up to its name. In that year, our fiscal deficit dropped from RMB 319.1 billion to RMB 300 billion, RMB 19.1 billion less year on year; its proportion of GDP went from 2.3% to 2.0%, down by 0.3 percentage points year on year. The long-term treasury debts for treasury debts for construction issued dropped from RMB 111 billion to 80 billion, RMB 31 billion less than the previous year.

The Central Economic Working Conference (CEWC), convened in late 2005, made the decision to continue the prudent policy in 2006. Based on that, our 2006 deficit is planned to go down to RMB 295 billion, 5 billion less than RMB 300 billion in 2005; our issuance of long-term construction treasure debt is planned to drop to RMB 50 billion, RMB 30 billion less than RMB 80 billion in 2005.

The prudent policy was more in name than in reality in 2004, officially lived up to its name in 2005 and will continue in 2006. The three-year experience tells us this policy transfer moves forward in a progressive way, significantly different from the last transfer, which seemly was accomplished overnight. This transfer highlights and attempts to obtain "double decreases" and an "appropriately tight" policy, but the actual "double decreases" per year is mere a drop in the bucket of RMB 3000 billion of the fiscal revenue and expenditure. One of its important features is that the policy inclines to be prudent and "appropriately tight" step by step.

This implies its proactive feature cannot be achieved in one action but in a long progressive process, no matter how we transfer to or continue the prudent policy.

2 Constraints of the prudence-oriented transfer

What are the factors that make the fiscal policy transfer to a prudent one? Probably the reasons are the following five aspects (Gao Peiyong, 2005).

In the seven years that a proactive policy was carried out, local governments at all levels spent funds raised from the sales of central long-term construction treasure debt and those supporting funds from local finances and banks on a series of key construction projects, some already done and some still in progress. A great amount of additional funds are needed for these ongoing debt-financed projects; no new projects are about to begin from now on; they will stay halfway completed or incomplete. This is the first reason.

In the seven years that a proactive policy was carried out, we kept arguing that the policy would boost economic growth by 1.5 to 2 percentage points per year and our counterevidence was that the annual GDP increase would drop 1.5 to 2 percentage points without the proactive policy. Our economic growth has been always heavily dependent on expansionary spending, and China needs a solid support for sustainable economic growth to solve a series of real economic and social problems which have emerged in the transition period. Thus, were the policy transfer over fast, it would be a material shock to our economic operation. This is the second reason.

Either to achieve "five balanced aspects" (balancing urban and rural development, balancing development among regions, balancing economic and social development, balancing development of humanity and nature and balancing domestic development and wider opening to the outside world) or to maintain the harmonic development of economy and society, it costs a huge amount of money. Conventionally the central government allocates the budget funds by drawing upon the incremental revenue while not using the stock. Hundreds of billions of revenue increment per year certainly fill in some gaps, but it's not an all-purpose solution. Besides, how much our future revenue can increase is still unpredictable. As a result, the important revenue source we have to count on is to issue additional treasury debt. This is the third reason.

Every amount of the fiscal revenue or spending has vested interests involved. Even if we put aside the stock but concentrate on the increment for the effective fund allocation, we cannot transfer the policy without adjusting the current pattern of vested interests. When we transfer the policy orientation, we have to avoid and minimize the accompanying social unrest and instability. This issue that we need to take seriously is the fourth reason.

The prominent features of this round of macro control include that we have to prevent inflation from rising and deflation from returning; insist on inhibiting investment demand and strive to expand consumption demand; firmly halt haphazard investment and low-level, redundant construction in some industries and focus on the weak links in economic and social development. Therefore, a prudent fiscal policy, unlike a simple one against either inflation or deflation, should be carried out for multiple economic and social purposes. This is the fifth reason.

Jin Renqing (2004) published *Prudent Fiscal Policy Should be Carried out to Promote Steady and Rapid Economic Development* right after the closing ceremony of the 2004 CEWC. He reviewed the constraints of the fiscal policy transfer in that paper. For instance, a policy should be relatively constant as debt-financed projects have their own construction cycles and those ongoing and halfway projects need additional investments; an instant brake will cause materially negative impacts on the economy when it grows fast and some industries and projects have heavy reliance on the funds from the sales of treasury debt; as there is still much backwardness measured against the goal of "five balanced aspects", it's necessary to maintain a deficit of a certain size so that we can centralize resources on such public sectors as agriculture, education, public health, social security and eco-environment; we are able to take a more active response to various complicated situations home and abroad if we maintain the intensity of macro control.

3 Possible measures

To guide the implementation of prudent fiscal policy, the finance ministry has proposed an updated 16-character principle of deficit control, structural adjustment, reform deepening, revenue increase and expenditure decrease (Jin Renqing, 2004). The 16-character principle should be interpreted under real circumstances.

By "deficit control", we mean reducing fiscal deficit and long-term construction treasure debt to an appropriate level. We won't do much to cut down either the deficit or long-term construction treasure debt due to both historical and real factors. At the moment there is nothing we can do but push forward reforms to achieve deficit control step by step.

By "structural adjustment", we mean optimizing government investment portfolios in accordance with the scientific outlook on development and the construction requirements on public finance. The adjustment will definitely be engaged with both flow and stock of the finance. No matter how we deal with problems individually or if we guarantee consumption demand and suppress investments as well, the structural adjustment should be aligned with reform measures and should be achieved through progressive reforms.

By "reform deepening", we mean giving up the economic growth that is supported or stimulated by fiscal expenditure but focusing on the public finance reform itself and the reform-oriented fiscal arrangements under the flag of "promoting growth and development by reforms" so as to propel the process of the overall reform.

By "revenue increase and expenditure decrease", we mean intensifying taxation by collecting taxes payable as much as possible, curbing the overgrowth of fiscal spending and improving the efficiency of financial funds. This is regular work for both finance and tax authorities and also a long-term goal to achieve through reforms.

The "16 Chinese characters" above logically blueprints the implementation of prudent fiscal policy and is full of the spirit of reform. Actually it will be carried out under the keynote of deepening reforms.

4 Summary: problems to be explored

The current situation of our macro economy and the operation law of fiscal revenue and expenditure indicate that prudent fiscal policy will stay with us throughout the Eleventh Five-Year Plan period. On the broad platform where prudent fiscal policy is carried out for the macroeconomic environment, how to accelerate those reforms that are under the proposed plan or urgent to be promoted is one of the focuses of our prudent policy and also one of the major works of our finance and taxation in the Eleventh Five-Year Plan period.

According to the *Suggestions of the Central Committee of the Communist Party of China on the Formulation of the Eleventh Five-Year Plan for National Economic and Social Development (2005)*, the major finance and taxation reforms that are under the proposed plan or urgent to be promoted are classified into three types. They include:

1 Focus reform on improving and implementing the system guarantee under the scientific outlook of development. For instance, we need to further improve the public finance system; rationally define the powers of governments at all levels; adjust and standardize the payment relation between the central and local governments and among local governments at all levels for the purpose of establishing sound finance and tax systems that are matched with their authorities; adjust the spending structure and accelerate the construction of public finance system; implement a finance and tax system that facilitates the transformation of the economic growth pattern, scientific advancement and energy and resource conservation.
2 Reform in finance and taxation. For instance, we need to improve the system of finance transfer payment between the central and provincial governments and straighten out finance management systems at the provincial level for the

purpose of the equilibrium of public services among regions; improve the value-added tax (VAT) system and strive to accomplish the VAT transition; unify all corporate income tax (CIT) systems that are applicable to various enterprises; carry out a personal income tax (PIT) system that combines the comprehensive type with the categorical type together; adjust and improve the resource tax, levy the fuel tax and carry out the property tax step by step; consolidate the achievements from the reform of rural taxes and administrative charges and press ahead with the overall rural reform; deepen the reforms on sector budgets, centralized treasury payment system, government purchase and revenue and expenditure budget management systems; and standardize the management of land leasing incomes.

3 Focus on supporting further improvement. For instance, reforms of the education system, social security system, health care system and income distribution system.

VI. Initiating a new round of taxation system reform

1 Contents

This taxation system reform is quite different from the last one in 1994. It's called a new round of taxation system reform. About its novelty, back early in October 2003, an overall description was made in Article 20 of the *Decisions of the Central Committee of the Communist Party of China on Some Issues Regarding the Improvement of the Socialist Market Economic System*, approved in the Third Plenary Session of the Sixteenth CPC Central Committee. Afterwards in October 2005, based on the previous description, the plans for taxation system reform throughout the Eleventh Five-Year Plan period were officially included in Article 24 of the *CPC Central Committee's Suggestions on the Formulation of the Eleventh Five-Year Plan for National Economic and Social Development on the Fifth Plenary Session of the Sixteenth CPC Central Committee.*

The contents of this new round of taxation system reform include the principle and the programs at two different layers.

Let's talk about the upper layer. Its principle is summarized into 12 Chinese characters of "a more simplified taxation system, a broader tax base, lower tax rates and stricter tax collection". Compared to the 1994 reform's 16-character principle of "unified tax law, fair tax liability, simplified tax system and rational decentralization", we will find the 2005 reform is unlike the 1994 reform which intended to establish a taxation system suited to the market economy and is not intended to make a fresh start but to concentrate on further improvement of our statutory tax system on the basis of the 1994 system framework. Thus the scale and influences of the new reform are smaller than their predecessors.

Let's talk about the lower layer. This new reform contains eight programs, namely, reforming the export debate system; unifying all CIT systems that are applicable to various enterprises; transforming VAT from the productive to a consumptive type by including equipment investment into the scope of VAT deduction;

improving consumption tax by broadening the tax base to a proper extent; reforming PIT by implementing a PIT system that combines the comprehensive type and the categorical type together; carrying out a tax-for-fee reform on urban construction by imposing a unified property tax on real estates while abolishing current charges in a proper time; empowering local governments with certain taxation powers under the unified tax administration; and creating a favorable environment for the progressive unification of rural and urban tax systems.

Among the projects, some have so far been started and made some progress during the Eleventh Five-Year Plan period. They are reforming the export debate system; raising the payroll deduction threshold, one of the contents of the PIT reform; launching the pilot project of transforming VAT from the productive to a consumptive type in three provinces and one city in Northeast China; and abolishing agriculture tax, an important step to unify rural and urban tax systems. Those projects that need to start and be completely finished within the Eleventh Five-Year Plan period are the VAT transformation, unifying all CIT systems that are applicable to various enterprises, implementing a PIT system that combines the comprehensive and categorical types together, adjusting and improving resource tax, levying fuel tax and pushing forward property tax.

2 Focal points

All projects noted earlier must be pressed ahead, but some of them should outweigh the others in the new round of taxation system reform throughout the Eleventh Five-Year Plan period as they are more significant to the overall reform. They are VAT, CIT and PIT. More will be discussed about the reforms on these three taxes in following sections.

(1) Value-added tax (VAT)

Our statutory VAT system was born in the early 1990s when inflation and shortage economy were the principal contradictions we kept saying over and over, so we were committed to inhibit inflation, consumption and investment demand. At that time, other major difficulties facing us were revenue shortfall and a low ratio of fiscal revenue to GDP, so we attempted to figure out how to boost fiscal revenue and its share of GDP. Any possible tools we could think and make use of were endowed with the nature of inflation and demand inhibition; any possible solutions we could take and implement were targeted at revenue increase. The VAT system, of course, should be put to good use for these purposes. In that case, we finally chose the productive tax base for the VAT system of the day, which meant no taxes on fixed asset purchase would be deductible, although VATs were usually calculated on the basis of the amount of the value added in production and operations, the amount of the non-value added (taxes paid on the purchase of fixed assets before) would be deductible, meanwhile the worldwide VAT tax base of the time was consumptive, which meant the value of purchased fixed assets was excluded from the tax base.

A few years ago when our inflationary macro economy was replaced by the deflationary economy and our fiscal revenue turned around to increase at least RMB 100 billion year over year, our statutory VAT system became no longer appropriate due to its consumption and investment inhibition. The public voices and desires for the adjustment of our current VAT system grew louder and stronger. Not disappointedly, our tax authority came up with relatively matured reform plans. On the Third Plenary Session of the Sixteenth CPC Central Committee convened in 2003, a consumptive-type VAT substituting for the productive-type VAT, one of the contents of the new round of taxation system reform, was stipulated in the *Decisions of the Central Committee of the Communist Party of China on Some Issues Regarding the Improvement of the Socialist Market Economic System*.

As VAT has a substantial impact on the tax system and overall revenue, its system reform matters significantly. A good idea about the VAT reform is to start a pilot project at first and then extend the experimental reform to the whole nation. Coincidently the strategy to revitalize Northeast China and other old industrial bases was about to be implemented, so we decided to try out the VAT reform measures first in Northeast China in the second half of 2004. It was the prologue to the VAT system reform.

The trial project of the VAT system reform has obtained some success as of today. It should have been the moment to extend the reform nationwide; however it's delayed due to the unsuccessful CIT reform, and another focus of our reforms. The process of the VAT reform relies on the successful CIT reform to a great extent.

(2) Corporate income tax (CIT)

When different CIT systems apply to domestic and foreign enterprises, the actual tax burden for domestic enterprises is higher than that for foreign enterprises by at least 10 percentage points. In the past several years, social sectors have made full elaborations of the necessity to unify the two CIT systems that are applicable to domestic, foreign and foreign-invested. There is a tax rate difference of 10 percentage points in the two CIT systems, under which a domestic enterprise has to pay higher tax than a foreign enterprise, so reform must be carried out to achieve an equal tax rate for both domestic and foreign enterprises. It must be stopped right now no matter how. Our tax-related authorities already have matured plans for reforming CIT systems for domestic and foreign enterprises in terms of the direction and contents.

However, the CIT reform is impeded and delayed again and again despite public voices, attempts and demonstrations for its start. One of the reasons on the table is the cut of tax preferences that are exclusive for foreign enterprises will hinder the introduction of foreign capital, but this reason has been repeatedly argued and proved to be false in the last few years.

China is one of the most attractive nations to invest in. It has topped the list of foreign direct investments for years. We keep thinking over why do foreign investments enter China? Tax preferences, of course, are very attractive, but such a small profit is far from decisive in the direction of foreign investments. Relatively speaking, political stability, robust economy, promising market and abundant and cheap labor are the most attractive to foreign capital. If it were the tax preferences that some businesses came to China for, they wouldn't be technically strong enough to boost our economic development. This is the first point.

In the early years of the reform and opening up when our economy was still in the toddler period, we indiscriminately absorbed foreign capital and believed the more the better. Now that our economy is booming and the national power is steadily rising, we deserve high-quality foreign investments. Today's Chinese economy cannot and shouldn't be unscrupulous about foreign investments as more doesn't necessarily lead to better. It's by any measure behind the times to follow the initial philosophy of the reform and opening up to attract foreign capital for today. This is the second point.

Due to some well-known causes, a large number of domestic enterprises have inherent problems of their own; what's worse, discriminatory high tax rates are intentionally imposed and tax laws and regulations have constraint effects. No doubt the development of domestic enterprises is restrained. None of domestic enterprises compete with foreign enterprises in a fair environment where taxes and other discriminative policies are gone for long. This is the third point.

The WTO doesn't reject granting "super-national treatment" to foreign enterprises in terms of taxes, but its fundamental principle is all enterprises enjoy indiscriminative "national treatment" and this is how every WTO member does it now. If we insist on granting tax privileges or "super-national treatment" to foreign enterprises, is it possible for us to cover the cost paid by profits returned?

After all, in today's China, the loud voices against the start of the unification of both CIT systems for domestic and foreign enterprises in due time come from the interest-involved administrative departments, whose political achievements are susceptible to the increase or decrease of foreign investments. The possible changes in regional tax preferences that have lasted for years may also cost some local governments the opportunities to enjoy their exclusive "differential land rents".

The complexity lies in the fact that CIT system unification is not just about only CIT, and its delay actually slows down the process of VAT reform and the new round of whole tax reform.

VAT reform is to alleviate burdens on taxpayers in general by downsizing its tax base. This reform is inclusively beneficial to all taxpayers, but CIT system unification reform is quite different. The CIT reform is to cut the tax rate for domestic enterprises but raise the rate for foreign enterprises in order to reach a compromise. It's doomed to fight against resistance. An effective option that can remove resistance, push forward the reform smoothly and have the least side effects is to reform both VAT and CIT simultaneously. In that case, the changes in tax burdens caused by one tax reform can offset those changes caused by the other, and will minimize the potential resistance to the CIT reform and garner the success of the new round of taxation system reform in return. If the solo VAT reform was conducted, it would undoubtedly gather wide popularity due to its effective alleviation of tax burdens for taxpayers, but we would lose the special opportunity to balance the tax burdens in the new round of taxation system reform, and it would be even more difficult to start the CIT reform, which might be deferred forever.

(3) Personal income tax (PIT)

As noted earlier, the tax exemption threshold, a content of the PIT reform, has already been raised, but the PIT still needs a comprehensive reform in the Eleventh Five-Year Plan period.

The reason is China's statutory PIT system has great effect in the regulation of personal income distribution and the existing PIT pattern.

As its name implies, PIT refers to the tax collected from individuals and imposed on their different sources of incomes. In reality, taxes can be collected based on the categories of income or the total sum of all income, or both. Accordingly, the PIT system can be classified into a categorical type, a comprehensive type and a hybrid type.

The current PIT system in China is actually a categorical one. PITs are collected from 11 categories in total. They are wages and salaries; individual household production or business operation incomes; incomes from contracted (or leased) operation of enterprises and institutions; remuneration from personal service; author's remuneration; loyalties; interests (dividends and bonuses); incomes from property rental; incomes from the transfer of property; incidental incomes; and others. Different tax-levying measures and tax rates apply to different income categories. Therefore, PIT looks like one tax, but actually it comprises 11 categories.

The tax system composed of multiple taxes is like a symphony orchestra. PIT contributes to government revenue but it also has a special task that is to regulate resident income distribution. We notice the increasingly wide gap in income distribution in China has already jeopardized the steady development of our economy and society in the long run to a considerable extent. We should strive to narrow down rather than widen the income distribution gap. It becomes our major strategic task in the period of Eleventh Five-Year Plan. As one of the most important means to regulate income distribution, PIT reform should aim to effectively adjust the gap in resident income distribution.

However, our current categorical income tax pattern is no longer suitable to regulate income distribution. The reason is very simple. Income inequality is the difference found in comprehensive incomes of individuals, including their all sources and categories of incomes, while our current taxes are levied on different categories of personal incomes. This measure helps eliminate evasion from the root and somehow narrow down the wealth gap, but it's far from exhaustive as it's not rooted in comprehensive income.

High earners are expected to pay more taxes than low earners in order to narrow down their income gaps. We should carry out a comprehensive income tax system such that taxes are collected based on personal consolidated income declared by individuals. This is the conventional development track of PIT systems in all nations, and this is where our PIT reform should go. On the Third Plenary Session of the Sixteenth CPC Central Committee, Article 20 of the Decisions on Some Issues Regarding the Improvement of the Socialist Market Economic System sets forth the objective of PIT reform as "reforming the PIT system is to combine both comprehensive and categorical types together".

3 Summary: problems to be explored

Based on the discussions about this new round of taxation system reform, we have arrived at several conclusions as follows.

1. A tax system in any country should be rooted in its actual economic and social environment and adapt to its changes. Our tax system was designed in 1993, implemented in 1994 and has developed for 12 years so far. We made some modifications but didn't change its fundamental pattern in the last 12 years. By contrast, the Chinese economic and social environment has experienced striking change. Today it's more apparent to us that our tax system is unsuited to economic and social conditions in China. It will impose more and more negative effects on our economy unless we reform our tax system to keep up with the times. It's the moment for us to start this new round of taxation system reform in a comprehensive way in the period of Eleventh Five-Year Plan.
2. The proposed tax reform will be carried out at the expense of fiscal revenue decrease. Both the VAT and CIT reforms are estimated to cut revenue by RMB 200 billion. It's a very big price. We should be cautious about reforms when our fiscal budget is not enough to cover every aspect. However, we cannot put the tax reform aside due to cautiousness. It cannot go on for long to delay the planned tax reform due to the worries about the fiscal revenue cut. If the long-awaited tax reform was not started until the day when our fiscal budget was big enough, the day would be far away and may never come. Now is the time that our tax revenue soars faster than ever. We should seize the "peak period" of revenue growth and spend off-budget tax revenue on this new round of taxation system reform. It should and must be an important choice in the Eleventh Five-Year Plan period.
3. Apart from the reasons on and off the record, whether we can overcome the difficulties in unifying the domestic and foreign CIT systems and starting the new round of taxation system reform, it's finally up to the interest-involved authorities and local governments. If only they put department and local interests aside and concentrate on state and macro interests, if only they get rid of obstructions from vested interest groups, all reforms under the proposed plan or those urgent to be promoted will break the ice. This law applies to the CIT reform and other reforms as well. It is common sense that we finally comprehend after a series of practices.

(Originally published in *Finance & Trade Economics*, Vol.1, 2006)

Notes

1 If RMB 128.8 billion of export rebates payable were credited into the fiscal revenue of this year, the national revenue would have been RMB 2767.179 billion, its increased amount being RMB 595.649 billion while its excessive amount of RMB 410.145 billion increased by 27.43 percentage points.
2 If the excessive fiscal revenue of this year to be spent were credited into the spending amount, the year of 2004 would have seen the earlier break of RMB 3000 billion in terms of the national spending.
3 Refer to *China Taxation News* (March 10, 2005) for more details about these six factors.
4 A prominent example is that the tax base and rates (17%) of the productive-type VAT are directly related to the design philosophy of budgeting liberally and spending sparingly.

Bibliography

CPC central committee's suggestions on the formulation of the eleventh five-year plan for national economic and social development. (2005, October 16). *People's Daily*.

Gao Peiyong. (2005). Transfer to prudence in carrying forward reforms – analysis of 2005 China fiscal policy orientation. *Taxation Research, 1*.

Jin Renqing. (2004, March 7). Prudent fiscal policy should be carried out to promote steady and rapid economic development. *People's Daily*.

Jin Renqing. (2005). Deepen the Reform, Adhere to the Scientific Development, and Compose a New Finance Epic – a Speech Delivered at the National Work Conference on Finance, National Work Conference on Finance, Beijing, December 19.

XuShanda. (2004). *Speech at China tax revenue forum*, April 24. Retrieved from www.finance.sina.com.cn/roll/20040424/1551737

10 On China's current fiscal tendency

China's current fiscal tendency just depends on the dynamic movement of several critical factors as the pattern of economic and social development does. For a good study of our fiscal tendency, an appropriate option is to gain insight into the overall operation of fiscal revenue and expenditure from the analysis of several key factors regarding fiscal systems and mechanisms.

As far as China's current operation pattern of fiscal revenue and expenditure is concerned, there are four critical factors regarding fiscal systems and mechanisms that impose great influences on the overall pattern.

I Scales of revenue and expenditure: "excessive revenue" dominant mechanism

The review of scales of China's fiscal revenue and expenditure in the last two or three years has drawn a promising prospect for fiscal systems and mechanisms. That is, no matter of whether central or local or summarized national fiscal data is concerned, its final scale in each annual financial statement is determined by the scale of "excessive" tax revenue. In other words, it's no other than sustainable huge "excessive" tax revenue that contributes most to the year-end financial scale, which is way larger than the budget scale of the same fiscal year.

Let's take our 2006 financial figures for instance to explain Figure 10.1.

In 2006, the national fiscal revenue and expenditure budgets were RMB 3542.338 billion and RMB 3837.338 billion respectively, but our final statements were RMB 3934.362 billion and RMB 4132.616 billion[1] respectively. The revenue exceeded its budget by RMB 392.024 billion, or 11.07 percentage points, while the expenditure exceeded by RMB 295.278 billion[2] or 7.69 percentage points.

On the surface, such a huge disparity lies between the budget and the final account because of "excessive" fiscal revenue, which leads to "excessive" expenditure and finally results in both scales being expanded. However, a further study indicates it's our current budget constraint mechanism that fundamentally accounts for the expanded scales.

When we prepare the revenue budgets including both overall income and tax income indices, we always raise those indices by several percentage points against a rainy day, usually 2 to 4 percentage points over the estimated GDP

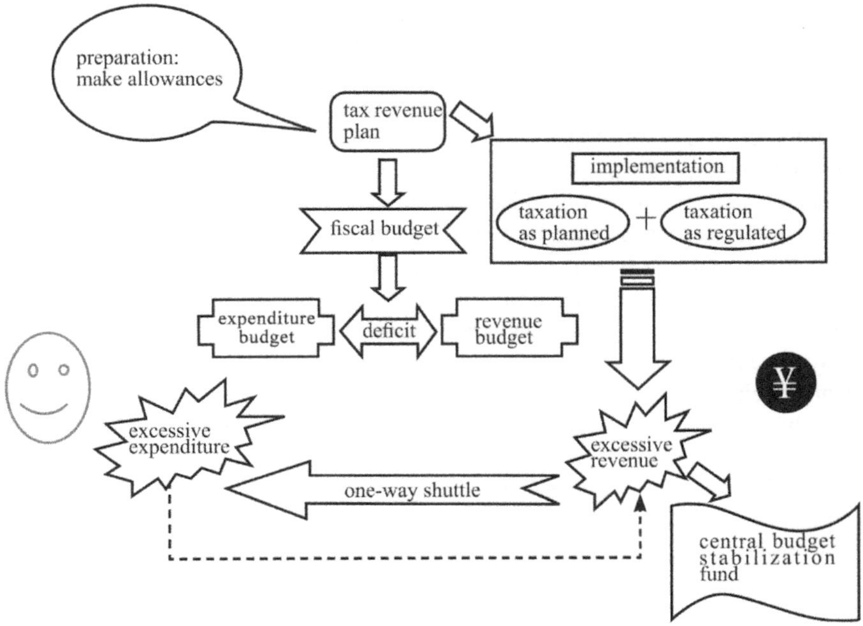

Figure 10.1 Scales of revenue and expenditure: "excessive revenue" means everything

increase. For instance, 2006 GDP is estimated to increase 8 percentage points, so the revenue budget is expected to have a 12% (= 8% + 4%) increase. It should be noted that, in the last 13 years, the annual tax revenue increase was up to 20.13% – almost twice as much as the annual GDP increase (10.14%) in the same period, the actual GDP increase was way higher than its estimated increase and the tax revenue accounted for over 95% of the revenue budget. These facts tell us there is much room left for "excessive revenue" in the stage of budget preparation whatever the reasons are.

In the stage of budget implementation, our tax authorities who are governed by our taxation management system do their routine jobs according to both the taxation plan and statutory taxation system. The mandatory taxation plan is broken down into multiple compulsory tasks to be fulfilled by taxation authorities at all levels. Besides, to collect all taxes payable according to our statutory taxation system is the duty that our taxation authorities should fulfill under the flag of regulation-based taxation. In short, we should collect taxes in accordance with both plan and regulation. The plan is strict and non-negotiable; the regulation looks strict but works flexibly, depending on the taxation capability. However the rapid development of taxation legal construction at the moment stops the possibility of arbitrary regulation. The actual disparity between the plan and the statutory system leaves much room for the "excessive revenue" reserved in budgeting for taxation authorities to "fulfill".

At the stage of budget approval, our statutory budget law holds an ambiguous attitude to both "excessive revenue" and "excessive expenditure".[3] The use of "excessive revenue" is usually decided under the administrative system and has no need to be approved by people's congresses beforehand. Even though formal procedures exist that how the excessive revenue is spent should be reported to and approved by the Standing Committee of the National People's Congress (NPC) in advance, the usual way is the spending goes ahead of its notification or coincides with its notification. Fiscal deficit and "excessive revenue" that should have conditioned each other turn out be completely separate and go their own ways. As a result, "excessive revenue" per year is almost completely translated into "excessive expenditure" of the same year. A one-way shuttle, as it were, goes from "excessive revenue" to "excessive expenditure".

Now we find "excessive revenue" is no longer what it used to be and people also change their attitude toward "excessive revenue". They do not passively accept but actively pursue "excessive revenue"; consequently "excessive revenue" tends to be normal (see Figures 10.2 and 10.3). "Excessive revenue" valued at hundreds of billions of RMB rolls in every year, attaches greater importance to fiscal revenue and results in larger scales of fiscal revenue and expenditure, even beyond the budget.

When all system and mechanism factors mentioned before interact with each other, our annual budgets for fiscal revenue and expenditure scale up in the way

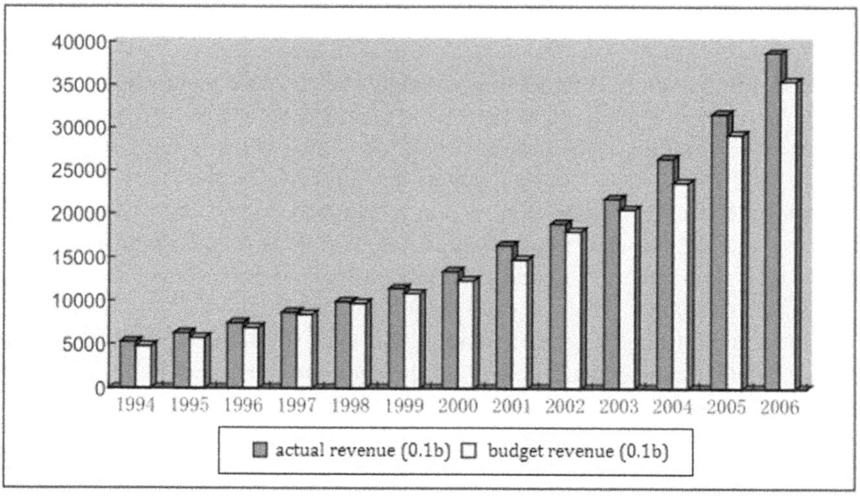

Figure 10.2 Excessive fiscal revenue is normalized (1994–2006)

Sources: Editorial Committee of China's Finance Year Book: 2004 Finance Year Book of China, *China State Finance Magazine*, 2004; National Bureau of Statistics: 2006 China Statistical Yearbook, China Statistics Press, 2006; National Bureau of Statistics: Statistical Communique of the People's Republic of China on the National Economic and Social Development, *Economic Daily*, March 1, 2007; Ministry of Finance: Reports on 2006 Central and Local Budget Performance & 2007 Central and Local Budget Draft, *Economic Daily*, March 19, 2007.

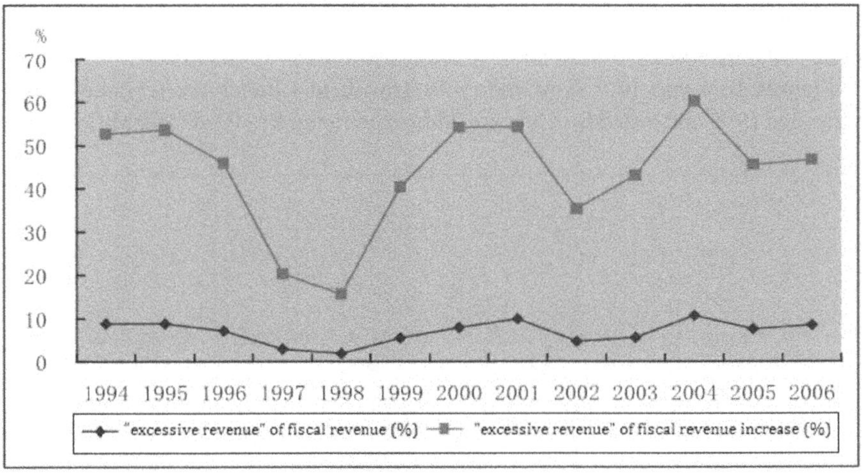

Figure 10.3 "Excessive revenue" ratio stays at a high level

Source: See Figure 10.2.

that "excessive" revenue is directly translated into "excessive expenditure", shown as Figure 10.1. In short, the actual fiscal revenue and expenditure equals their budgets plus their excessive amounts respectively.

There is only one exception for now. The abovementioned factors had a kind of loose transmission in 2006. The taxation plan, one of the working principles for taxation authorities, became less mandatory but more instructive; not all "excessive revenue" went to "excessive expenditure" as it allocated RMB 50 billion for the "central budget stabilization fund" and RMB 20 billion for fiscal deficit offset. The one-way shuttle effect was thus weakened in the way that is interpreted as the funnel at right corner of Figure 10.1.

Our scales of fiscal revenue and expenditure have their own way of working themselves out. They go along the path of "budgeting → budget implementation → excessive tax revenue → excessive fiscal expenditure → final scale". Our way is believed to be different from general principles in textbooks and regular practices of typical market economies as well. Our way is an atypical one featured with "transition". It means the mechanism by which "excessive revenue" dominates our scales of fiscal revenue and expenditure probably stays with us unless the abovementioned system and mechanism factors are completely changed and we transition to a standard fiscal budget system that fits the market economy.

After all, how China's scales of revenue and expenditure will head forward in the future depends on the process of fiscal budget system reform. It should be a very important clue for us in studying China's current fiscal tendency.

II Tax revenue growth: repeats the history

When the mechanism that "excessive revenue" dominates the scales of fiscal revenue and expenditure works, tax revenue growth plays a critical role.

Figures 10.4 and 10.5 show the rapid growth of China's tax revenue, which started in 1994 and lasted for 13 years. The tax revenue was RMB 100 billion in the

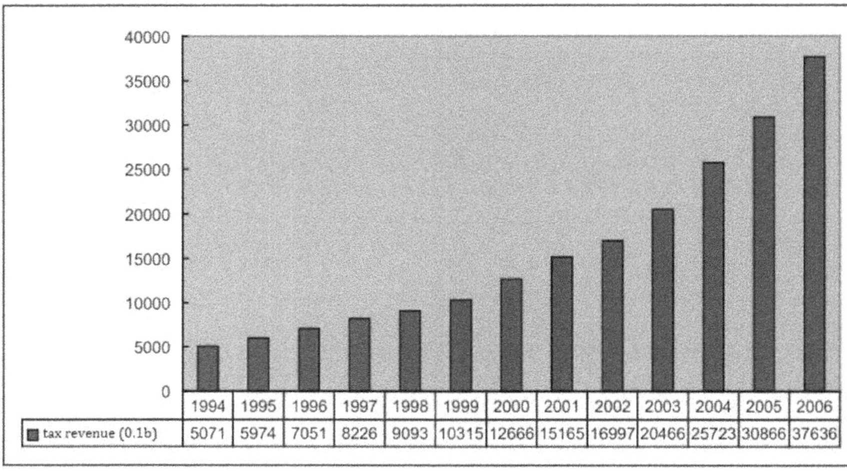

Figure 10.4 Constant rapid growth of tax revenue (1994–2006)

Sources: Editorial Committee of China's Tax Year Book: 2005 China Taxation Yearbook, China Taxation Publishing House, 2005; National Bureau of Statistics: 2006 China Statistical Yearbook, China Statistics Press, 2006; National Bureau of Statistics: Statistical Communique of the People's Republic of China on the National Economic and Social Development, *Economic Daily*, March 1, 2007.

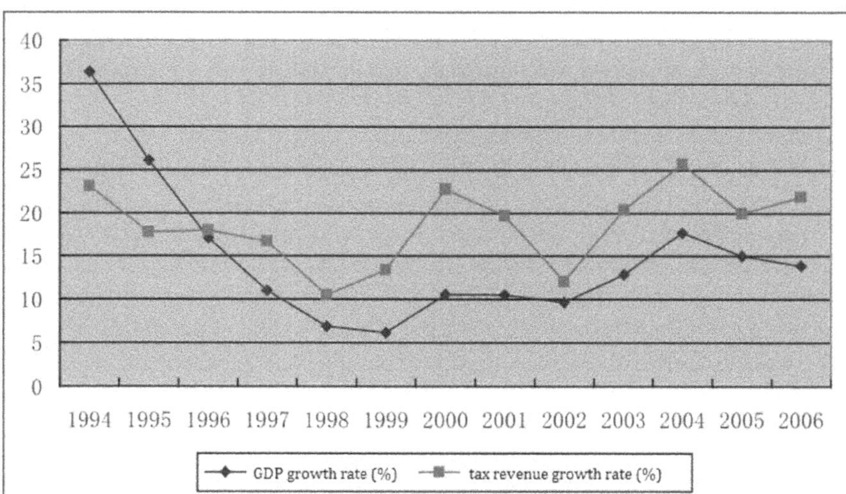

Figure 10.5 Tax revenue and GDP growth rate (1994–2006)

Source: See Figure 10.4.

first few years and rose to RMB 200 billion, RMB 300 billion, RMB 500 billion and RMB 700 billion in the following years, reaching a higher and higher level. The 2006 national tax revenue reached RMB 3763.6 billion, which is 9.14 times the 1993 national tax revenue. The annual growth rate of tax revenue (20.13%)[4] in the 13 years is almost more than twice the GDP growth rate (10.14%).

Similar to what decides the scales of fiscal revenue and expenditure, the so-called "tri-archic theory" (Jin Renqing, 2002) or "multi-factor theory" (Xie Xuren, 2006; Li Fangwang, 2006) could account for the phenomenon of constant rapid growth of tax revenue, but our statutory taxation system is still the underlying cause.

If we look into the histories of both China and global taxation, we find that the 13-year rapid growth of the tax revenue is exclusive in China and even the world. This is an exception that can be hardly explained by general rules and factors, such as economic growth, policy adjustment, price rise or the progressive rate system, taxation intensification, or the structural disparity between GDP and tax revenue and influences of foreign trades on GDP and tax revenue growth. So far all of them have never ever caused such a rapid growth elsewhere but China.

Two analytic reports (Xu Shanda, 2004; The Plan and Statistics Department of State Administration of Taxation (SAT), 2006) from SAT show that the comprehensive tax collection rate in China, computed as the actual collected taxes[5] divided by the statutory taxes, rose from 50% in 1994 up to 70% in 2003, an increase of 20 percentage points over 10 years. The actual collection rate of VAT (see Figure 10.6), i.e. the first tax, rose from 57.45% in 1994 to 85.73% in 2004, an increase of 28.28 percentage points over the past 11 years. Such a rise in the actual tax collection rate reveals that Chinese tax authorities hold tremendous "scope of tax collection" and have the impressive capability of tax collection. It's the great efforts made

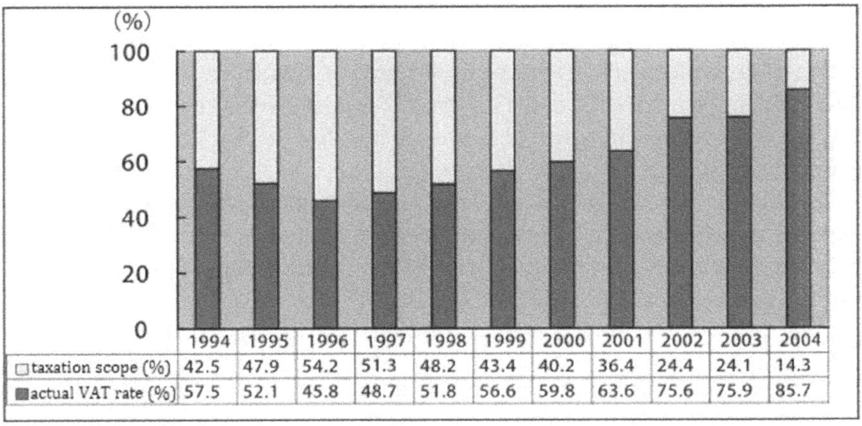

	1994	1995	1996	1997	1998	1999	2000	2001	2002	2003	2004
□taxation scope (%)	42.5	47.9	54.2	51.3	48.2	43.4	40.2	36.4	24.4	24.1	14.3
■actual VAT rate (%)	57.5	52.1	45.8	48.7	51.8	56.6	59.8	63.6	75.6	75.9	85.7

Figure 10.6 Steady rise of actual VAT rate (1994–2004)

Source: Quoted from Macro Analysis of Changes of VAT Rate and Results of Golden Taxation Project (Phase 2), Plan and Statistics Department, SAT

by Chinese tax authorities to intensify taxation that give powerful and sustainable impetus to the tax revenue growth.

We should notice that our tax revenue started to grow immediately after the birth of our statutory tax system. It means the 1994 tax reform changed the history of our tax revenue. As far as the "scope of tax collection" is concerned, we should dig into the breeding and birth backgrounds of our statutory tax system, which was born in the period from 1993 to 1994 and is branded with three marks of that time (Gao Peiyong, 2006).

First, serious inflation. All possible means including the tax system design were mobilized to curb the high inflation rate, up to 20% then. Our statutory tax system was designed to be anti-inflationary; for instance, VAT used the productive tax base that inhibited impulsive investments from enterprises and was loose in defining taxable targets.

Second, severe financial constraint. To prevent the fiscal revenue to GDP ratio from dropping at that time, it was not enough to maintain the original taxes at the same level. We had to achieve a huge "revenue increase". Our statutory tax system was designed to boost tax revenue and targeted at realizing its established scale.

Finally, the lower tax collection rate. To achieve the established goal of tax revenue, our statutory tax system was designed to offset the effects of the lower tax collection rate. It must be flexible so that an "economical" scale of tax revenue could be ensured under a "loose" tax system.

Multiple factors interacted with each other and finally determined the pattern of our current tax system. During that period, even if we targeted for tax revenue of RMB 500 billion, we had to establish a tax system with a taxable capacity of RMB 1000 billion, considering the facts including "investment enthusiasm inhibition", "revenue increase" and "lower tax collection rate". In other words, the massive "scope of tax collection" that Chinese tax authorities possess was actually reserved at the birth of our current tax system. It's the tremendous expansion potential that pushes China's tax revenue onto the track of constant rapid growth.

It is not difficult to find that China's tax revenue developed in the last 13 years in the way of "current tax system → scope of tax collection → taxation intensification → tax collection rate → tax revenue growth". When we are aware that this development path starts from the current tax system, we are bold enough to say China's tax revenue will repeat its history in next few years unless we change the current tax system.

To sum up, how will China's tax revenue go in the future? Specifically, will its rapid growth continue? Those questions are ultimately solved in the process of new taxation system reform. This is another important clue for us in studying China's current fiscal tendency.

III "System restoration": spending-to-GDP ratio shows a V-shaped curve

Both "excessive fiscal revenue" and constant rapid growth of tax revenue are financial sources for governments engaged in financial operation. When we look away from "excessive fiscal revenue" and tax revenue growth, turn to government expenditure and finally focus on the allocation pattern of all social resources, we will find both are amazingly identical in their development tracks in the previous 13 years; consequently, the scale of fiscal expenditure expands and the allocation pattern of all social resources shows a momentum of "system restoration".

Figure 10.7 shows our scale of fiscal expenditure has increased sharply since 1994. The national spending was barely RMB 579.262 billion in 1994, reached RMB 1000 billion, a record high in 1998, two years later, RMB 1500 billion, another record high in 2000, RMB 2200 billion in 2002, RMB 2800 billion in 2004, RMB 3393.028 billion 2005 and RMB 4132.616 billion in 2006, a new record high.

When we compare the annual growth rate of fiscal expenditure (19.94%) with that of GDP (10.14%) for the same period, it's obvious that the former is twice as much as the latter. As a result, the GDP distribution pattern is definitely increasingly favorable to the government. The share of fiscal spending to GDP rose from 12.0% in 1994 to 19.73% in 2006.

If we extend our vision to the 28-year history of the reform and opening up, we will find from Figure 10.8 that the share of fiscal spending to GDP, basically a reflection of the allocation pattern of social resources, has an asymmetric V-shaped move. At the beginning of the reform, we aimed at decreasing the share, which was 31.0% in 1978 and falling for several years, down to 11.2% in 1996. It was a year of a turning point. After that, the share started to rise again and reached 19.73% in 2006. In the future, this share is expected to soar under the stimulus of the robust growth of tax revenue, especially the massive "excessive revenue".

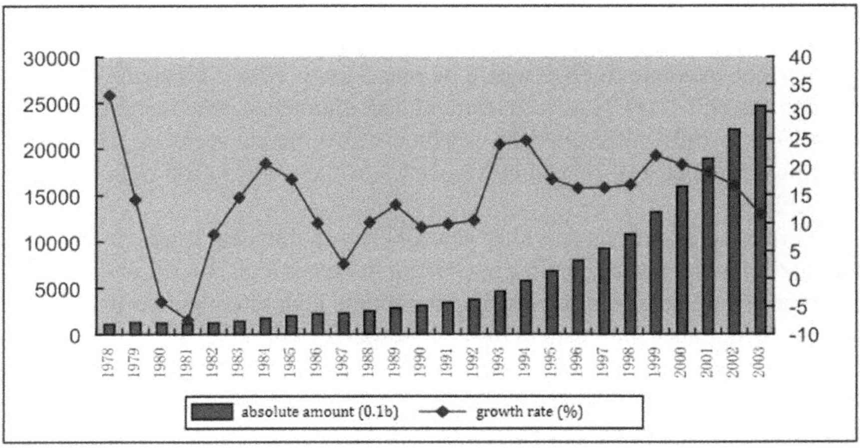

Figure 10.7 Fiscal expenditure development (1978–2003)

Source: See Figure 10.2

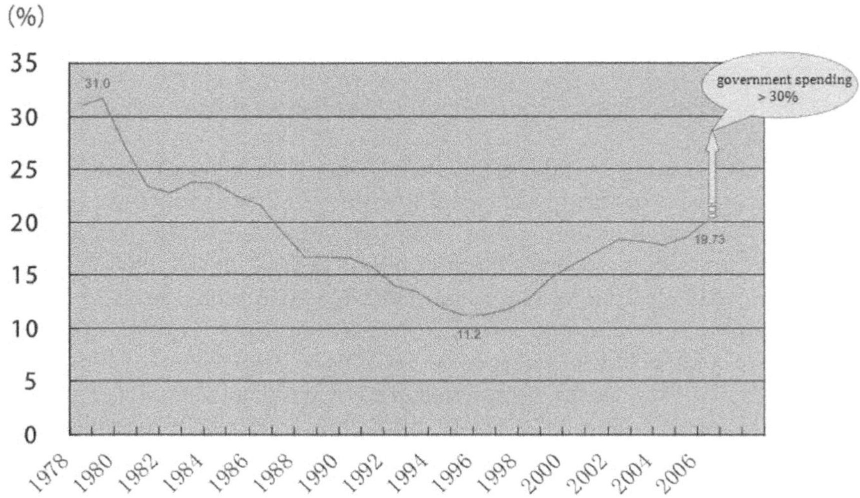

Figure 10.8 System restoration: steady rise in the share of fiscal expenditure to GDP (1978–2006)

Source: See Figure 10.2

The complexity is that things are different from what they were at the beginning of the reform and opening up. To be specific, the fiscal spending in China is within the budget's scope and is just a part of the whole government spending. If we took the actual government spending as the numerator, its proportion in the GDP would be raised. For instance, the actual spending in 2006 included RMB 4132.616 billion in fiscal spending and even the off-budget payment on debt due in the current year, the social security expenses on balancing the interests of all parties, the off-budget and the beyond-system expenses.[6] If so, the share of actual government spending to GDP would be raised up to 30%. This figure is almost close to the 1978 level. Now an interesting fact is unveiled, that during the period from 1978 to 2006, the proportion of Chinese government spending to GDP has an almost symmetric V-shaped move, shown as the arrow in top right corner of Figure 10.8.

A further study tells us that after new China was founded, it was in 1960 that the share of government spending to GDP hit its record high, 39.3%, and the share left from the starting point is reaching an all-time high after the reform. It's time to reassess our allocation pattern of social resources and our goals.

It is noticed that the scale of government spending expanded very quickly in the last 13 years. The reasons are the fast growth of tax revenue, the unstandardized fiscal budget system and their interactive effects. It's the fast growth of tax revenue that loosens the restrictions on the expansion of government spending; it's the unstandardized fiscal budget system that directly leads to liberal spending behaviors. As a result, government spending is able to expand quickly and the allocation pattern of social resources starts to show the tendency of "system restoration". All factors involved in the expansion are related to systems and mechanisms and rooted in our current taxation system and fiscal budget system. The allocation pattern of social resources is likely to continue its momentum of "system restoration"; what's worse, its consequences probably contradict what the reform and opening up intended at the beginning, unless the new tax reform proposed begins in an all-around way and the fiscal budget system is standardized.

By the same token, if we try to figure out how the Chinese government spends and the allocation pattern of social resources in the future, we can find the answers in the process of reforms that make relevant systems more adaptive to the market economy. This is the third important clue for us in studying China's current fiscal tendency.

IV Taxation system reform: substantial practices in 2008

With regard to the tax reform, we cannot miss the blueprint of a new round of tax reform, drawn out in the Third Plenary Session of the Sixteenth CPC Central Committee and in the "Eleventh Five-Year Plan".

Article 20 of the *Decisions of the Central Committee of the Communist Party of China on Some Issues Regarding the Improvement of the Socialist Market Economic System (2003)*, approved in the Third Plenary Session of the Sixteenth CPC Central Committee, defines eight programs for tax reform: to reform the export debate system, unify all corporate income tax (CIT) systems applicable to various enterprises, transform VAT from the productive to consumptive type by including equipment investment into the scope of VAT deduction, improve consumption tax by broadening the tax base to a proper extent, reform personal income tax by implementing a personal income tax system that combines the comprehensive type and the categorical type together, carry out a tax-for-fee reform on urban construction by imposing a unified property tax on real estates while abolishing current charges in a proper time, empower local governments with certain taxation powers under the unified tax administration and create a favorable environment for the progressive unification of rural and urban tax systems.

On that basis, section 2 of Chapter 32 in the *Outline of the Eleventh Five-Year Plan of National Economic and Social Development of the People's Republic of China*, published in the Fourth Session of the Tenth NPC (2006), extends the contents of taxation system reform that is intended to start in the Eleventh Five-Year Plan period to 10 programs: to transform VAT from a productive to consumptive type on a national scale, adjust the collection scope of consumption tax to an appropriate extent by rationally regulating the tax burden and the collection of some taxable items, begin to collect fuel tax in a proper time, appropriately adjust the collection scope and categories of business tax, improve the export tax rebate system, unify all CIT systems that are applicable to various enterprises, implement a personal income tax system that combines the comprehensive type and the categorical type together, reform the real estate tax system by carrying forward the property step by step and abolishing relevant fees, reform the resource tax system and improve urban maintenance and construction tax, farmland conversion tax and stamp tax.

Up to now, the programs that have been started and made some progresses are: reforming the export tax rebate system; reforming personal income tax by raising its threshold and requiring income declaration filed by high-income taxpayers themselves; making experiments on transforming VAT from the productive to a consumptive type in three provinces and one city in Northeast China; and taking an important step in unifying both urban and rural tax systems by abolishing agricultural tax, adjusting consumption tax and unifying the vehicle and vessel tax system. The programs that have started are more than expected and do cover a wide scope; when we peel off the outside and dig deeper, we will discover that real tax reform is not yet coming.

In fact, the reason is that VAT and CIT reforms (CIT reform is to launch a new CIT law that unifies the two CIT systems that are applicable to domestic enterprises, foreign enterprises and foreign-invested enterprises respectively) are placed at the center of the blueprint of this new round of taxation system reform. The two reforms result in the biggest change in tax revenue, get most taxpayers involved and have a most far-reaching influence on economic and social lives. From the very beginning, the most importance is to them and their slight moves will surely affect the overall situation.

Take the year of 2006 for instance (see Figure 10.9). VAT, VAT from imports, CIT and CIT from foreign-invested and foreign enterprises contribute respectively 34.3%, 13.0%, 14.7% and 4.1%, or totally 66.1%, to the national tax revenue of

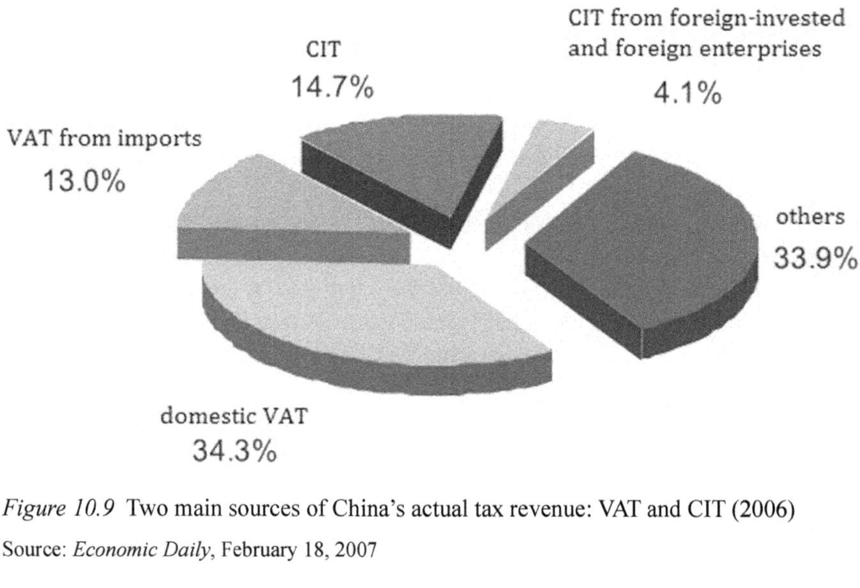

Figure 10.9 Two main sources of China's actual tax revenue: VAT and CIT (2006)

Source: *Economic Daily*, February 18, 2007

3763.6 billion. As both VAT and CIT are now in the process of reforms, it can be asserted that they are the main sources of China's actual tax revenue.

For this reason, the government departments are quite cautious about VAT and CIT reforms and make great efforts to get well-planned. The final solution is to launch both VAT and CIT reforms together in a proper time.

Why should the two reforms be launched together? The reason is that VAT reform intends to transform from the productive to a consumptive type, which is a feature of the decreased tax base. Despite frequent compromises under the pressure of "fiscal revenue cut-down", VAT transition still intends to relieve the burden on taxpayers. It's like a generalized system of preferences, beneficial to almost all taxpayers. No doubt, it meets no lions in the way. However, CIT reform intends for "unification", that different CIT systems for domestic and foreign enterprises are unified into a standard one. Theoretically there are three options to achieve "unification", namely the lower threshold overriding the higher (cutting the tax burden of domestic enterprise down to the level of foreign enterprise), the higher overriding the lower (raising the tax burden of foreign enterprise up to the level of domestic enterprise) and the compromised threshold (drawing both taxes closer to the middle by cutting down that of domestic enterprise and raising that of foreign enterprise). In fact, the third option, a compromised threshold, is finally chosen due to the high cost of taxation system reform and our weak financial capacity. Obstacles are right there to stop its start as it alleviates burdens on domestic enterprise while increasing burdens on foreign enterprises. In order to remove possible obstacles and push forward the reform successfully, an effective solution with fewer side effects is to introduce both VAT and CIT reforms at the same time. If so, taxpayers would enjoy some tax benefits from two reforms, although partially offset by some increased taxes. Possible hindrances to CIT reform will be consequently minimized, and the success of the new round of taxation system reform will be close at hand.

As a result, the two reforms were carried out almost at the same time indeed, but their progresses were jaw-droppingly surprising. The VAT reform went quite well. Its pilot projects first started in eight industries in three provinces and one city of Northeast China in July 2004, and were carried out throughout the country one year later. However, things turned out to be different for the CIT reform. It was planned to get approval in the 2005 NPC and come into effect together with the VAT reform in 2006, but the plan fell through. It was hoped to get an approval in the 2006 NPC and start in 2007, but finally disappointed. Not until March 2007 when the Fifth Session of the Tenth NPC was closed, the CIT reform was submitted for approval and eventually approved by a majority of votes. Now the long-awaited CIT reform is expected to officially start in 2008.

It's the fourth year that the postponed VAT reform waits for the readiness of the CIT reform by continuing its experimental projects. How is it developing now? Actually there have been two options for the VAT reform since 2006. One is that it stops waiting and starts alone. It will, of course, gain wide popularity soon as it does, reducing many taxes for taxpayers, but the CIT reform will be more difficult to carry out and even probably be postponed forever once it loses this special opportunity to offset its effect of increased taxes. The other is that it continues to wait until the CIT reform is ready to start. In that case, the complete VAT collection and deduction mechanism will suffer from a great shock; moreover, tax evasions will be evoked due to the long-term VAT policy differences between the pilot and other areas. The outcomes challenge tax collection and management activities. To wait or not to wait, it's an awkward dilemma, but the VAT reform was eager to start long before. Therefore, when the CIT reform officially begins in January 2008, the VAT reform is expected to extend to the whole nation unless the macroeconomy has a big change.

Given the special positions and roles of VAT and CIT, given the reduced taxes of the two reforms (RMB 90 billion and 200 billion respectively, calculated based on 2006 figures) accounting for the majority of the cost of the new round of taxation system reform, and given the potential increased revenue or little revenue cut from other reforms, it's estimated that the new round of taxation system reform is about to enter its high-tide period at the moment of the start of two tax reforms.

Studying China's current fiscal tendency from the clue of "CIT reform → VAT transition → a new round of taxation system reform → fiscal budget system reform", we will have an optimistic estimation on our future operation of fiscal revenue and expenditure.

V Conclusions

This paper starts with several system and mechanism factors that determine China's current pattern of fiscal revenue and expenditure operation, reveals its law of operation against the real background and finds out those clues to the current tendency of fiscal operation.

All discussions indicate China's hope for a sound and rapid financial development now lies in rationalizing the operation systems and mechanisms of fiscal revenue and expenditure and removing all possible system and mechanism obstacles. All of this is determined by the success of relevant system reforms that are urgent or have been proposed.

(Originally published in *Finance & Trade Economics*, Vol.4, 2007)

Notes

1 The figures resulted from adjustment. For example, RMB 4132.616 billion = 4021.316 billion of national fiscal expenditure + 61.3 billion of the payment for export rebates + 50 billion of the payment for central budget stabilization fund.
2 RMB 96.746 billion of the gap between excessive revenue and expenditure includes 20.005 billion of central fiscal deficit decline and 76.741 billion of local fiscal surplus or carry forward.
3 A literal expression from our statutory budget law is "previous-year budgetary surpluses of all governments at various levels could be spent on the carry forwards next year; if a balance remains, it could supplement to the budget turnover funds; if still remains, it could be spent on necessary items in budget next year".
4 The growth rates in the 13 years were: 23.1% (1994), 17.8% (1995), 18% (1996), 16.7% (1997), 10.5% (1998), 13.4% (1999), 22.8% (2000), 19.7% (2001), 12.1% (2002), 20.4% (2003), 25.7% (2004), 20% (2005) and 21.9% (2006).

5 The statutory taxes are what should be collected under the statutory taxation system; the actual collected taxes are what can be collected by tax authorities and within the tax capacity. Their disparity depends on the tax collection rate. Thus, the statutory taxes are computed as the tax base multiplied by the statutory tax rate, while the actual collected taxes are computed as the tax base multiplied by both statutory tax rate and tax collection rate.

6 Calculated on the basis of figures in *China Statistical Yearbook* and *Finance Year Book of China*, the four types of expenses in 2005 were RMB 392.337 billion, 760 billion, 435.171 billion and 400 billion respectively.

Bibliography

Decisions of the central committee of the communist party of China on some issues regarding the improvement of the socialist market economic system. (2003). Beijing: People's Publishing House.

Gao Peiyong. (2006). Mystery of the constant rapid growth of China's tax revenue. *Economic Research Journal, 12.*

JinRenqing. (2002). *On China contemporary taxation.* Beijing: People's Publishing House.

Li Fangwang. (2006). Quantitative characteristics of 2000–2005 China's tax revenue growth and the new taxation system reform. *Taxation Research, 8.*

Ministry of finance, reports on 2006 central and local budget performance & 2007 central and local budget draft. (2007, March 19). *Economic Daily.*

Outline of the eleventh five-year plan of national economic and social development of the people's Republic of China. (2007, March 17). *Economic Daily.*

Plan and Statistics Department, SAT, Macro Analysis of Changes of VAT Collection Rate and Results of Golden Taxation Project (Phase 2), 2006.

XieXuren. (2006, June 13). XieXuren meets the press. *China Financial and Economic News.*

XuShanda. (2004). *A speech at China tax revenue forum*, April 24. Retrieved from www.finance.sina.com.cn/roll/20040424/1551737

11 Analysis of current major taxation issues*

Preface

In different historical periods, no matter the development course of the whole economy and society or a specific economic and social sector, it always encounters different important factors and even changes that exert significant influences on the overall situation. When we get a good grasp of these factors or changes, we are able to observe and solve a series of major economic and social issues.

Taxation is unexceptional. In recent years, the significant factors and changes in taxation, an economic and social sector that has been updated with the times throughout human history, not only determine taxation activities but also unveil to us a series of unprecedented issues that can be hardly figured out within the framework of the existing theories. These new taxation issues may be challenges or opportunities. They cannot be evaded and should be answered and solved.

Taxation issues, especially major taxation issues, should be studied not only from the microscopic but also from the macroscopic perspective. This is a truth that both history and reality keep telling us. Only when we make a so-called equilibrium analysis of taxation from the macroscopic perspective and pinpoint taxation from its interrelation and interaction with other relevant factors are we likely to arrive at realistic judgments and have a global insight. Only when all this is done are we able to establish a new theoretical taxation framework that is rooted in China's national conditions.

When we carefully review the global operation of China's current taxation from the macroscopic perspective, we will find that although the zigzag contradictions in the taxation sector are frequently changed, only several issues are assessed as "major" issues against a benchmark of the "butterfly effect". They are tax revenue growth, tax collection and management, tax burden, the share of tax revenue to GDP and the new round of tax system reform.

In view of the above mentioned, this paper aims at two interrelated tasks. One is to answer and solve the current major taxation issues aforementioned from the macroscopic perspective; the other is to improve the existing theoretical taxation framework based on the first task.

I Sources of tax revenue growth

Interestingly, we have never stopped rephrasing its growth since 1994 when our tax revenue accelerated. At first we said "rapid growth", then "over growth", and "supercharged growth" later. The growth rate of our tax revenue soared up to 30% in 2007. Then a "super speed growth" prevailed.

The expressions from "rapid growth", "over growth", "high speed growth" to "super speed growth" in fact reflect our confusion about the constant rapid growth of China's tax revenue. A second thought is that it doesn't mean we dislike it. Let's consider an extreme case. Suppose that the tax revenue growth rate reaches 300% or even 3000% and all other factors are not considered, it's not bad for all of us. We are confused because tax revenue is not a windfall after all. We cannot discuss its growth without any consideration of the macroeconomic situations. If we attempted to do it, we would find that our tax revenue growth in reality could not be well explained under the existing theoretical framework.

All economic textbooks and reference books tell us that the economy determines tax revenue and tax revenue comes from the economy. It's translated as the economy is the source of tax revenue or the tax revenue growth gets solid support only from the economic growth. However, these theories in books are challenged by the reality of our tax revenue growth. Take the first six months of 2008 for instance. Our national tax revenue grew at 30.5% but our GDP grew at 10.4% during that period. If the economy is the source of tax revenue, where does the extra 20.1% of tax revenue come from? Even if the inflation is considered, our GDP growth rate that is based on current prices will be 18.3%,[1] a sum of original 10.4% and 7.9% (CPI over the same period). They still have a gap of 12.2%, almost half of the tax revenue growth rate. What can account for this difference?

Apparently, China's actual tax revenue has other sources in addition to the economic growth.[2] We have to look into non-economic factors that contribute to the difference between both growth rates. As our actual tax revenue growth comes from only economic and non-economic sources, and all economic sources are common and can be well explained within the existing theoretical framework, we should only focus on non-economic factors to figure out the reasons behind this.

Nevertheless, the tax departments on the front lines can hardly detail the non-economic factors that drive the constant rapid growth. We can read between the lines of the growth causes summarized so far by the officials.

Since the end of the 1990s the tax departments have tried to collect all possible explanations for the wide social doubt on tax revenue growth. In summary, all explanations are classified into either the "three-factor theory" or "multi-factor theory". Under the former theory, China's actual tax revenue grows thanks to economic growth, policy adjustment and taxation enhancement (Jin Renqing, 1992); under the latter theory, it grows as a result of the interaction of economic growth, price rises, structural difference between GDP and tax revenue, progressive tax system, taxation enhancement, differential influences of foreign trade on the GDP growth and tax revenue growth (Xie Xuren, 2006).[3]

Recently, the fiscal department (Tax Affairs Department, Ministry of Finance (MOF), 2008) published a report of Correct Views on Tax Revenue Growing over GDP. This report argues that tax revenue grows over GDP due to differences in price references, statistical bases and accounting measures, differences between the GDP and tax revenue structures, and the progressive systems for several taxes.

Among the possible causes listed above, tax collection and management and the progressive tax system should be classified into the non-economic sector, if there are only economic and non-economic camps.

How tax collection and management affect tax revenue growth has no answers in our existing theoretical framework yet. The practices of tax collection and management in China and even other countries prove again and again that, based on our current tax system, our tax departments' hard work on taxation enhancement will somehow decrease tax avoidances and evasions, improve the collection and management level and raise the tax collection rate by means of updating technologies, perfecting management mechanisms, improving quality of their employees or even elevating their skilled level. In the end, tax revenue will grow beyond doubt. It means that, due to the interaction of both subjective and objective factors, the tax collection and management level of tax departments inclines to ascend. If it keeps ascendant (not descendant), tax revenue will always grow faster than GDP.

When the progressive tax system is considered, how it affects the tax revenue growth has definitive statements in our existing theoretical framework. Nowadays, the tax structures in all countries, though they vary in their formats, consist of a progressive income tax, maybe larger or maybe smaller. The progressive income tax highlights the fact that tax rates applicable to taxpayers rise as their incomes or profits grow. In other words, the progressive income tax is taking a greater share of the incomes or profits of taxpayers. Therefore, once the progressive tax system works, tax revenue will always grow faster than GDP.[4] This is a general law of tax revenue growth written in the tax economics.

When we study our actual growth in tax revenue based on the abovementioned theoretical analysis, we find it's not too much that the progressive tax system contributes to our tax revenue. For instance, income taxes were 25.9% of the national tax revenue in 2007. Among that, personal income taxes (PITs) with a share of 6.4% were collected from 11 categories and not all of these categories were taxed at a progressive tax rate. Corporate income taxes (CITs) with a share of 15.6% were mainly collected at a single proportional tax rate, despite two rates available; CITs[5] from foreign-invested and foreign enterprises with a share of 3.9% were mainly collected at a proportional tax rate, although various tax deductions were available. In this case, the share that comes from the progressive tax system is absolutely a small part of China's actual tax revenue.

Under such circumstances, the either-or fact is the other non-economic factor that contributes most to our tax revenue growth cannot be anything but tax collection and management. This assertion is solidly demonstrated by what our tax departments have achieved by enhancing tax collection and management. The State Administration of Taxation (SAT) measured (2005) the VAT collection rate was raised from 57.45% in 1994 to 85.73% in 2004, an increase of 28.28 percentage points over 11 years. That means after 1994 there is up to RMB 366.812 billion of tax increments that come from VAT and are collected due to enhanced tax collection and management.

Conclusion 1: When we study China's actual tax revenue growth, a do-less-for-more option is to not only pay attention to its overall growth rate but also focus on its difference from the GDP growth rate.

Conclusion 2: Both economic and non-economic factors work together to boost the growth of China's actual tax revenue. We can start with the non-economic factors and their contributions to figure out why tax revenue and GDP grow at different rates.

Conclusion 3: At present tax collection and management becomes the main non-economic factor boosting China's tax revenue growth. And it's the constantly improving level of tax collection and management that contributes most to the fact that the tax revenue growth rate is way ahead of the GDP's.

II Magic of tax collection and management

Traditionally, we study tax collection and management from the perspectives of management, technology or methodology, not at the macro level or within the macroeconomic framework. Thus, when the magic of tax collection and management outshines and provides a vital source of tax revenue growth, we cannot find mature answers within our existing theoretical framework.

The booming activities of tax collection and management bring new things or changes to us one by one and also surprisingly remind us with fresh examples that tax collection and management is a very important macro variable. The previous analysis already indicates that, based on the fixed tax arrangements or the unchanged tax system, the efforts to enhance tax collection and management are also able to result in tax revenue increase and the changed GDP distribution pattern, and achieve fruits from investment and consumption adjustment and macroeconomic control.

This is a significant logical conclusion, from which we infer two rules as follows.

First, for the intended macro achievements, there is more than one way to increase tax revenue. For instance, enhancing tax collection and management is as effective as changing the tax system (such as adding tax types, increasing tax rate and expanding tax base). Both measures are the same or similar propellers in the hands of the government to boost tax revenue.

Then, the level of tax collection and management is meant to ascend and never descend. Moreover, it is one of major responsibilities of the tax departments to enhance tax collection and management by collecting all taxes payable from as many as possible; thus it is an inexhaustible source for the government to get tax revenue that grows faster than GDP.

Why do tax collection and management have such beautiful magic? We need to dig out the special story from the macro perspective.

Before we go, we need to answer two questions as follows.

First, is it an exclusive case in China or a worldwide case that tax collection and management can drive tax revenue?

Available documents, published by worldwide tax departments, say that no one at present can achieve a tax collection rate of 100% and no one does not have some "taxation room". They differ from each other in the actual tax collection rate or the taxation room. Those who have more advanced taxation technologies, more mature measures, richer experience and better taxation mechanisms have a higher tax collection rate –otherwise, a lower rate. Nevertheless, the fact is that as long as the tax collection rate is not 100% and the tax departments have some taxation room, any efforts they make to enhance tax collection and management are able to gain the result that tax revenue grows faster than GDP, regardless of nations and their phases of economic development.

Then, throughout worldwide tax history, we are the only case where tax collection and management is so closely interrelated with tax revenue under the circumstances of the unchanged tax system. Tax collection and management in all countries has the same or similar "gene", but why does it burst with so much power only in China? Is there any special reason? If it is, what is that?

Looking into the fact that tax collection and management with the same or similar "gene" has different effects on tax revenue growth in different lands, we ascribe it to the different forcing space, the basic breeding environment for tax collection and management. The more forcing space, the more room for maneuver, the more power released; the less forcing space, the less room for maneuver, the less power released. According to this, China's tax collection and management is more magically powerful than any others to boost tax revenue, just because our tax departments have more "taxation room" where "statutory tax burdens" are far distant from "actual tax burdens".[6] If no such huge "taxation room" exists, no matter how much harder they work to enhance tax collection and management or what they are capable of, they are unable to make so high non-economic factor contribution that leads to a wide difference of growth rates between tax revenue and GDP.

The next question is why do Chinese tax departments have so much "taxation room"?

The "taxation room" is obviously dependent on its root, the tax system. In other words, how far tax departments can go to collect taxes is actually the result of arrangements of the tax system, while the arrangements are directly dependent on the basic environment for tax collection and management.

In 1994 when our current tax system was born, tax departments were not skilled at collection and management while taxpayers were not quite honest. Consequently the actual tax collection rate was quite low then. In such a basic environment, in order to realize the established goal of tax revenue, the statutory tax system was designed to impose a higher burden of statutory taxes. For instance, the government set the tax revenue target of RMB 500 billion in that year, but it had to establish a tax framework with a nominal revenue of at least RMB 1000 billion if the actual collection rate was only 50% (Xu Shanda, 2004). It means tax revenue of RMB 500 billion can only be ensured by a tax framework of RMB

1000 billion. The actual burden is less than the statutory rate by 50%, which is just the available room left by our current tax system for tax departments, and also the ground on which tax collection and management can play an effective role or perform magic.

The abovementioned examples of the VAT collection rate can also indicate that in recent years especially since the year 2000, our tax departments have made great progress in their collection capability and taxpayers have become more honest. It's the great improvement in those two aspects that drives our tax collection rate to rise and narrow down the gap between the statutory and the actual tax burdens. In this way, the factor of collection and management contributes more and more to the tax revenue growth.

The binding relationship between tax collection and management and our current tax system is an important clue for us to analyze and study the magic of tax collection and management in China and its future trend.

Conclusion 4: Tax collection and management is another major macro variable of the government. It will increase tax revenue, provide an inexhaustible source for tax revenue to grow over GDP and even change the GDP distribution pattern and achieve the goals of macro control policies by enhancing collection and management.

Conclusion 5: The extraordinary magic of our tax collection and management comes from the huge "taxation room" left by our current tax system. It's because of the massive "taxation room" that China's tax collection and management is more effective in boosting the tax revenue than any other nations. The unusual growth of China's tax revenue is seemingly attributed to the extraordinary magic of tax revenue administration, but actually it is derived from the huge 'space' provided by the currently existing tax system.

III Judgment on tax burden

With regard to China's tax burden, the so-called Tax Misery Index comes to our mind. It is another expression of the tax burden. Forbes ranked China second and third in the Global Tax Misery Index respectively in 2005 and 2007. Certainly we disagree on such a ranking, as it cannot show how heavy the actual burden is. Nevertheless, two questions should be answered as to why Forbes gave China such rankings and is China's tax burden heavy or light on earth.

Forbes measures the Tax Misery Index by total max marginal statutory rates of all main taxes including CIT, PIT, property tax, employers' social insurance, employees' social insurance and value-added tax (VAT) (or sales tax) in one country. For instance China's index is 160, equivalent to the sum of max statutory rates of CIT (33%), PIT (45%), property tax (0%), employers' social insurance (44.5%), employees' social insurance (20.5%) and VAT (17%) (Shu Qiming & Liu Xinli, 2006).

This is almost opposite to our measurement of the tax burden. We usually measure by the share of tax revenue to GDP. It is equivalent to tax revenue divided by

GDP of the same year. For instance in 2007 the tax burden was 19.82%, computed as national tax revenue (RMB 4944.9 billion) divided by the GDP of the same year (RMB 24953 billion).

The differences between the two measurements and their results tell us there may be at least two benchmarks for the tax burden. They are the statutory and the actual burdens. What astonish people are the two totally opposite results, which come from two different benchmarks to measure China's tax burden in reality. In today's world, our tax burden is at a very high level if measured on the benchmark of the statutory tax burden, but at an absolutely low level if measured on the benchmark of the actual tax burden.

Again, so large a contrast between the high level and the low level justifies to us the important real national condition that there is a huge gap between the statutory and the actual tax burdens in China. It's the wide disparity that misleads people's thoughts about China's tax burden.

When we have a further understanding, we discover the reason that the tax burden has been controversial for years is that people confuse the statutory and the actual tax burdens.

Since the moment when the current tax system was put into effect we have been trapped in some contradictions. On the one hand, complaints from enterprises and residents about the heavier tax burden never stop; on the other hand, governments assert that no actions have been taken to increase taxes. The first thought occurs to us that at least either party is likely to have a misunderstanding, but when we stand in both parties' shoes and give a second thought, we will realize they are telling the truth. Tax burdens for enterprises and residents are increased for sure; but governments never carry out any tax system adjustment that intends to increase taxes. So, why do enterprises and residents have heavier burdens under the unchanged tax system? The answer to the paradox cannot be anything but the fact that the gap between our statutory and actual burdens is narrowed down when our tax collection capability is improved. In other words, increased tax burdens for enterprises and residents refer to the increased actual not the statutory burdens; unchanged tax burdens declared by governments refer to the consistent statutory not the actual burdens. In brief, the coincidence of the unchanged statutory burden and increased actual burden is the very important real fact in China.

Conclusion 6: The two benchmarks do not exclusively measure China's real tax burden. Our tax burden will be concluded as a heavy one if measured on the benchmark of the statutory burden, but as a light one if measured on the benchmark of the actual burden. No matter which benchmark prevails, the conclusion is just one-sided, not comprehensive or objective, unless two benchmarks prevail at the same time.

Conclusion 7: We should notice the fact that the statutory and actual burdens are closer and closer when we judge China's real tax burden. We can truly understand our real tax burden only when we have a dynamic insight into the narrowing gap of both burdens.

IV Tax revenue and GDP distribution pattern

Most people are delighted and excited about the tax revenue growth especially the rapid growth but are astounded and worried about the revenue decrease, and even about a small decline in the revenue growth.

Such cases and their frequencies of occurrences are related to people's observational perspectives. For governments, the more tax revenue the better, no matter how revenue or expenditure is concerned; but if we change perspective and observe from the viewpoint of the whole economy and society, we'll find more is not necessarily better. Tax revenue is not a windfall but it eventually has its own purposes.

Tax revenue is all about distribution after all. People will find tax revenue is just a component of GDP if they go to the source. It is more like, for instance, a "shutoff valve" on the GDP distribution "pipeline". It shuts off some nodes in the GDP distribution pipeline and then transfers a part of GDP to the pockets of governments. Under a given GDP scale, tax revenue rises and the incomes of enterprises and residents decline; tax revenue grows faster and the incomes of enterprises and residents grow slower; tax revenue takes a larger share and the incomes of enterprises and residents take a smaller share, vice versa. When we consider the irreversibly proportional relationship between both the growth rates of tax revenue and GDP, their difference, no matter positive or negative, is an important issue for our attention.

Let's take the last five years for instance. The growth rate differences between tax revenue and GDP (based on current prices) were 7.5%, 8.0%, 5.0%, 7.2% and 14.7% respectively from 2003 to 2007; accordingly, the growth rate differences between urban household PCDI (per capita disposable income) and GDP (based on current prices) were –2.9%, –6.5%, –3.6%, –2.6% and 0.5% respectively; the growth rate differences between rural household PCNI (per capita net income) and GDP (based on current prices) were –7%, –5.7%, –4.2%, –4.5% and –1.3% respectively.[7] The share of tax revenue to GDP, a definitely far-reaching figure, also has some highly relevant changes, rising from 15.1% to 16.1%, 16.8%, 18.0% and 19.82% year by year. Comparing all these figures, it's not difficult to find which side GDP distribution favors and what are the driving sources for tax revenue to grow faster than GDP.

In fact not all records of the history are positive. At least at the beginning of the reform and opening up, the tax revenue to GDP ratio was dropping step by step. When we look through the 30 years of the reform and opening up, things are quite dramatic. They are totally opposite in both 15-year periods before and after 1994.

Given that tax revenue is a component of fiscal revenue after all, and the significance of tax revenue to fiscal revenue has undergone tremendous changes[8] before, during and after the reform, we might as well take the fiscal-to-GDP ratio as a benchmark for the sake of comparability.

When the reform and opening up started, in order to increase the role of market in social resource allocation, we were determined to pursue the reform goal that we should decrease the share of fiscal revenue to GDP. Thus, we introduced a series of reform movements, which aimed at "reducing taxes on enterprises and allowing them to retain more profits" and "granting decision-making powers to enterprises and allowing them to retain more profits". When these actions worked, the fiscal-to-GDP ratio fell from 31.2% in 1978, to 25.5% in 1980, 22.2% in 1985, 15.7% in 1990, 12.3% in 1993, and finally 10.8% in 1994, a decrease of 20.4 percentage points over the 15 years.

Against the background of weakening macro control and increasingly severe fiscal difficulties, the 1994 finance and tax reform came out in order to enhance macro control of the government and turn the fiscal situation for the better. Its significant achievement is that the fiscal-to-GDP ratio was turned around from the bottom. This ratio ascended from 10.3% in 1995, to 11% in 1997, 13.5% in 2000, 17.2% in 2005 and 20.09% in 2007, an increase of 9.29 percentage points over the 14 years.

Aligning the changing track in the first 15 years with the one in the last 15 years, it obviously looks like an asymmetric "V" shape.

Things are tricky as they are different from what they used to be before the reform and opening up. The fiscal revenue we talk about here is not all of government revenue. Even when we discuss the scale of all kinds of budgets that are on the record and submitted by finance departments to the people's congresses, fiscal revenue is just regular budget revenue. In addition, there are some types of "below-the-line" revenue that are in parallel with the regular budget revenue, including fund budget revenue, liability budget revenue and off-budget revenue from earmarked financial accounts. If we totaled up all kinds of budget revenue and the incomes out of system and budget, the share of government revenue to GDP would rise to 30%, which is almost the 1978 level.

In this context, we are astonished to find the aligned changing tracks in the first and the last 15 years is a completely symmetric "V" shape. In other words, when the market-oriented reform has gone through 30 years from 1978 to 2007, we now come back to its starting point where the share of public revenue to GDP is concerned.

However things have not yet ended. The macro economy in 2008 had profound changes and tax revenue and fiscal revenue growth began to fall, but the growth rates of both tax revenue and fiscal revenue in first three quarters still stayed at high levels, respectively 24% and 25.8%. Their growth rates in the fourth quarter are likely to fall more, nevertheless tax revenue and fiscal revenue in the whole year will certainly exceed RMB 6000 billion respectively, even reach a higher record.[9] Moreover, if there were no surprises or no extensive adjustment to our current tax system, the situation that both tax revenue and fiscal revenue grow faster than GDP would stay with us for a period from now on. It means we will still head forward along the right trail of the "V" shape.

When we get down to see the "system restoration" in China's resource allocation pattern, we are somewhat at sea. In addition, there are some other problems such as the relative PCDI decline, higher saving rate and lower domestic consumption rate, so we inevitably feel urgent to solve all.

Now when the reform and opening up has gone through 30 years, it seems we have to reemphasize the basic balance formula for GDP (i.e. GDP = consumption +

investment + government expenditure = consumption + savings + tax revenue). The formula tells us we need to analyze GDP from both the supply and demand sides. On the supply side, GDP equals to the sum of consumption, savings and tax revenue; on the demand side, GDP equals the sum of consumption, investment and government expenditure. When GDP is a fixed amount, one is more and the others are less. Any discussions about tax revenue, the tax revenue growth rate and the share of tax revenue to GDP cannot be divorced from this basic balance formula. Otherwise, our estimates of situations may be wrong; our movements may contradict the intentions of our macroeconomic and social policies.

Conclusion 8: Tax revenue is not a windfall. The differences between the growth rates of tax revenue and GDP are rooted in the GDP distribution pattern. Unavoidably it's not all-inclusive to talk about the tax revenue growth without considering the GDP distribution pattern.

Conclusion 9: We should analyze such macro variables as tax revenue growth at the macro level. If only we consider the general interests of government, enterprises and residents, if only we consider what matters to the overall economic and social development, we are able to have realistic and appropriate assessments of their potential influences on our economy and society.

Conclusion 10: When we review the changes of the share of tax revenue to GDP in the last 30 years after the reform and opening up, we will find the fact that it's the time to review the allocation pattern of social resources and reassess its objectives.

V Reasons for tax system reform

At least on the day when the Third Plenary Session of the Sixteenth CPC Central Committee officially put forward its intention to "implement the tax system reform step by step" in 2003,[10] we began to applaud and cry out for the start of a new round of tax system reform. We always say it is extremely urgent to start the new tax reform, but its process seems more like "much said and little done", thus people are sure to ask whether there are good reasons for a new round of tax system reform.

Generally speaking, to define reasons for the tax reform, it's probably necessary to recognize and understand the following facts.

First of all, tax reform is an eternal theme in the world and in the history of human social development. The tax system changes more frequently than any other economic system around us.

Secondly, as to why the tax reform is an eternal theme and why the tax system changes most frequently, it's simply because the tax system has to be rooted in the economic and social environment at that time and keep pace with changes in the economic and social environment.

In addition, China's current tax system was born in 1994 and already has a history of 15 years. During that period, its fundamental pattern has yet not changed, despite some amendments, while China's economic and social environment has had some earth-shaking changes. That means our current tax system has deviated from our real economic and social environment.

Finally, it becomes increasingly clear that China's tax system at the moment no longer matches up with its root, the economic and social environment. It will definitely hinder economic and social development, and even have more and more negative outcomes, unless it changes with the times.

Specifically, there would be a long list of reasons that vary from each other. From the perspective of carrying out the scientific outlook on development and constructing a socialist harmonious society, we have some examples as follows.

Let's begin with the tax system compositions. Indirect taxes constitute the major part of our current tax system. The turnover tax revenue makes up about 70% of the whole tax revenue. Such a tax pattern is relatively good for the government to effectively obtain revenue, but not good to effectively bridge the gap between the rich and the poor. It's the tax system that is composed of all tax categories and works like a symphony orchestra. Each category, of course, is meant to gain income, but also has its own position where it undertakes different tasks from others. Relatively, direct taxes are more functional than indirect taxes in adjustment, but indirect taxes are more functional than direct taxes in revenue collection. Therefore, we should progressively increase the share of direct taxes and decrease the share of indirect taxes relative to the whole tax revenue. Our tax reform should move forward in the direction that we will gradually improve the function of our taxes in narrowing down the wealth gap and providing a solid source of income as well.

Then let's move to the composition of indirect taxes. At present, the majority of our direct taxes are PITs at the level of flow. So far China has had no property taxes yet in a real sense. The existing estate tax and urban house tax are not collected from individuals, although they are included in the group of property taxes nominally. The two taxes are definitely not direct taxes as their payers are conventional "institutions". Given that the wealth disparity among individuals is reflected in the both indices of flow and stock, and the stock is fundamental and decides the flow to some extent, we should collect property taxes as soon as possible and end the situation that no taxes are imposed on properties held. Thereby it should be put on schedule that a direct tax system shall be established to levy taxes on incomes and properties for the purpose of bridging the wealth gap.

Then let's examine the system design for a specific tax system. Our current PIT is collected by category. It seems to be one tax but is made up of 11 categories. Such a tax system features more collection but less adjustment as it helps greatly to collect taxes from the sources and minimize tax avoidance and evasions, but helps little to eliminate income disparity. When we measure the income disparity among individuals, we actually compare their comprehensive incomes, including those incomes from all sources and categorical items. Therefore, it will be absolutely effective to impose taxes on different categories of personal incomes in adjustment, but its effects are far from being inclusive. If high earners are required to pay more taxes than low earners for the purpose of bridging their income gap, we should implement the comprehensive income tax system that individuals declare their own incomes and pay their taxes on a tax base of all their own income. This is how the PIT system evolves in every country and also the direction of our reform of the PIT system.

Finally, let's look at the design of tax burden. We had to set a higher "statutory tax burden" in order to achieve a lower "actual tax burden" 15 years ago; but we don't need such massive "taxation room" 15 years later when the tax authorities have improved their collection ability, taxpayers are more honest than ever before and the gap between the "actual burden" and "statutory burden" is already narrowed down. What's more, given that the seventeenth CPC National Congress already set forth the goal of "raising the proportion of residents' incomes to national income distribution", given that it's the moment to relieve burdens on enterprises and residents after our current macroeconomic situations have changed, it's quite necessary and absolutely possible to cut down the higher "statutory tax burden" and thus turn our tax revenue back to the normal growth track that aligns with our macroeconomy.

That's what accounts for the start and the completion of a new round of tax reform. And all causes are reasonable. The remaining task for us is to seize opportunities and carry out the blueprint of the new round of tax reform, drawn in the Eleventh Five-Year Plan, through the updated tax reforms.

Conclusion 11: We may list many reasons to start anew round of tax reform, but the fundamental reason is that our current tax system already deviates from its roots, the economic and social environment.

Conclusion 12: We should eliminate tax system factors that hinder economic and social development after careful thought and then establish a tax system that can catch up and keep pace with our economic and social environment. This is a very important task for China to complete as soon as possible.

(Originally published in *Taxation Research*, Vol.11, 2008)

Notes

* A companion volume to the author's *Macro Views on Tax – Analysis of Several Current Major Tax Issues*, in 2002.

1 In reality, the released GDP growth rate is calculated based on fixed prices but the tax revenue growth rate is calculated based on current prices. Before comparing the two rates, the former shall be adjusted. The GDP growth rate based on current prices equals the GDP growth rate based on fixed prices and CPI (consumer price index).

2 The opinion that many people believe "the growth rate of tax revenue cannot be directly compared with the GDP rate" may be more reasonable.

3 Refer to "XieXuren Meets the Press" for more details, *China Financial and Economic News*, June 13, 2006.

4 According to Yang Bin (2008), the tax revenue elasticity is always more than one if only the multiple-tax system prevails.

5 Since 2008 CITs and income taxes from foreign-invested and foreign enterprises have been consolidated into "CIT".

6 The statutory tax burden and the actual tax burden are two opposite concepts. The former refers to the taxes that should be theoretically collected under the stipulated tax system; the latter refers to the taxes that the tax departments are able to collect in reality.

7 The GDP growth rate is adjusted on the basis of current prices because it has to be compared with tax revenue growth rate and resident income growth rate. The comparison method was already discussed before.
8 Based on the comparable benchmark, the share of tax revenue relative to fiscal revenue was 45.9% in 1978, 57.7% in 1984, 94.9% in 1991, 93.4% in 2001, 90.1% in 2005 and 89.1% in 2007.
9 Figure s come from *People's Daily Online*, October 24, 2008.
10 Article 20 of the Decisions of the Central Committee of the Communist Party of China on Some Issues Regarding the Improvement of the Socialist Market Economic System (2003), approved in the Third Plenary Session of the Sixteenth CPC Central Committee, defines eight programs for the tax reform. They are to reform the export debate system; to unify all corporate income tax systems that are applicable to various enterprises; to transform VAT from the productive to a consumptive type by including equipment investments into the scope of VAT deduction; to improve consumption tax by broadening the tax base to a proper extent; to reform personal income tax by implementing a personal income tax system that combines the comprehensive type and the categorical type together; to carry out a tax-for-fee reform on urban construction by imposing a unified property tax on real estates while abolishing current charges in a proper time; to empower local governments with certain taxation powers under the unified tax administration; and to create a favorable environment for the progressive unification of rural and urban tax systems.

Bibliography

China statistical yearbook (2008). (2008). Beijing: China Statistics Press.

Gao Peiyong. (2002). Macro views on taxation. *Taxation Research, 2–3.*

Integrated planning division, *MOFinistry of finance, China, China finance statistics (1950–1991)*. (1994). Beijing: Science Press.

Jin Renqing. (1992). *Comments on Chinese contemporary tax revenue*. Beijing: People's Publishing House.

Plan and Statistics Division (2005). SAT, Macro Analysis of Changes of VAT Collection Rate and Results of Golden Taxation Project (Phase 2).

ShuQiming,& Liu Xinli. (2006. Tax Misery Index Is Unaccountable for the Actual Tax Burden, Website of the Administration of Taxation (SAT), March 9, 2006.

Taxation Division, Ministry of Finance. (2008). Correct Views on Tax Revenue Growing over GDP, MOF Website, September 11, 2008.

XieXuren. (2006, June 13). XieXuren meets the press. *China Financial and Economic News*.

XuShanda. (2004). *Speech at 2004 China tax revenue forum*. Retrieved from www.finance.sina.com.cn/roll/20040424/1551737

Yang Bin. (2008). Questions to the theory of synchronized growth of tax revenue and GDP. *Taxation Research, 9.*

12 Several major changes in China's macroeconomic policy pattern

As the 2012 Central Economic Work Conference (CEWC) concluded, China's macroeconomic policy pattern has changed significantly in at least four aspects. Such changes determine China's economy to a great extent in 2013 and a period in the future and also have a material impact on China's economic and social development process.

I Macroeconomic policy positioning: achieving "healthy and sustainable economic development and social harmony and stability"

As far as the functional positioning of our macroeconomic policy pattern is concerned in the past, we always based ourselves in the sectors related to economic development and highlighted or focused on rapid economic growth. Our reviews on the previous CEWCs discover that the economic philosophy was defined as "sustainable, rapid and healthy" in the 1990s, and as "sustainable, rapid, coordinated and healthy", "steady and fast", "fast and sound", "sound and fast" and then "steady and fast" one after another in the 21 st century. In short, our macroeconomic policy always aims at fast economic growth.

However, the 2012 CEWC employs a different expression for the functional positioning of our macroeconomic policy. It is to "achieve healthy and sustainable economic development and social harmony and stability". This is the first time policy makers have overlooked fast growth and extended our macroeconomic policy into the social development sector. Obviously this change is of epoch-making significance.

"Healthy and sustainable" replaces "steady and fast" as our objective for economic growth, and "social harmony and stability" and "healthy and sustainable economic development" stay side by side regarding the functional positioning of our macroeconomic policy. Such changes unfold to us at least the following facts.

First, our economic growth has decelerated from a high rate to a medium rate, and then to a single-digit rate as our industrialization enters into its middle and later periods. On this regular phenomenon, people have gradually arrived at a consensus.

Second, with the evolution of the global financial crisis, people also have gradually reached a consensus on its persistence and profundity. For instance, people believe the worldwide economy will remain at a low growth rate and when this crisis will end is still unpredictable now; when the global economic climate has changed a great deal in its connotations and conditions, the important strategic opportunities for our economic growth no longer come from the international division of labor, export expansion and investment acceleration. We are forced to create new opportunities by boosting domestic demand, improving our innovation capability and accelerating the transfer of our economic development mode; we must be aware of and get well prepared for the unexpected under the conditions of economic slowdown and production overcapacity.

Third, as its growth slows down, the economy should anchor itself in quality and efficiency improvement, and turn to seek for a quality, efficient and sustainable growth that abides by economic law. This is the third consensus people have already arrived at. Based on that, five specific measurements of economic growth come into being. They are growth of high quality, growth accompanied by employment increase, growth synchronized with resident income increase, growth accompanied by efficiency improvement and by sustainable resources and environment.

Finally, as various social conflicts in current China break out frequently and distinctly, people have reached a vast consensus on the relation between economic growth and social stability, and among development, stability and reform as well. "Social harmony and stability" is upgraded to the same level of "healthy and sustainable economic development". Both are taken as functional objectives of our macroeconomic policy. In this way, economic sectors are aligned with social sectors. The move to integrate healthy and sustainable economic development with social harmony and stability becomes a very significant option and is of course incorporated into our macroeconomic policy.

II Macroeconomic policy function: integrating "counter-cyclical regulation with structural adjustment promotion"

Macroeconomic policies in the sense of conventional economics are usually used as a counter-cyclical tool. Its macro control efforts could be summarized as "acting against the wind" that the expansionary measures are taken in economic recession while tight measures in the inflationary times. In our history, at least after the Asian financial crisis in 1998, macroeconomic policies in different periods are all made for counter-cyclical regulation, no matter a "proactive fiscal and appropriate monetary" policy package, or a "proactive and prudent" package and a "dual prudent" package, or a "proactive and moderately loose" package and a "proactive and prudent" package in recent years.

Our macroeconomic policies used to play an exclusive role of counter-cyclical regulation, but on the 2012 CEWC it is described to "give full play to counter-cyclical regulation and structural adjustment promotion". In other words, the

2013 policy must have the effects of both counter-cyclical regulation and structural adjustment promotion. It has thoughtful causes and considerations.

First, as the global economy keeps going up and down, and serious unbalanced, inharmonious and unsustainable problems are emerging, more and more facts have proved that this round of global financial crisis is an outcome of both periodic and structural factors and is mainly caused by an unbalanced economic structure. A recovery in a real sense will never come unless the existing economic structure changes. For this reason, we have to intensify strategic adjustment of our economic structure and completely transform our economic development mode in order to get our economy back on the track of healthy and sustainable development.

Second, now our economy is trapped in a vicious cycle where the downward pressure on economic growth and the production overcapacity contradict each other. Macro control measures against either one will lead to ineffective alleviation, unless they are applied to the both at the same time. As long as a two-pronged strategy is developed to have an effect on both counter-cyclical regulation and structural economic adjustment, the macroeconomic policy arrangements will finally match our economic reality.

Finally, in order to avoid altering economic structure during the anti-crisis process, or not gain the anti-crisis goals at the price of economic structure alteration, almost the only option left for us at present is to start from industrial structure adjustment and finally promote economic growth with structural adjustment or obtain the goal of economic growth compatible with structural adjustment by addressing production overcapacity and relieving economic downward pressure.

III Macroeconomic policy's objective: realizing "steady growth, structural adjustment, price control and risk prevention"

In this anti-crisis fight, our macroeconomic policy was initially targeted at "maintaining growth". When it overrode any other tasks, we could concentrate our resources with determination and spare no efforts to pursue it. Later when the economic situation eased and changed, we substituted "steady growth" for "maintaining growth", and also then supplemented additional objectives of macroeconomic policies into the original bracket. Besides "steady growth", "price control" was added due to the inflation driven by excess liquidity, and then "structural adjustment" was added due to the increasingly serious issues concerning economic structure. Up to now, the so-called triple target has taken shape, consisting of "steady growth, structural adjustment and price control".

The year of 2013 sees the hidden risks of financial sectors increasingly visible as a variety of debts that were borrowed through anti-crisis measures a few years ago are due in succession. It becomes an important task of macro-control enhancement and improvement to defend the bottom line that no systematic or regional financial risks should break out. The 2012 CEWC thereupon adds "risk prevention" into the objectives bracket of our macroeconomic policy. The triple target evolves into a quadruple target, consisting of "steady growth, price control, structural adjustment and risk prevention".

The new problem is when we have more than one objective, such as three, four or even more; we have to de-concentrate our macro-control resources, attempt to attack and conquer all fronts at once and obtain multiple objectives. It actually delivers us several messages as follows.

First, due to our dispersed forces, our macro-control actions in 2013 should and have to be flexible to achieve steady growth, structural adjustment, price control and risk prevention. It means the effective room for macro control is compressed to a great extent and is relatively narrow now.

Second, given the pressing necessity for steady growth and given that steady growth is required to be placed in a more important position, we cannot spare no efforts or devote most of our energy to steady growth like we used to, but we must achieve or balance several objectives at once.

Finally, our current macro control that is pinned by multiple objectives is more like a tug of war. Either side that is under greater pressure (more difficult situation) will receive more resources allocated through macro control. Inevitably it's hard to decide the objective priority or the major force of our macro control.

IV Macroeconomic policy package: tending to a prudent policy under the name of a "proactive and prudent" package

When the 2012 CEWC decides to continue to implement proactive fiscal policy and prudent monetary policy, our "proactive and prudent" macroeconomic policy package that lasted for two years comes to its third year. However this "proactive and prudent" package is not what it was. Our macroeconomic policy has never lived up to its name yet. They contain different material contents even under the same name. Looking into all arrangements made at the 2012 CEWC, we discover the 2013 "proactive and prudent" package tends to be prudent compared to the previous ones.

First, most developed economies like the EU, USA and Japan are introducing a new series of quantitative easing policies one after another, thereby the major currencies worldwide will be devalued due to extra money printed, and the pressure on potential inflation and asset forms will increase, resulting in an overflow effect on our economy eventually. Given the accumulated and increased hidden risks of our financial sectors, new local governments are likely eager to establish new local financing platforms after they take office; given that the previous inflationary pressure caused by excess liquidity is not relieved yet, a new round of inflationary pressure input from the outside and created from the inside is being generated. Against this background, the functional room of monetary policy is therefore constrained or compressed to a great extent, so we have to devote most of our efforts to price control and risk prevention.

Second, let's analyze from the three pivots of proactive fiscal policy. They are deficit increase, tax cuts and expenditure expansion. Despite the 2013 fiscal deficit increases, it has to be controlled under the international safety line of 3%, in the shadow of European sovereign-debt crisis, the US fiscal cliff and the hidden risks of our financial sectors. Tax cuts become evidently the main carrier of 2013 proactive fiscal policy, but our common sense tells us, compared to expenditure expansion, its expansionary effect is less and more indirect. Expenditure expansion, although useful and available, has to be restrained in 2013. Our governments at all levels should economize by strictly controlling regular expenses and also spend every coin wisely on important matters that have to be done. All factors will mitigate the expansionary effect of proactive fiscal policy to some extent.

Finally, the efficacy of expansionary measures has declined according to the law of diminishing marginal utility. It means, on the one hand, the overdosing and massive economic expansionary measures won't be as effective as they were in 2008 and 2009; on the other, in order to obtain high-quality, efficient and sustainable economic growth, or healthy and sustainable economic growth during the process of constant transition of our economic development mode and constant optimization of our economic structure, we have to balance multiple objectives, namely steady growth, structural adjustment, price control and risk prevention, and find a harmonious and coordinated solution to regulate counter-cyclical economy and promote structural adjustment.

(Originally published in *Economic Daily*,
February 8, 2013)

13 Tax reduction

Complexity in China

Nowadays, there is no doubt that the supply-side structural reform has been a frequently used concept in China. With regard to how to carry out this reform, especially how the government should push this reform, simply there are two kinds of basic prescriptions given by people: streamline administration and institute decentralization, and tax cuts. Of course, the former belongs to the reform level and needs to be implemented with the help of reform measures, while the latter is often included in the policy level, and reflected in choices related to macroeconomic policies. During implementation, the former inevitably affects the pattern of vested interests, and cannot come into effect within a short term, while the latter is mainly limited to policy adjustment and can come into effect within a relatively short term. Therefore, tax cutting is regarded as the preferred measure for the supply-side structural reform, even as the general therapy for solving the current contradictions and problems.

However, facing current national conditions and the taxation situation of China, when calming down, we'll find that the actual situation is not as simple as the above discussion, and also may be more complex than expected by many people.

It's natural that tax cuts involve the evaluation of the tax burden situation in China. The macro-tax burden, i.e. the proportion of tax revenue in the GDP of the same year, is an international general evaluation index of tax burden. Once this index is used to evaluate the tax burden situation in China, the first trouble to be emerge is "unified statement", which means that the macro-tax burden has to be adjusted and transformed into "macro-tax and fee burden".

It's because the revenue collected from taxpayers by the government is not all called tax in present China. Besides tax revenue, there are also various fees, funds, fines, etc. In addition, the budget listed by the government does not mean the general public budget only. Besides the general public budget revenue, it also includes the budget revenue from governmental funds, operation of state-owned capital and social insurance funds. In the face of numerous government revenue forms and government budget revenue types, there has always been a controversial issue of which part or parts should be included in sub-items of the macro-tax burden index. Out of different considerations and from different points of view, some people tend to the "narrow statement", which means that only the government revenue nominally called tax should be included in the range of macro-tax burden; some people prefer the "medium statement", which means that only the general public budget revenue should be included in the range of macro-tax burden; others persist in the "wide statement", which means that all government revenues should be included in the range of macro-tax burden. People have continually argued about the three different statements for years. There is much to be said on both sides. In the situation where the arguments are almost on a par, people's cognition about which level China's macro-tax burden is in the world has always been in a chaotic state, and China hasn't set up a unified and widely accepted statistical index related to macro-tax burden yet.

It is gratifying that with the official implementation of the new budget law since January 2015, it seems that the argument about the issue of macro-tax burden can come to a conclusion. Different from the former budget law, it is clearly specified in the new budget law that all the government revenues and expenditures shall be included in the budget, and the government budget is a unity integrating the general public budget, governmental fund budget, state-owned capital budget and social insurance fund budget. It is recognized that in nature, all the four types of government budget revenue belong to the revenue collected from taxpayers by the government, ceded by taxpayers to the government and composed of taxpayers' hard-earned money, and are merely different in name or form. Therefore, it has become a measure following the laws of reform and development of human history to include various forms and names of government revenue all in the statistical range of macro-tax burden.

Once the standard of "wide statement" is used to evaluate the tax burden situation in China, it will be further found that in 2014 as an example, the ratio of the source of government revenue nominally called tax to the source of government revenue denoted with other names was about 53:47. Unless studying on the issue seriously, we'll never learn the truth that the scale of government revenue from other sources except the tax is so large that if this part of government revenue is indulgently excluded from the statistical range of macro-tax burden, it will hinder the proper evaluation of the tax burden situation in China, blur the vision of common people and even tend to distort the government's macro decision-making. In order to avoid the recurrence of such matter, or to absolutely cut off the logical chain of recurrence of such matter, it is undoubtedly necessary to uniformly call various non-tax revenue sources as "fees", so as to adjust and transform the "macro-tax burden" into the "macro-tax and fee burden", and use "macro-tax and fee burden" as the applicable index to evaluate the tax burden situation in China.

According to the calculation based on statistical figures of 2014, if tax revenue and non-tax revenue were combined, or the general public budget revenue was combined with the budget revenue from governmental funds, operation of state-owned capital and social insurance funds, with the repeated parts being eliminated, the total government revenue would be RMB 22.557 trillion, accounting for 35.42% of GDP of the same year. The figure is equal to about 39% of the average tax burden in industrialized countries, at an above-average level in the world today.

What's more, tax cuts also involve the choice over whose taxes should be reduced and which taxes should be reduced, because tax revenue is a general term composed of taxes from different taxpayers of different natures. In China today, both aspects have distinctive characteristics depending on the national conditions and taxation situation of China.

For the former, let's take 2014 as an example: the proportion of tax revenue paid by state-owned enterprises, collective enterprises, joint-equity cooperative enterprises, joint-stock companies, private enterprises, etc. in the total national tax revenue amounting to RMB 11.9158 trillion reached 90%. In addition, the proportion of tax revenue from non-enterprise sources, namely paid by resident natural persons, was less than 10%. The ratio of revenue sourced from enterprises to that sourced from resident natural persons was about 90:10. If the tax revenue shares paid by private economy were deducted from the revenue sourced from resident natural persons, the revenue sourced from resident natural persons would only account for about 6%. As a result, the ratio of revenue sourced from enterprises to that sourced from resident natural persons was about 94:6.

We can learn from such an out-of-balance structure of tax revenue sources that in today's world, though the macrotax and fee burden of China is merely at an above-average level, the tax and fee burden of China's enterprises is far higher than the macrotax and fee burden. One of the main causes is that the macrotax burden of China is mainly imposed on enterprises. Regardless of the problem that taxes and fees which should have been paid by enterprises are often transferred through various channels, as it were, the tax and fee burden in China is generally borne by enterprises themselves.

For the latter, let's still take 2014 as an example, the proportion of indirect tax revenue from domestic value-added tax, domestic consumption tax, business tax, value-added tax and consumption tax of imported goods, vehicle purchase tax, etc. in the total national tax revenue amounting to RMB 11.9158 trillion reached 64.2%. If other local taxes with the strong indirect tax characteristic were added, the proportion of whole indirect tax revenue in the total tax revenue would exceed 70%. In addition, the proportion of direct tax revenue from enterprise income tax, individual income tax, etc. was only 26.2%. The ratio of indirect tax revenue to direct tax revenue was about 70:30. The indirect tax, as it were, plays a dominant role in China's tax revenue.

We can gain enlightenment from such an out-of-balance structure of tax revenue types in the world today. Though the macro-tax and fee burden of China is at an above-average level, the majority of China's tax revenue can be openly embedded in the price of various commodities and elements as one of the factors of price. Since this part of tax revenue is invisible and impalpable, its corresponding tax burden can be handled in the same way. However, due to its large shares and great influence on the price of commodities and elements, it only significantly raises the price level of commodities and elements, which inevitably reduces the price competitiveness of commodities and elements, but also binds the rise and fall in price together with the change of taxation system and the level of tax burden, which also inevitably distorts the normal formation of the price mechanism.

Furthermore, with a different interactive mechanism from direct tax, indirect tax has no direct correlation with the surplus-deficit status. Thus, even an enterprise running at a loss should pay the indirect tax as usual without any leeway.

It means to rub salt into the wounds of the enterprise running at a loss that is urgently exploring a way out to break through the dilemma.

On the one hand, the tax and fee burden in China is generally borne by enterprises solely. On the other hand, indirect tax plays a dominant role in China's tax burden. Considering the respective functions of and the interaction between both two forces mentioned above from the perspective of supply-side structural reform, we can easily understand that as a result of the overall accounting, even if the macro-tax and fee burden of China fails to be at an above-average level in the world today, it is still severely out-of-balance no matter the sources and types when the detailed accounting is carried out by getting rid of the limitations of total quantity and deepening it to the internal structure. The inevitable result caused by this out-of-balance structure is the imbalance of the tax and fee burden level among relevant taxpayers and among different tax types and categories. Specifically, the tax burden of enterprises is heavier than that of resident natural persons; the tax burden of indirect tax is heavier than that of direct tax.

We can hereby give a brief summary of the discussion in this paper as follows.

First, though tax cutting apparently belongs to the category of macroeconomic policy arrangement, it is actually a significant initiative concerning the supply-side structural reform, for which efforts need be made at both levels of policy arrangement and reform promotion. Therefore, the proper choice for ensuring the implementation of tax cuts into the supply-side structural reform is to systematically make plans for various relevant deployments related to tax cuts at both levels of macroeconomic policy arrangement and comprehensive in-depth reform promotion on both demand and supply sides.

Second, both tax cuts and fee reductions are required in the overall planning of promoting the supply-side structural reform. It has been noticed that there are great differences in standardization between the current mechanisms of taxes and fees in China. The standardization of taxes is far higher than that of fees, while the undue interference from fees is far higher than that of taxes; thus, relatively speaking, fee reduction is more important. Therefore, for promoting supply-side structural reform, we can yield twice the result with half the effort by taking the opportunity of formal implementation of the new budget law, continually carrying forward the taxes and fees reform implemented since the late 1990s of the last century, and making efforts to achieve new breakthroughs through the standardization of government revenue behaviors and mechanism.

Finally, under the banner of tax cuts and fee reduction, it is necessary to classify the involved tax and fee items or types, so as to define the priorities of implementation. For instance, as far as the overall planning of taxes and fees, fee reduction should be given the priority relative to tax cuts; as far as tax cuts, tax cuts for enterprises should be given the priority relative to that for resident natural persons; and it is a better choice to reduce the indirect tax than the direct tax. In other words, the emphases of tax cutting measures focusing on the supply-side structural reform should and must be laid on fee reduction, tax cuts for enterprises and indirect tax cuts.

(Originally published in *International Taxation in China*, 2016: 1)

14 Chinese finance under the "new normal"

Several tendency changes

More and more facts repeatedly show that, as economic development entered the "new normal", Chinese financial operation has changed significantly. Among these changes, there must be some contingent ones, but most of them are tendencies. We might even say that they resulted from the effect of the economic development law.

These tendency changes repeatedly show that Chinese finance, as a mirror and the inevitable result of economic development speed, structural adjustment and kinetic energy conversion, has transformed from its previous habitual operational state to a new different operational orbit.

In the face of these tendency changes, on the one hand, we should profoundly understand and accurately grasp them on the basis of comprehensive summary and systematical analysis; on the other hand, we should adjust the previous habitual series of concepts, thoughts and strategies comprehensively in a proper time and actively adapt to and lead the Chinese financial operational new pattern under the "new normal" of economic development with a new series of concepts, thoughts and strategies that differ from previous ones.

Tendency change no. 1: sharp slowdown of fiscal revenue growth speed and rapid decline of tax elasticity coefficient

The basic theory of economics makes us realize that there is a strong corresponding relation between economic growth and fiscal revenues (Romer et al., 2007). Moreover, the development experiences of relevant states also show that economic growth will drive fiscal revenues to increase more significantly and economic downturns will cause a more significant decline of fiscal revenue (IMF, 2015). In the past several years, Chinese fiscal revenues have apparently experienced this operational orbit.

As shown in Figure 14.1, with the constant slowdown of economic growth, the growth rate of Chinese general public budget revenue sharply decreased after reaching 24.8% in 2011, except for the peak value of 32.4% in 2007. It was 12.9%, 10.2%, 8.6% and 8.4% respectively in 2012, 2013, 2014 and 2015. In other words, it only took four years for the growth rate of general public budget revenue to sharply slow down from 24.8% to 8.4%. It decreased from a two-digit

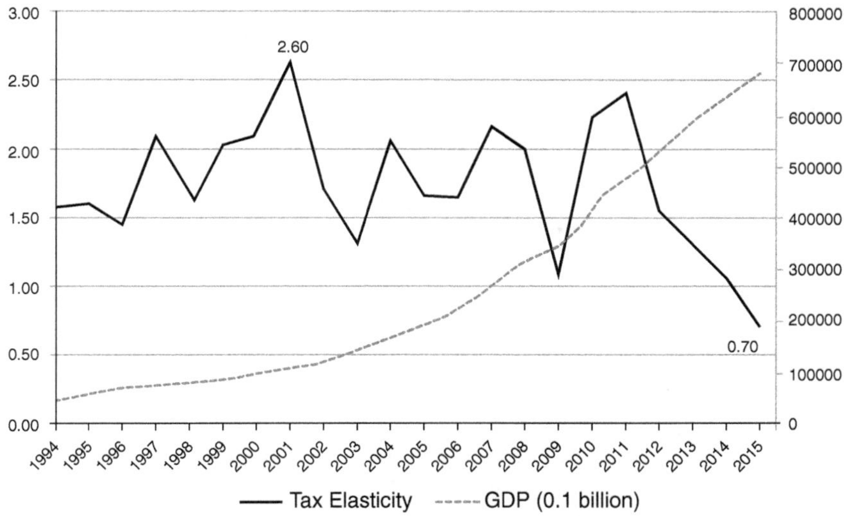

Figure 14.1 Fluctuation tendency of fiscal revenue growth rate (1994–2015)

Data sources: National Bureau of Statistics of the People's Republic of China: 2015 Chinese Statistics Yearbook, China Statistics Press; Ministry of Finance: Report on 2015 Central and Local Budget Enforcement and 2016 Central and Local Budget Proposals (on *People's Daily*, March 18, 2016); Ministry of Finance: Chinese Financial Yearbooks (1994 to 2015), *China Financial Magazine*.

number to a single-digit number, equivalent to about one-third of that of four years ago. The rapid slowdown speed is astonishing.

Further, 8.4% of 2015 is just a nominal value. There are two necessary subtractions from nominal growth rate to actual growth rate: First, the 11 items of governmental fund revenues transferred from the governmental fund budget shall be deducted. Thus, the actual growth rate is 5.8% if calculated according to comparable caliber. This number is far less than one-fourth of that of four years ago, and also less than the budget increase rate by 1.5%. This is the second consecutive year fiscal revenues did not achieve the budget goal. Second, some special income-increasing measures taken on the basis of consideration for a balanced budget shall be deducted, for instance, increasing the profit delivery scale for specific state-owned enterprises and institutions. Therefore, 5.8% also needs to be discounted. The slowdown of the fiscal revenue growth rate may be considered as a cliff.

The more severe problem was that this slowdown momentum was just a beginning and there is still no sign of bottoming at present. Looking forward into 2016 and several years into the future, the factor change values in the following aspects shall be paid special attention to.

First, economy determines finance. In the situation of continuous global economic downturn, with the promotion of Chinese supply side's structural reform, the five tasks including "de-capacity", "de-stocking", "de-leverage", "cost-reduction" and "short board improvement" were implemented into practice, thus, the pressure on the economic slowdown increases without decrease. The further slowdown of the fiscal revenue growth rate is sure to occur if there are no non-regular special income-increasing measures to be taken.

Second, as the main revenues of Chinese fiscal revenues, the tax revenues under the current tax system mainly come from added-value tax, consumption tax, business tax and other indirect taxes. This kind of "indirect taxes–oriented" tax revenue pattern means that, with the economic slowdown and continuous decline and even negative growth of PPI, it is expected that the growth rate of fiscal revenues will slow down at the amplitude higher than GDP deceleration.

The reason why we made this judgment is that many researches have proved that: among the factors affecting Chinese tax revenues, economic fluctuation and price fluctuation are two main aspects (Gao Peiyong, 2006; LvBingyang et al., 2007; Zhou Li'an et al., 2012). It has been the first time that the growth rate of tax revenues in 2015 (4.8%) was lower than GDP growth rate (6.9%) since 1994. Besides, in the whole year of 2015, the monthly growth rate of tax revenues did not exceed 5%, and even was lower than 3% in the first half year. The growth rate of tax revenues in each month was lower than the corresponding-period GDP growth rate. For this, there is a more reliable explanation: the indirect taxes–oriented tax system structure with the industrial added value as the tax calculation basis is highly correlated to price. Under the influence of the long-term downturn of PPI and other price indexes, the growth kinetic energy of fiscal revenues has obviously declined.

Third, in recent years, with increasing pressure on the economic downturn, the Chinese tax elasticity coefficient has shown a tendency for rapid decrease. The ratio between tax revenues and GDP growth rate is called as the tax elasticity coefficient, which is an important standard for measuring tax revenue increase capacity (Craig & Heins, 1979). In the past several years, Chinese tax revenues are elastic (more than 1) as shown in Figure 14.2. From 1994 to 2015, the average tax elasticity coefficient was 1.72. For eight years during this period, the tax elasticity coefficient even exceeded 2. For instance, in 2011, the tax elasticity coefficient even was 2.38. However, after 2011, the tax elasticity coefficient began to decline. It was 1.57 in 2012, declining by 0.81 within a year. It was 1.28 and 1.07 in 2013 and 2014 respectively. In 2015, it even fell below the critical point – 1 and further declined to 0.7. It only takes five years for the tax elasticity coefficient to change from elastic to inelastic.

Fourth, the slowdown of tax revenue growth rate is also a main cause for increasing contribution degree of the non-tax revenue growth rate for the overall fiscal revenue growth rate (Table 14.1). From March, 2014 to now, the monthly average growth rate of non-tax revenues reached 23.61%, no lower than two-digit level. The monthly average growth rate of tax revenues in the same period was just 5.58%. In 2015, the non-tax revenues were RMB 2,732.5 billion, increasing by 28.9% and 10.6% than the previous statistics by the same method and scope. Since the volume of non-tax revenues is far less than that of tax revenues, the non-tax revenues still cannot change the slowdown tendency of the overall fiscal

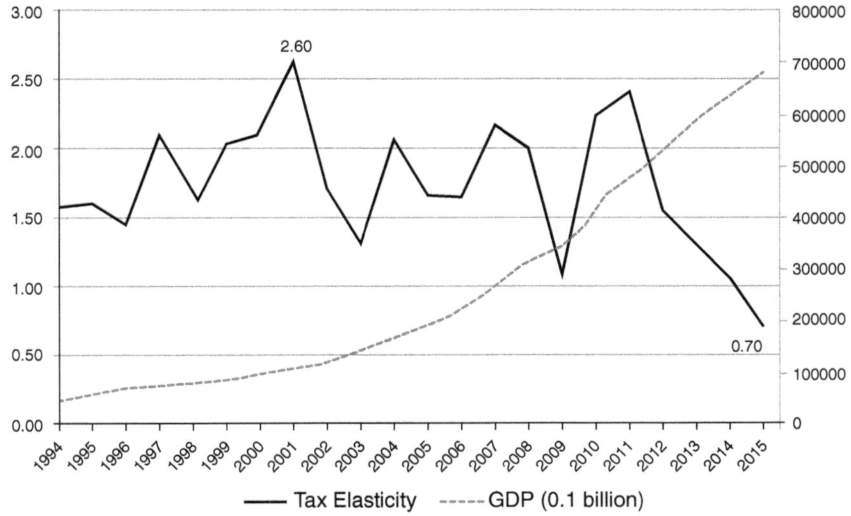

Figure 14.2 Change tendencies of tax elasticity and GDP (1994–2015)

Data sources: National Bureau of Statistics of the People's Republic of China: 2015 Chinese Statistics Yearbook, China Statistics Press; Ministry of Finance: Report on 2015 Central and Local Budget Enforcement and 2016 Central and Local Budget Proposals (on *People's Daily*, March 18, 2016); Ministry of Finance: Chinese Financial Yearbooks (1994 to 2015), *China Financial Magazine*.

Table 14.1 Change tendencies of tax revenues and non-tax revenues (2007–2015)

	Proportion between non-tax revenues and general public budget revenues	*Proportion between tax revenues and general public budget revenues*
2007	11%	89%
2008	12%	88%
2009	13%	87%
2010	12%	88%
2011	14%	86%
2012	14%	86%
2013	14%	86%
2014	15%	85%
2015	18%	82%

Data sources: Ministry of Finance: Report on 2015 Central and Local Budget Enforcement and 2016 Central and Local Budget Proposals (on *People's Daily*, March 18, 2016); Ministry of Finance: Chinese Financial Yearbooks (1994 to 2015), *China Financial Magazine*.

revenues although the contribution degree increase of the non-tax revenues would fill a part of the gap caused by the reduction of tax revenues.

Fifth, during the period of the overall slowdown of fiscal revenues growth rate, there were great differences in the growth rate slowdown amplitude among different areas as well as between central government and local areas. For the provinces dependent on resources and energy, such as three provinces in Northeast China, Shanxi, etc., their growth rate of fiscal revenues slowed down, even presented negative growth. The slowdown amplitude of central fiscal revenue growth rate was greater, because the central fiscal revenues' dependence degree for indirect-tax revenues is higher than local areas'. This unbalanced state among different areas as well as the central government and local areas worsened the fiscal revenues in the growth rate slowdown tendency.

Finally, due to the needs to stabilize growth and promote supply-side structural reform, in the list of measures available for proactive fiscal policies, tax abatement has replaced the traditional expenditure increase to become the preferred operation. Whether a large-scale tax abatement represented by changing business tax to value-added tax is implemented comprehensively or the tax abatement for small and micro enterprises is carried out, as long as the direct tax reform which focuses on individual income tax and real estate tax and tends to tax increase cannot be implemented simultaneously, unless the direct tax reform is carried out simultaneously but the tax increase strength is less than that of tax abatement, resulting in imbalance between increase and abatement effects, the slowdown amplitude of the fiscal revenue growth rate will be further increased.

Under the interactions among the above factors, for 2015, the fiscal revenue growth rate calculated with the price change factor deducted in comparison is likely to slow down if there are no special revenue increase measures or important reform actions to be taken in other respects.

Tendency change no. 2: fiscal expenditures increase against the trend, and the rigid growth pattern increasingly strengthens

At the same time, fiscal expenditures increased. Generally, expenditures in various respects did not deviate from the general trend where they decreased correspondingly with the decline in disposable financial resources (Romer et al. 2008). With the slowdown in economic growth, the need to increase expenditure for stabilizing growth, promoting reform, benefiting people's livelihood, preventing risks, etc. and social security expenditures for pension, medical care, etc. presented a sharp increase in momentum under the effect of inertia, and mid–long-term expenditure pressure became greater.

In 2015, even though the speed of GDP increase slowed down to 6.9%, the nationwide general public budget expenditure growth rate still reached 15.8%. The difference between them was more than 8.9%. Through the comparison between revenue growth rate and expenditure growth rate in a longer time sequence, we can also find, during the 50 months from February 2012 to April 2016, there were only three scattered months where the expenditure growth rate was lower than revenue growth rate. In the rest of the months, the expenditure increase amplitude was higher than that of revenues.

A more severe problem was: looking forward to 2016 and several years into the future, the pressure of the above various expenditures will increase without decrease and tend to further increase.

First, Chinese fiscal expenditures always have a tradition of counter-cyclical regulation for economic slowdown. In 1998 and 2008, two rounds of proactive fiscal policies realized economic stabilization through expenditure expansion (Gao Peiyong, 2010). Against the background of the "comprehensively establishing the well-off society" overall deployment strategy put forward on the Fifth Plenary Session of the Eighteenth CPC Central Committee, by 2020, GDP and per-capita income of urban and rural residents shall double those of 2010, to realize the economic growth goal of the annual average no lower than 6.5%, the financial policies, as the governmental first-level regulatory tool, will continue playing an important role. It can be expected that, at least during "the Thirteenth Five-Year Plan" period, the Chinese fiscal policy layout will remain in a state of expansion.

In this context, it will be inevitable for financial deficits to expand and the proportion between financial deficits and GDP to increase year by year. In 2015, the growth rate of fiscal expenditures was higher than that of fiscal revenues by 6.27%, and fiscal expenditures exceeded fiscal revenues by RMB 2355.1 billion. The actual deficit rate reached 3.48%. In 2016, the Chinese budget deficit rate is expected to be 3%, and the arranged budget deficit is RMB 2.18 trillion, increasing by RMB 560 billion more the prior year's budget deficit. The Chinese deficit must be more than 3% if the other respective factors which are nominally included in the deficit but not different from deficit influence are essentially covered according to the same method and scope as the current internationally calculated statistics.

Second, even though no strong stimulation policies are being carried out, the supply-side structural reform also needs be promoted on the basis of the corresponding increase in fiscal revenues. To achieve the goals of keeping macro policies stable and creating a steady macroeconomic environment, "de-capacity", "de-stocking", "de-leverage", "cost reduction" and "short board improvement" need to be supported by an increase in fiscal expenditures.

Third, if the mitigation of economic fluctuation to relieve the economic downturn is considered as a short-term expenditure increase cause under fiscal counter-cyclical regulation, the structural change in economic and social development is the direct cause of the long-term rigid growth of fiscal expenditures. Structural changes in population, the development of long-term transformation and the conversion of international status once significantly promoted the rigid growth of fiscal expenditures in many states (Liu Xiahui, 2013). Nowadays, China is experiencing similar economic and social development reform. In 2010, the Chinese working-age population started to decline after reaching its peak, and the demographic dividend officially disappeared (Cai Fang, 2010). In 2014, China became the second largest economy in the world; thus international responsibilities increased accordingly (Xi Jinping, 2015). In 2015, China comprehensively implemented structural reform and took innovative development as the first priority (Li Keqiang, 2016). Seen from the perspective of the long-term tendency, the growth rate of Chinese fiscal expenditures has been never lower than the GDP growth rate since 1994 (Figure 14.3). Even in the situation where the growth rate

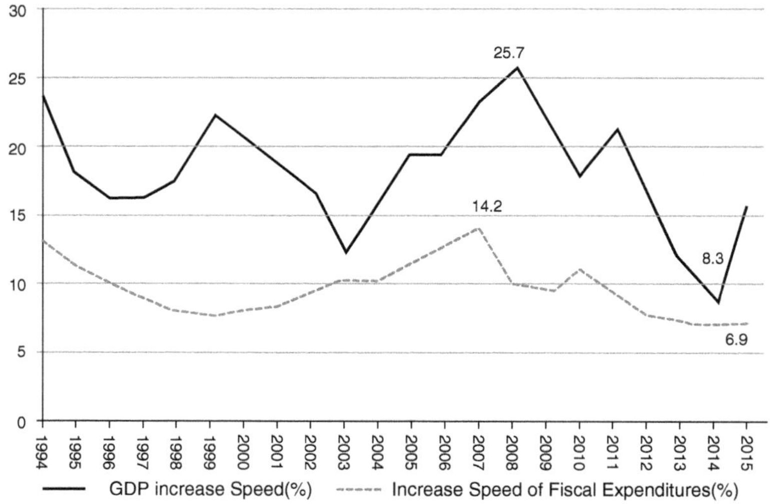

Figure 14.3 Comparison of change tendency of GDP growth rate and fiscal expenditure growth rate (1994–2015)

Data sources: National Bureau of Statistics of the People's Republic of China: 2015 Chinese Statistics Yearbook, China Statistics Press; Ministry of Finance: Report on 2015 Central and Local Budget Enforcement and 2016 Central and Local Budget Proposals (on *People's Daily*, March 18, 2016); Ministry of Finance: Chinese Financial Yearbooks (1994 to 2015), *China Financial Magazine*.

of fiscal revenues was lower than the GDP growth rate in 2015, the growth rate of fiscal expenditures still doubled the GDP growth rate.

Finally, macroeconomic analysis shows that fiscal expenditures always present a continuous growth tendency no matter whether during high-speed economic growth, low-speed economic growth or medium-speed economic growth, which has been written in textbooks as a law of economics. In other words, whatever the economic trend and fiscal revenue situation is in 2016 and in the future, the rigid growth momentum of fiscal expenditures will not change and is likely to become strengthened.

Tendency change no. 3: turning "over-budget revenues" into "shortage of fiscal revenues" due to the increasing role of the non-general public budget

In the past few years, how to distribute and employ the "extra fiscal revenues" as the result of budget implementation was a daily problem for Chinese budget management. Since the scale of "extra fiscal revenues" was large and the phenomenon had persisted for a long period, the decision about the allocation and employment of "the extra fiscal revenues" attracted much attention. Moreover, the decision mechanism and its economic and social influence, etc. during the process have been disputed.

However, as of 2015, as the growth rate of fiscal revenues gradually slowed down, the fiscal "over-budget revenues" lasting for several years changed to "shortage of budget revenues". Calculated according to the same method and scope as the previous statistics, the general public budget revenue growth goal and the actual growth rate were 7.3% and 5.8% respectively in 2015 with a difference of 1.5% between them. The result of the budget revenue increase scale deducted from the actual revenue increase scale is the "shortage of fiscal revenues" – 208.3 billion, accounting for 1.37% of the general public budget revenues for that year.

Actually, this turning point from "over-budget revenues" to "shortage of fiscal revenues" may be traced to 2014 regardless of the influence of special revenue increase factors. As mentioned above, the fiscal revenue growth rate (8.6%) of that year was reached on the basis of a series of special measures, including increasing profits handed by partial financial institutions, etc. It is very likely for budget to not reach the 2014 budget index – national fiscal revenues increase by 8% if no special measures are actively taken regardless of the slowdown in the growth of fiscal revenues. In that way, the "shortage of fiscal revenues" will occur a year in advance.

As shown in Figure 14.4, the turning point from "over-budget revenues" to "shortage of fiscal revenues" occurred in 2015, but this change was not accomplished in one stroke. Before this, as the economic downturn gradually formed and became prominent, the reduction in fiscal revenues lasted for several years, resulting in "over-budget revenues". In 2013 and 2014, the amounts of national "extra

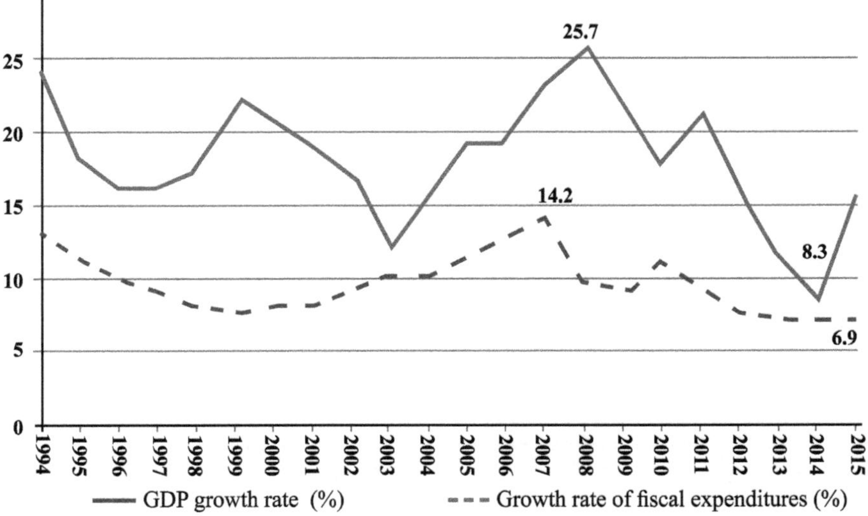

Figure 14.4 Comparison between national actual fiscal revenue and fiscal budget revenue from 1994

Data source: Ministry of Finance: Reports on the Central and Local Budget Implementations in the Last Year and the Budget Proposals of the Next Year submitted by Ministry of Finance to National People's Congress for deliberation from 1994 to 2015, www.mof.gov.cn/zhengwuxinxi/caizhengshuju/.

fiscal revenues" were RMB 257.9 billion and 84 billion respectively. Compared with the previous situations, both the scale of "extra fiscal revenues" and the proportion of "over-budget revenues" showed a tendency of continuous reduction.

A more severe problem was that the reduction in the scale of "extra fiscal revenues" would finally change to "shortage of fiscal revenues" for both central and local budgets. The "shortage of fiscal revenues" is not a temporary phenomenon and very likely to become normal, and even aggravate. Figure 14.5 shows, from the viewpoints of central and local-level general public budgets, the proportion between "extra fiscal revenues" and central and local revenues changed dramatically. Prior to 2013, these two curves (of the proportion between "extra fiscal revenues" and central fiscal revenues and the proportion between "extra fiscal revenues" and local fiscal revenues) were basically circulating towards space. However, in recent years, they were below 0%. In 2015, regardless of the comparison by the same method and scope as the previous statistics and special revenue increase factors, the central fiscal revenues declined by 0.5%, local fiscal revenues' increase rate was lower than the budget increase rate by 2.5%, and the fiscal revenues of some provinces dependent on resources and energy showed a negative growth tendency.

The change from "how to distribute and employ the extra fiscal revenues" to "how to cope with and make up the deficits caused by shortage of fiscal revenues" is very important in Chinese budget management. It means that it is very easy to divide the sections of fiscal budget revenues according to actual fiscal revenues, which may even be a highly possible event in most years with the "new normal"

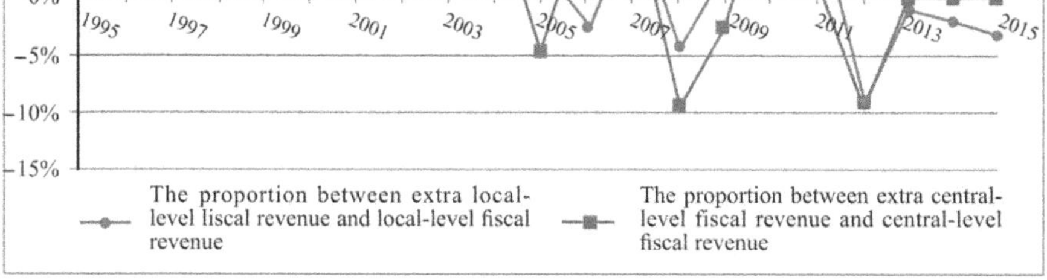

Figure 14.5 Proportion between central and local extra fiscal revenues and their general public budget revenues

Data sources: Ministry of Finance: National Financial Settlement (2010 to 2014) www.mof.gov.cn/zhengwuxin xi/caizhengshuju/; Ministry of Finance: Report on 2015 Central and Local Budget Enforcement and 2016 Central and Local Budget Proposals (on *People's Daily*, March 18, 2016).

of economic development. Therefore, how to make up the fiscal gap between revenues and expenditures after the emergence of "shortage of fiscal revenues" will become more and more important in Chinese budget management.

Thus, dramatic change occurred, resulting in a profound consequence: the non-general public budget revenue gradually becomes an important factor influencing budget management and fiscal revenue and expenditure balance.

In previous years, the budget management mentioned by people mainly referred to the general public budget unless there was some special background or significance. Actually, in China, except for general public budget, the governmental fund budget, social insurance fund budget and state-owned capital operation budget can and shall be included in the governmental revenue and expenditure range. The thought of "carrying out all-revenues (the total of general public budget revenues and non-general public budget revenues) budget bill management" put forward at the Third Plenary Session of the Sixteenth CPC Central Committee in 2003 was established on the basis of the budget conception and governmental revenue and expenditure pattern. Several years after that, this reform deployment remained in the planning stage and was not put into practice indeed.

However, with the formation of the "shortage of fiscal revenues" and the need to make up the fiscal gap between revenues and expenditures due to "shortage of fiscal revenues", against the background of comprehensively deepening reform, the new Budget Law of the People's Republic of China implemented as of January 1, 2015 officially expanded the budget concept to an all-revenue governmental budget system containing a general public budget, governmental fund budget, social insurance fund budget and state-owned capital operation budget. In this context, the significance of non-general public budget revenues to governmental revenue and expenditure balance gradually became important. In 2013, general public budget revenues accounted for 58.95% of the total governmental revenues; however, prior to 2012 (included), this proportion was above 60% (in Figure 14.6). Correspondingly, the proportion between the non-general public budget revenues, including the governmental fund budget, social insurance fund budget and state-owned capital operation budget and the total budget revenues showed a rising tendency. Therefore, financial revenue and expenditure balance increasingly depends on non-general public budget revenues. It is necessary to pay more attention to non-general public budgets' management and strengthen the coordination between the general public budget and non-general public budgets.

Tendency change no. 4: periodical expansion of fiscal policies and significance of assessment on all-revenues effect

Chinese fiscal management has always been implemented carefully, which was shown in the selection of fiscal policy orientation. In the past, both the decision to implement expansion or austerity and the degree of expansion or austerity implementation are generally discussed yearly. Even though the decision is to keep the original fiscal policy pattern, statements such as "continue implementing the active fiscal policies in the next year" or "continue implementing the sound fiscal

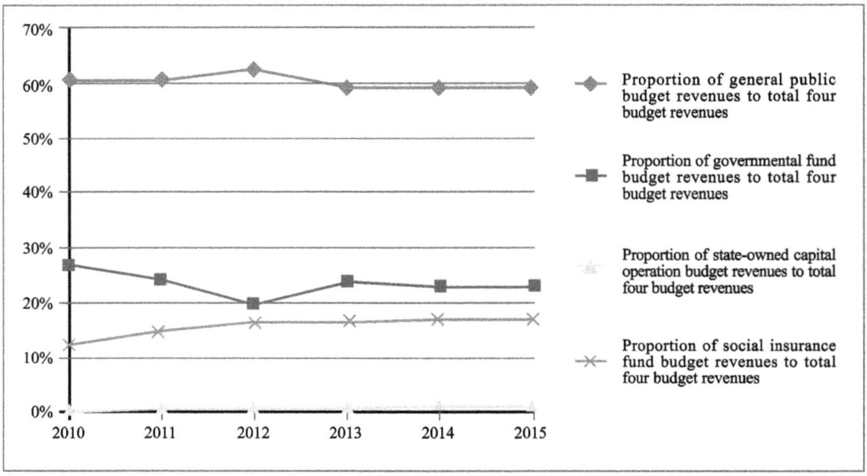

Figure 14.6 Proportions between four budget revenues and the total governmental revenues (2010–2015)

Data sources: Ministry of Finance: National Financial Settlement (2010 to 2014), www.mof.gov.cn/zhengwuxinxi/caizhengshuju/; Ministry of Finance: Report on 2015 Central and Local Budget Enforcement and 2016 Central and Local Budget Proposals (on *People's Daily*, March 18, 2016).

policies in the next year" must be made at the Central Economic Working Conference held at the end of each year.

However, with the emergence of change in the economic situation, on the one hand, economy develops a downturn and pressure increases constantly; on the other hand, to realize the strategy goal of comprehensively establishing a well-off society, the GDP growth rate must be kept above 6.5%. Moreover, the promotion of supply-side structural reform needs to create a steady macroeconomic environment. Those respects require that Chinese macroeconomic policies, especially fiscal policies, must be extended during the long period of macroeconomic operation, at least during "the Thirteenth Five-Year Plan" period. In other words, different from the previous fiscal policy orientation decision made yearly, Chinese fiscal policies have formed a phenomenon of periodic expansion.

Moreover, in the meantime as the fiscal policy shows cyclical expansion, intensity of fiscal expansion also increases gradually. A prominent phenomenon could be observed from the change in words used for the statement of fiscal policy orientation at the Central Economic Working Conference – for instance, "continue the implementation of positive fiscal policy" in 2015, "positive fiscal policy shall be powerful" in 2015 and "intensify the positive fiscal policy" in 2016.

Against this background, both the level of the financial deficit and scale of the national debts will see a large increase. As a result, as two indexes for managing and controlling financial and economic risks, the rate of deficit (proportion of the financial deficit to GDP) and debt ratio (proportion of the national debts to GDP) will also be improved obviously. For instance, in 2016, the financial deficit of RMB 2.18 trillion listed in the general public budget is RMB 560 billion more than in the year 2015, with the rate of deficit increased from 2.3% to 3%. In addition, the financial deficit of the central government is RMB 1.4 trillion and the local financial deficit is RMB 780 billion in 2016. Both of them are increased by RMB 280 billion as compared with the year 2015. The quota of the national debts balance of central finance is RMB 12.590835 trillion, with an increase of RMB 1.4 trillion compared with 2015, and the quota of the general debt balance of the local governments is RMB 10.70724 trillion, which is a net increase on the basis of zero.

In fact, tracing back to 2012, it can be seen from Figures 14.7 and 14.8 that the phenomenon of the continuously enlarged level of financial deficit and scale of national debts has lasted for four years, and just overlaps with the period of economic slowdown. After prospecting for the basic outlook of the macroeconomic situation during the "Thirteenth Five-Year Plan", one may be assured that the situation will not weaken, but will be further intensified possibly.

Similar to the analysis above, such change in the general public budget shall naturally act on the non-general public budget under conditions of implementing the new Budget Law, so as to reflect the full-covered government budget including the general public budget and governmental fund budget, social insurance fund budget and budget of operation of state-owned capital. Therefore, in view of the fully covered government budget, the estimation and control of financial and economic risks through the fully covered financial deficit and fully covered

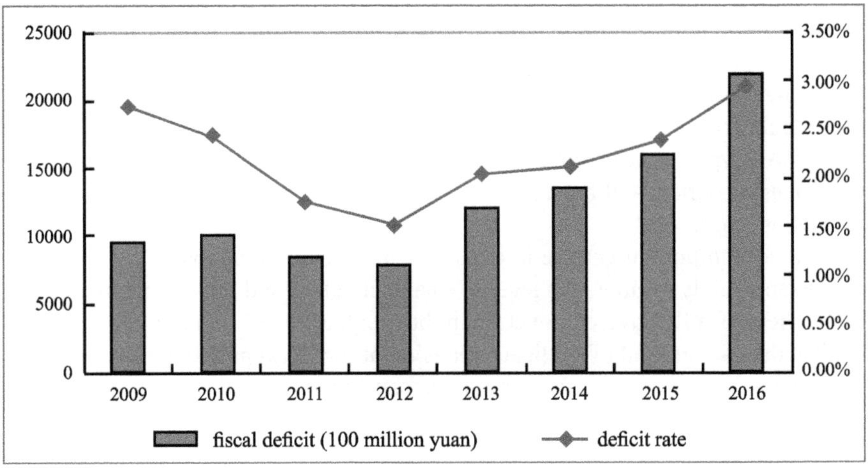

Figure 14.7 Financial deficits and their proportion of GDP

Data sources: Ministry of Finance: Report on Central and Local Budget Enforcement of the Previous Year and Budget Proposals of the Next Year reviewed by the National People's Congress proposed by Ministry of Finance from 2009–2016, www.mof.gov.cn/zhengwuxinxi/caizhengshuju/; National Bureau of Statistics of the People's Republic of China: 2015 Chinese Statistics Yearbook, China Statistics Press.

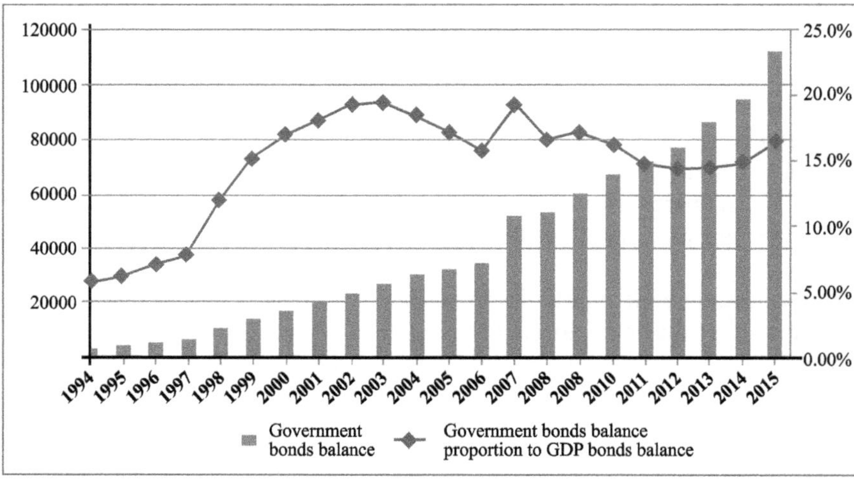

Figure 14.8 National debt balance and its proportion of GDP

Data sources: Ministry of Finance: Report on Central and Local Budget Enforcement of the Previous Year and Budget Proposals of the Next Year reviewed by the National People's Congress proposed by Ministry of Finance from 1994–2016, www.mof.gov.cn/zhengwuxinxi/caizhengshuju/; National Bureau of Statistics of the People's Republic of China: 2015 Chinese Statistics Yearbook, China Statistics Press.

national debts will also become a new trend and new normal based on the cyclical expansion of the fiscal policy.

From Figure 14.9, it can be seen that in 2015, the proportion of the general public budget deficit of RMB 1.62 trillion to GDP is 2.39%. On this basis, conduct the calculation in view of the fully covered government budget after adding the other three types of government budgetary income and expenditure. As a result, the financial deficit will be reduced to RMB 1.11319 trillion, whose proportion to GDP is 1.65%.

As a very important change in tendency, it indicates to us that it's very necessary to accurately estimate the level of financial deficit and scale of national debts in the view of fully covered government budget but not the general public budget against the background of cyclical expansion of the fiscal policy. It not only helps us evaluate intensity of the fiscal policy expansion and the macroeconomic effect in a comprehensive and systematic way, but also helps us control the relevant financial and economic risks properly.

Tendency change no. 5: changing the pattern from a centralized system to a tax-sharing system

Throughout historical experience, the relation between central finance and local finance is just like a financial transaction between two generations in a family. If

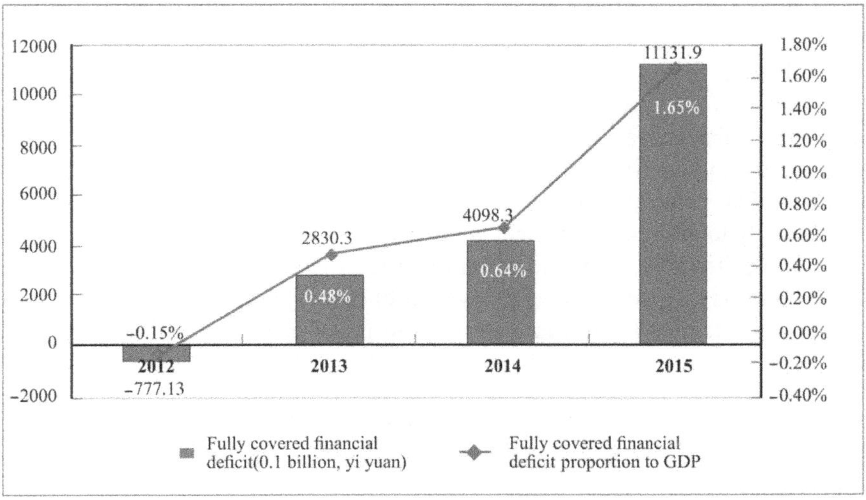

Figure 14.9 Basic situation of the fully covered financial deficit (2012–2015)

Data sources: Ministry of Finance: Report on 2015 Central and Local Budget Enforcement and 2016 Central and Local Budget Proposals (on *People's Daily*, March 18, 2016); Ministry of Finance: National Government Final Accounts (2012–2014) www.mof.gov.cn/zhengwuxinxi/caizhengshuju/.

the parents are capable of undertaking the demands of their children due to good financial condition or strong financial ability, it is natural selection or a normal phenomenon that the parents directly intervene or strictly control the arrangement of financial affairs for their children by giving money. However, if the parents have no ability or cannot undertake the demands of their children anymore due to a deteriorated financial condition or financial stress, their ability to intervene and control the arrangements for their children will decline with the decrease in the strength of their financial support.

This principle can be applied to the relationship between central finance and local finance. Since 1994, with the increase in the proportion of central fiscal revenue to China's total fiscal revenue and the increase in the scale of transfer payments from central finance to local finance, although China still advocates the "tax-sharing system" in the fiscal system, it is actually inclined more to concentration of power than decentralization as an elementary feature of the evolution of the relationship between central finance and local finance over 20 years. It can be verified from many perspectives. For instance, the "combination of financial power and administrative power" is replaced with "matching financial power and administrative power" as the basic principle for handling the relationship between central finance and local finance; in the division of tax categories, partial local taxes and even the main local tax types are transferred to the tax shared by central and local governments, with the latter accounting for more than 80%; in the adjustment of the transfer payment system, there is the slow standardized process and "department communication for obtaining projects and capital"; in the implementation of classified fiscal management, there is the long-term "absence" of revenue and expenditure management power and revenue and expenditure balance of power in local finance. In fact, it has the nature of "finance passing by" and so on.

However, we have already seen that the centralized pattern very closely associated with China's financial system for the long term has slightly changed since at least 2015, under the conditions of financial revenue slowing down, increased contradiction between financial revenue and expenditure and especially the increasingly tough central finance.

Example: Transfer payments. From Figures 14.10 and 14.11, on the one hand, the proportion of general transfer payment to central transfer payment and total amount of tax returns increases steadily, to reach 53.44% in 2014, about 3% higher than that of 2013; on the other hand, from 2011, the proportion of central transfer payment and total amount of tax returns to the general central public budget expenditure does not increase anymore, and shows a trend of continuous decrease. The proportion is 70.74% in 2011, 70.11% in 2012 and 69.57% in 2014. It decreases 1.17% in three years.

Take the local national debts as another example. Upon implementation of the new *Budget Law and Issuance of the Opinions of the State Council for Strengthening Local National Debts Management (GF [2014] No. 43)*, the Ministry of Finance continuously issues the *Notice on Printing the 'Interim Procedures for the Issuance Management of General Debt of Local Government' (CK [2015]*

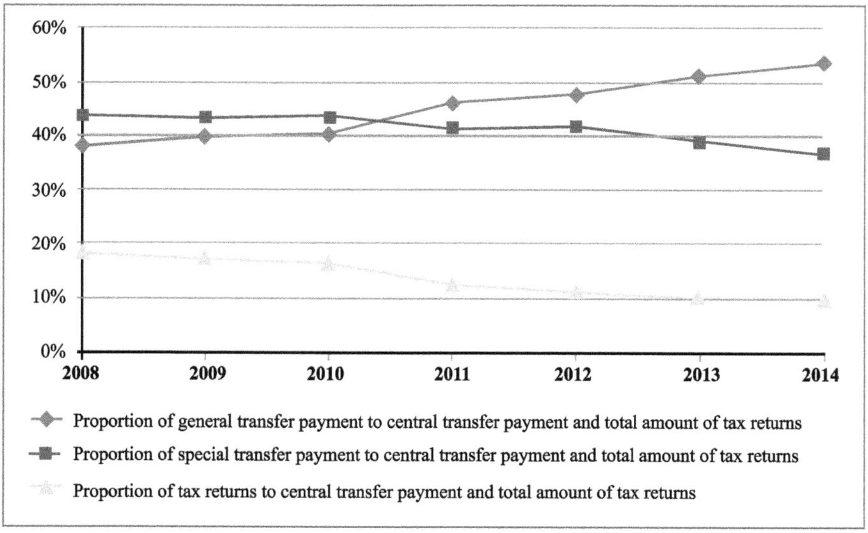

Figure 14.10 Trend of structural change in transfer payments from central government to local government

Data source: Ministry of Finance: National Government Final Accounts (2008–2015) www.mof.gov.cn/zhengwuxinxi/caizhengshuju/.

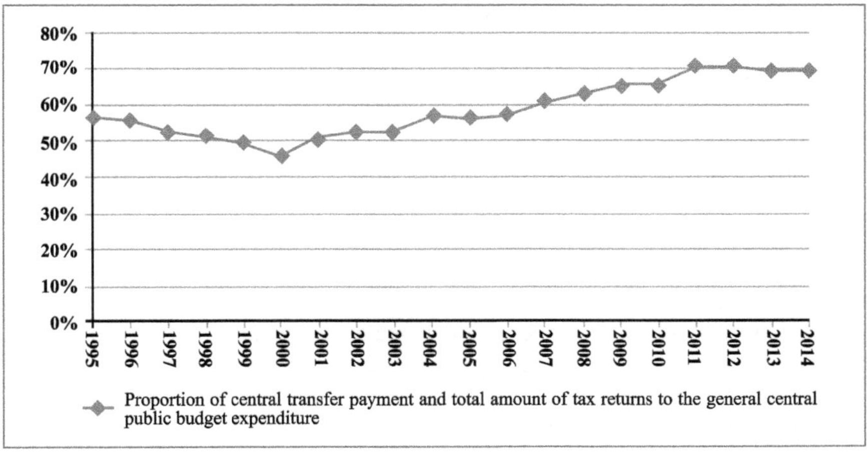

Figure 14.11 Proportion of central transfer payment and total amount of tax returns to general central public budget expenditure

Data sources: Ministry of Finance: Chinese Financial Yearbooks (1995–2007), *China State Finance Magazine*; Ministry of Finance: National Government Final Accounts (2007–2015) www.mof.gov.cn/zhengwuxinxi/caizhengshuju/.

No. 64) and the *Notice on Printing the 'Interim Procedures for the Issuance Management of Dedicated Debt of Local Government (CK [2015] No. 83)*. Taking this as an opportunity, the control of local national debts has changed slightly, and local issuance and return are allowed. Normalization and institutionalization of financing for debt of local government has formally stepped to our life.

It can be considered that the long troubled centralized pattern of the financial system may show a further change under such tendency, or even return to the road of the tax-sharing system. In this process, the prospects of gradually perfecting the local fiscal system, arousing the enthusiasm of the local government, comprehensively deepening reform of the financial system under the reform background and actually implementing the deployment may be seen.

Tendency change no. 6: forcing reform through financial difficulties and the appearance of new power for financial and tax reform

Through the study of the history of the reform of financial and tax systems at all times and in all places, all major reforms of financial and tax systems appeared in periods of financial difficulties but not periods of financial sufficiency. The greater gap between financial revenue and expenditure will make financial balance more difficult and a harder financial period, provide more motivation for reform, more easily reduce resistance and obstacles to reform and start the reform of the financial and tax system more easily.

Reform of the financial and tax system in China in 1994 can be taken as a highlighted example. In the final analysis, reform of the financial and tax system was determined smoothly and began on an unprecedented scale, because finance at that time had fallen into an extremely difficult situation and was unable to develop by following the original system. Through the date curve for the proportion of financial revenue to GDP over the years, it can be seen clearly that a deep V-shaped track is shown from 1978 to 2015, with the lowest point around the year 1994. As shown in Figure 14.12, the proportion of financial revenue to GDP is 31.02% in 1987 and 10.77% in 1994. Financial revenues and expenditures at all levels are difficult to maintain, especially those of the central government. The most basic budget enforcement was once affected by the increasingly reduced proportion of its revenue to the national financial revenue (Figure 14.13). In a manner of speaking, the increasingly intensified financial difficulty urges and finally hastens financial and tax reform.

On this basis, we inspect the current status of the reform of the financial and tax system and find that if the promotion of this round of reform of the financial and tax system over the past two years is slower than our original expectation, causing an inability to have effects in many aspects, it can be seen that difficulties extremely different from the previous time are shown in the recent period of time. With the sharply reduced growth of financial revenue, growth of financial expenditure against trend and increased financial deficit and scale of national debts, the consensus of relevant financial and tax reform is to be reached, the factors forcing

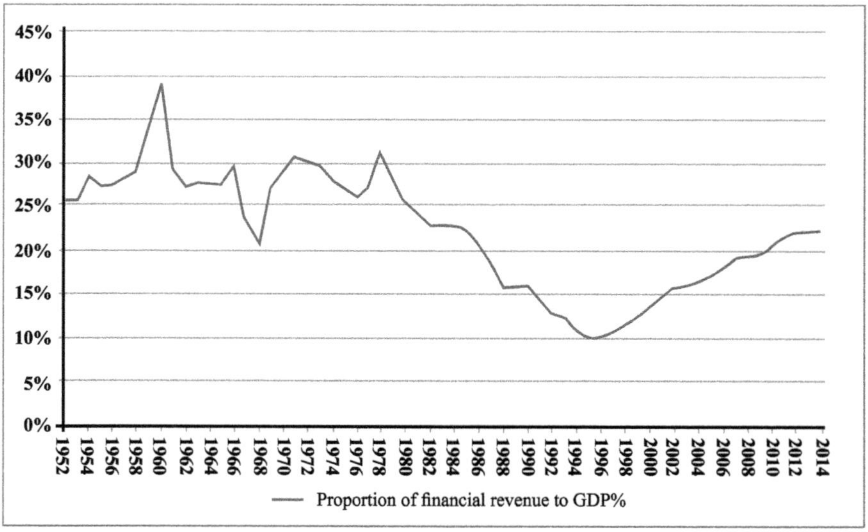

Figure 14.12 Change in the proportion of financial revenue to GDP around financial and tax reform in 1994

Data sources: National Bureau of Statistics of the People's Republic of China: 2015 Chinese Statistics Yearbook, China Statistics Press; Ministry of Finance: Chinese Financial Yearbooks (1994 to 2015), *China Financial Magazine*.

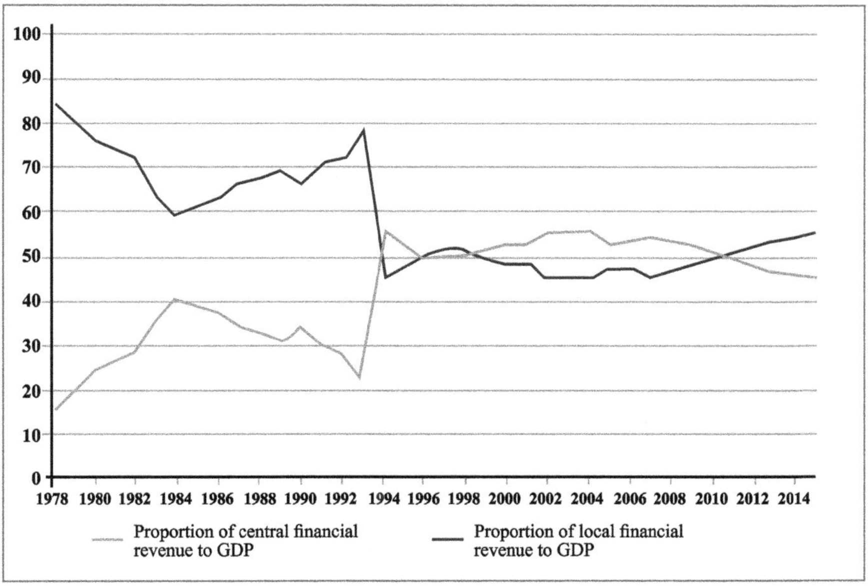

Figure 14.13 Change in the proportion of central and local financial revenues to GDP around financial and tax reform in 1994

Data sources: Ministry of Finance: Report on 2015 Central and Local Budget Enforcement and 2016 Central and Local Budget Proposals (on *People's Daily*, March 18, 2016); Ministry of Finance: Chinese Financial Yearbooks (1994 to 2015), *China Financial Magazine*.

financial and tax reform are gradually gathered, the power promoting financial and tax reform is rapidly generated and financial and tax reform of the relevant fields is accelerated.

For instance, the comprehensive change from business tax to added-value tax started as a result of reforms deployed in 2012 is regarded as a transitional measure for macro-control policy and reform of the financial and tax system after a four-year marathon and four-month suspension, and was finally launched nationwide in May 2016 in a formal way. On this basis, the overall plan for the reform of central and local revenue division and guidelines for the reform of the division of administrative powers and expenditure responsibilities between central and local governments are to be issued with the formation of a transitional scheme for the division of central and local revenues. Moreover, under the objective of stabilizing tax bearing, it may force the reform of direct tax represented by individual income tax and land tax with the gradual release of the effect of tax cutting of about RMB 500 billion during the comprehensive change from business tax to added-value tax.

Another example is that the fully covered government budget management provided with reforms deployed in 2003 fails to make any progress since it may impair the interest of relevant departments. However, since the general public budget faces enormous pressure and has been unable to complete the revenue budget in two consecutive years, 16 governmental fund budgets have been transferred to general public budgets from 2015 to now, and are regarded as necessary measures for relieving financial pressure and balancing general public budget revenues and expenditures, beginning the progress of making an overall plan for governmental fund revenue. The 16 governmental fund budgets include local additional education tax, culture construction fee, disabled employment security fund, irrigation and water conservancy construction and education capital from local land leasing income, income from transferring the right of charging for government loan forgiveness road, woods-raising fund, the fee for forest re-vegetation, foundation for water works, harbor dues on vessels, charge for waterway maintenance of Yangtze Estuary, soil and water conservation compensation, housing fund of the government, radio frequency occupation fee, railway asset liquidation income and income from liquidation of the reserved assets of power reform.

For instance, after experiencing a dozen years of revising state dates, suspensions due to difficulties and more revised start dates, the new Budget Law was finally passed in August 2014 and was formally implemented on January 1, 2015.

Against such a background, the Ministry of Finance continuously releases information on the reform of financial and tax system: "The budget reform obtains decisive progress, tax reform advances [in an] orderly [way], and the reform of financial system is actively promoted" (Ministry of Finance, 2016). During such period, measures shall be taken to promote the reform of financial and tax system as much as is possible.

It can be hereby estimated that it is possible for us to welcome the long expected climax of the new round of reform of financial and tax system in 2016 and the coming years.

(Originally published on the *Public Finance Research*, Vol.6. 2016)

Bibliography

Cai Fang. (2010). Demographic transition, demographic dividend and Lewisian turning point. *Economic Research*, (4), 4–13.

Craig, E. D., & Heins, A. J. (1979). The effect of tax elasticity on government spending. *Public Choice*, *35*(35), 267–275.

Gao Peiyong. (2006). Puzzle of continuously rapid growth of China's tax. *Economic Research*, (12), 13–23.

Gao Peiyong. (2010). A new round of positive fiscal policy: Progress inventory and trend prospect. *Economics of Finance and Trade*, (1), 5–12.

Gao Peiyong. (2014a). Discussion on the construction of fundamental fiscal theory under modern framework of national governance. *Social Sciences in China*, (12), 102–122.

Gao Peiyong. (2014b). From the adaption to the market economy system to the matching to national governance system: Discussion on the basic orientation of the new round of reform of financial and tax system. *Economics of Finance and Trade*, (3), 5–20.6.

IMF. (2015). *Fiscal monitor: Now is the time fiscal policies for sustainable growth.* Retrieved from www.imf.org/external/pubs/ft/fm/2015/01/fmindex.htm

Li Keqiang. (2016). Report on the government work. *Xinhua News Agency*, March 5. Retrieved from www.gov.cn/guowuyuan/2016-03/05/content_5049372.htm

Liu Xiahui. (2013). Macroeconomic management at supply side. *Economic Perspectives*, (10), 9–19.

Lv Bingyang, & Li Feng. (2007). Real example explanation to the puzzle of extraordinary GDP growth of China's tax. *Economics of Finance and Trade*, (3), 29–36.

Ministry of Finance. (2016, March 16). Report on 2015 central and local budget enforcement and 2016 central and local budget proposals. *People's Daily*.

Romer, C. D., & Romer, D. H. (2007). The macroeconomic effects of tax changes: Estimates based on a new measure of fiscal shocks. *American Economic Review*, 2007, *100*(3), 763–801.

Romer, C. D., Romer, D. H., Chetty, R., et al. (2008). Do tax cuts starve the beast? The effect of tax changes on government spending, manuscript. *Brookings Papers on Economic Activity*, 2008, *9*(1), 139–214.

Xi Jinping. (2015). A great power means greater duty, but not greater monopoly. *Xinhua News Agency*, March 38. Retrieved from http://news.xinhuanet.com/fortune/2015-03/28/c_127631629.htm

Zhou Li'an, Liu Chong, & Li Xing. (2012). Tax effort, tax agency and the puzzle of tax revenue growth. *Economics (Quarterly Publication)*, *11*(1), 1–18.

Index

Page numbers in italic indicate a figure and page numbers in bold indicate a table on the corresponding page.

For Product Safety Concerns and Information please contact our EU
representative GPSR@taylorandfrancis.com
Taylor & Francis Verlag GmbH, Kaufingerstraße 24, 80331 München, Germany

www.ingramcontent.com/pod-product-compliance
Ingram Content Group UK Ltd.
Pitfield, Milton Keynes, MK11 3LW, UK
UKHW022124190926
475702UK00013B/1642
* 9 7 8 0 3 6 7 5 9 0 5 7 4 *